RIVAL WISDOMS

## The wife of Bathes tale.

☞ That he is gentle that doth gentle deedis.
And therfore deare husbond, I thus conclude,
All were it that mine auncetors were rude,
Yet may that high God, and so hope I,
Graunt me grace to liue vertuously:
☞ Then am I gentle, when I begin
To liue vertuously, and leauen sin.
And there as ye of pouertie me repreue,
The high God, on whom that we belieue,
In wilfull pouerte chese to lead his life:
And certes, euery man, maid, and wife
May vnderstond, Iesu heauen king
Ne would not chese a vicious liuing.
☞ Glad pouert is an honest thing certaine,
This woll Seneck and other clerkes saine,
☞ Who so would hold him paid of his pouert,
I hold him rich, all had he not a sheert.
☞ He that coueteth is a full poore wight,
For he would han that is not in his might.
☞ But who y nought hath, ne coueteth to haue,
Is rich, although ye hold him but a knaue.
Uery pouert is sinne properly.
Iuuenall faith of pouert merrily:
☞ The poore man when he goeth by the way
Before theeues, he may sing and play.
☞ Pouert is hatefull good: and as I geffe,
A full great bringer out of businesse:
A great amender eke of sapience,
To him that taketh it in patience.
Pouert is, although it seeme elenge,
Possession that no wight woll challenge.
☞ Pouerte full often, when a man is low,
Maketh him God, and eke himselfe to know.
☞ Pouert a spectacle is, as thinketh me,
Through which one may his very friendys see.
And therfore, since that I you not greue,
Of my pouert no more me repreue.
Now sir, che of elde ye repreued me:
And certes sir, though none authorite
Were in no booke, ye gentles of honour
Saine, that men should an old wight honour,
And clepe hem father for her gentlenesse,
And authors shall I find, as I geffe.
Now there as ye saine y I am foule and old,
Then drede you not to been a cokewold.
☞ For filth, elthe, and foule, all so mote I thee,
Ben great wardeins vpon chastite.
But natheles, since I know your delite,
I shall fulfill your worldly appetite.
Chese now (qd she) one of thyse things twey,
To haue me foule and old till that I dey,
And be to you a true humble wife,
And neuer you displease in all my life:
Or els woll you haue me yong and faire,
And take your auenture of the repaire,
That shall come to your house because of me,
Or in some other place may well be.
Now chese your selue whether y you liketh,

This knight auiseth him, and sore siketh,
But at the last he said in this manere:
My lady and my loue, and wife so dere,
I put me in your wise gouernaunce,
Cheseth your selfe which may bee more plea-
And most honour to you and me also,  (saunce
I do no force whether of the two:
For as you liketh, it sufficeth me.
Then haue I got of you the mastry (qd. she)
Since I may chese and gouerne as me lest:
Ye certes wife (qd. he) I hold it for the best.
Kisse me (qd. she) we be no lenger wroth:
For vp my truth, I woll be to you both,
This is to say, to be both faire and good,
I pray to God that I mote sterue wood,
But I to you be also good and trew,
As euer was wife, sithen the world was new:
And but I be to morrow as faire to seene,
As any Lady, Emprelle, or Queene,
That is betweene East and eke the West,
Doth with my life right as you lest.
Cast vp the courtein, and looke how it is.
And when this knight saw verily all this,
That she so faire was, and so young thereto,
For ioy he hent her in his armes two:
His hart bathed in the bath of blisse,
A thousand times a row he gan her kisse:
And she obeyed him in euery thing,
That mought done him pleasure or liking,
And thus they liued vnto her liues end
In perfit ioy, and Iesu Christ vs send
Hulbonds meeke and yong, and fresh abed,
And grace to ouerliue hem that we wed,
And I pray to God to short her liues,
That will not be gouerned by her wiues.
And old and angry niggards of dispence,
God send hem soone a very pestilence.

¶ The Friers Prologue.

His worthy limitour, this no-
ble Frere
He made alway a maner lou-
ring chere
Upon the Sompner, but for
honeste
No villainies word as yet to him spake he:
But at the last he said to the wife,
Dame, God yeue you right good life,
Ye haue touched here, all so mote I thee,
In schole matter, a full great difficulte,
Ye haue said much thing right well I say:
But dame, here as we riden by the way,
Us needeth not to speaken but of game,
And let authorities a Gods name
To preaching, and to schoole of clargie.
But if it like vnto this companie,
I woll you of a Sompner tell a game,

Parde

# RIVAL WISDOMS

Reading Proverbs in the *Canterbury Tales*

*Nancy Mason Bradbury*

THE PENNSYLVANIA STATE UNIVERSITY PRESS
UNIVERSITY PARK, PENNSYLVANIA

Frontispiece: *The Workes of our Antient and Lerned English Poet, Geffrey Chaucer, Newly Printed*, edited by Thomas Speght (London: Adam Islip, 1602), fol. 36v. Mortimer Rare Book Collection, Smith College Special Collections, Northampton, MA.

Library of Congress Cataloging-in-Publication Data

Names: Bradbury, Nancy M., author.
Title: Rival wisdoms : reading proverbs in the Canterbury tales / Nancy Mason Bradbury.
Description: University Park, Pennsylvania : The Pennsylvania State University Press, [2024] | Includes bibliographical references and index.
Summary: "Situates Chaucer's proverbs in their premodern cultural and intellectual contexts, arguing that Chaucer places proverbs at the center of the interpretive possibilities the Canterbury Tales extends to its readers"— Provided by publisher.
Identifiers: LCCN 2023045205 | ISBN 9780271096889 (hardback) | ISBN 9780271096896 (paper)
Subjects: LCSH: Chaucer, Geoffrey, -1400. Canterbury tales. | Proverbs in literature. | Proverbs—History and criticism.
Classification: LCC PR1875.P76 2024 | DDC 821/.1—dc23/eng /20231220
LC record available at https://lccn.loc.gov/2023045205

Copyright © 2024 Nancy Mason Bradbury
All rights reserved
Printed in the United Stated of America
Published by The Pennsylvania State University Press, University Park, PA 16802–1003

The Pennsylvania State University Press is a member of the Association of University Presses.

It is the policy of The Pennsylvania State University Press to use acid-free paper. Publications on uncoated stock satisfy the minimum requirements of American National Standard for Information Sciences—Permanence of Paper for Printed Library Material, ANSI Z39.48–1992.

*To Scott and Mason*

CONTENTS

*Acknowledgments* | ix

Introduction: Reading Proverbially | 1

1 Proverbs and Premodern Reading Practices | 10

2 The Rival Wisdoms of Clerks and *Cherles* | 43

3 The Rival Wisdoms of Clerks and Women | 84

4 Proverb and Story in the *Tale of Melibee* | 125

Conclusion: Putting Proverbs in Their Places | 157

*Notes* | 175
*Bibliography* | 193
*Index* | 205

ACKNOWLEDGMENTS

Over the course of a long project, I have incurred many debts, and it is a pleasure to acknowledge them here. I am grateful to Smith College for giving me my undergraduate education and for providing moral and material support to me as a professor in the English department for over three decades. Much more than a workplace, the College has afforded an intellectual home, stimulating colleagues, bright and dedicated students, and cherished friends.

For generous help in bringing this book to fruition, I am indebted to Jenny Adams, Brigitte Buettner, Carolyn Collette, Eglal Doss-Quinby, and Nadia Margolis. William Oram read the entire manuscript one chapter at a time and responded with great kindness and astute suggestions; our conversations have left their mark on the final version. An anonymous reader for Penn State University Press responded in generous and knowledgeable detail; David Raybin's thoughtful and constructive suggestions exceeded all expectations for peer review. I thank Scott Bradbury for reading the completed manuscript cover to cover with a careful eye to inconsistencies and stylistic lapses. All of the above have helped to make this a better book. I am also grateful for the erudition of the many distinguished scholarly predecessors who make current work on Chaucer possible. Chaucer scholars know that we stand on the shoulders of innumerable giants whenever we write, and our debt necessarily extends well beyond the capacity of any single Works Cited list. To this day, I rarely read Chaucer without thinking of something said or written by the late Charles Muscatine, sadly missed by colleagues and former students.

I thank also my two able research assistants, Teresa Pandolfo and Katie Ciurleo, with special mention of the latter for meticulous counting of hundreds of pointing hands in Thomas Speght's 1602 Chaucer edition. For the gift of a copy of that edition, along with many other books of value, to the Mortimer Rare Book Collection at Smith College, I thank Judith Raymo, generous donor of the extensive Chaucer collection assembled by her late husband, Robert R. Raymo. A page from the Raymo copy of Speght's edition serves here as a frontispiece. Martin Antonetti and Shannon Supple, successive Curators of Rare Books, have supported the study of Chaucer at Smith College with generosity and enthusiasm. At Penn State University Press, my thanks to Ellie Goodman, Maddie Caso, Brian Beer, and Alex Ramos.

For drafts read, invitations to give talks or contribute to edited volumes, and other acts of collegiality, some of them long ago, my warm thanks to Mark Amodio, David Benson, Heather Blatt, Betsy Bowden, Neil Cartlidge, Mary Carruthers, Howell Chickering, Arlyn Diamond, Vincent DiMarco, Thomas DuBois, Susan Etheredge, Thomas Farrell, Susanna Fein, Rosalind Field, the late John Miles Foley, Michael Gorra, Richard Firth Green, Thomas Hahn, Stephen Harris, Valerie Johnson, Barbara Klaas, Carl Lindahl, the late Ron McDonald, Richard Millington, Ingrid Nelson, Douglas Patey, Cornelia Pearsall, Nicholas Perkins, Karl Persson, Rhiannon Purdie, Corinne Saunders, Lynn Staley, Michael Thurston, Delia Warner, and Jocelyn Wogan-Browne.

Finally, to Scott Bradbury (again) and to our son Mason, possessors of very different but equally valued wisdoms, my ongoing appreciation and admiration.

INTRODUCTION

*Reading Proverbially*

In the domain of literature, it is sometimes
the smallest things which have the greatest
intellectual value.
—ERASMUS, *Adages* I.V

The spark that ignited this book is an apology from Thomas Speght, Elizabethan schoolmaster, to the readers of his 1598 edition of the works of Geoffrey Chaucer. Speght came late to the editorial project, and he wrote that in the rush to publication, certain desirable features had to be forgone, including the marking of Chaucer's "sentences" (from Latin *sententia*) or wisdom expressions. In a prefatory note "To the Readers," he includes "Sentences noted" in a rueful list of projects "undertaken, although never as yet fully finished." He returns to this regret at the end of the book: "Sentences also, which are many and excellent in this Poet, might have ben noted in the margent with some marke, which now must be left to the search of the Reader." A revised edition published in 1602 made good on the omission; its title page proclaims, "Sentences and Prouerbes noted," and a revised letter "To the Readers" reiterates, "Prouerbes and Sentences marked."[1]

Speght's 1598 apology for leaving these expressions "to the search of the Reader" hints at a vanished premodern reading practice. What reader today searches a poem or a work of fiction for its proverbial wisdom? His belief that readers would miss his absent markings in the first edition and welcome them in the second accords with the special attention that Chaucer himself often draws to the abundant supply of "sentences and proverbes" in his work.[2] As the first book-length study to place Chaucer's proverb use in the context of a widespread and still growing zeal for proverbs, *Rival Wisdoms* attempts to recover something of the now-alien reading practice that Speght's 1602 edition supports.[3] It argues that a proverb-conscious encounter with the *Canterbury Tales* reveals fresh emphases and meaningful structures in Chaucer's last and most ambitious work. Attending to Chaucer's proverbs, as it turns out, brings to light some larger issues about how meaning was made in premodern fiction, as chapter 4 and the conclusion of this book seek to demonstrate.

Speght was not the first to flag proverbs in Chaucer but he was by far the most thorough: at his direction, printers added to the 1602 revised edition many hundreds of marginal pointing hands, also called fists or manicules (☞ from Latin *manicula*, 'little hand'), about 776 of them in the *Canterbury Tales* alone.[4] A page from this edition illustrating a particularly dense cluster of these markings serves as the frontispiece to this book. Marking Chaucer's proverbs was hardly a new development in 1602: from the earliest textual witnesses onward, the manuscripts of Chaucer and his contemporaries bear marginal indicators such as the English word *proverbe*, or, in Latin, the imperative *nota* or *nota proverbium*; some offer Latin equivalents for recognizable sayings, and some identify sources, especially the Bible, the Church fathers, and the Latin classics. In addition to verbal indicators, scribes and readers used various marks to emphasize portions of manuscript texts, including the hand-drawn ancestors of the printer's fists in Speght's edition, sometimes sketched with preternaturally long pointing fingers, carefully articulated fingernails, or elaborate cuffs and sleeves. The "index" finger with which they point was already so called in Chaucer's day: his near-contemporary John Trevisa writes that "the second [finger] is called index . . . with it we announce and show and teach all things."[5] With the advent of the new technology, the hand-drawn manicules in manuscripts were soon adapted as printer's devices.[6]

Marking wisdom expressions in printed books in English was not unusual in the period 1500–1660. It served to emphasize the erudition of works in an emerging vernacular, and it supported the prevalent practice of compiling quotations for commonplace books.[7] Because other indicators such as commas, inverted commas, or font changes were more common than manicules for this purpose, Joseph A. Dane speculates that Speght's choice of manicules might have been influenced by those that mark scattered passages in Chaucer's *House of Fame* in the printer's copy from which Speght's 1602 edition was typeset. Dane demonstrates that its printers worked not from Speght's 1598 edition, as one might expect, but from a copy of a 1561 edition by John Stow, annotated by hand.[8] Whether premodern readers searched out "sentences and proverbes" for themselves in Speght's 1598 edition or were directed to them by manicules in the 1602 revision, my question is how this proverb-conscious reading would have affected their experience of the *Canterbury Tales*.

For insight into the reading practice implied by Speght's apology and his later editorial markings, I have benefitted in particular from two sources, one pre- and one post-Chaucer. The first is the thirteenth-century Latin proverb collection assembled by Albertanus of Brescia, translated in the fourteenth century, first into French and then by Chaucer into English as the *Tale of Melibee* (discussed in chapter 4). The second is the work of the preeminent international scholar Desiderius Erasmus (ca. 1466–1536), who spent a good portion of his career scouring ancient Greek and Latin works for "sentences and proverbs." Erasmus's masterwork, eventually called the *Adagiorum chiliades* (*Thousands of Adages*, henceforth the *Adages*), began its long publishing history in 1500, a century after Chaucer's death in 1400 brought an end to the *Canterbury Tales*. The intellectual world inhabited by Erasmus shared with the earlier centuries of Albertanus and Chaucer a veneration for the proverb that extended back to classical antiquity.

With humanistic ardor, Erasmus sought in his readings the Greek and Latin proverbs that he thought of as preserving the distilled wisdom of the ancients. Nearly as important as the wisdom contained in the proverb itself, he makes clear, is the dexterity with which a speaker or writer introduces it into a new context. From his invaluable introduction to the *Adages*, we learn that when skillfully applied, a proverb "will wake interest by its novelty, bring delight by its concision, convince by its decisive power." A proverb possesses "some native authentic power of truth." It secures precious past wisdom that might otherwise be lost: "What vanishes from written sources, what could not be preserved by inscriptions, colossal statues, and marble tablets, is preserved intact in a proverb."[9] By following Speght's pointing fingers, reading proverbially to the extent it is still possible, I hope to show that in the *Canterbury Tales*, Chaucer, too, acknowledges these powers of the proverb, reflecting on its capacity for good and also for harm, and on its potential to expand and deepen—but also to regulate and constrict—the complex multiple meanings of his stories.

Given the prominence accorded to proverbs in the medieval and early modern reception of Chaucer's work—no other stylistic or rhetorical feature of his poetry was ever singled out in the same way—it is noteworthy that the last book-length treatment of this topic was B. J. Whiting's *Chaucer's Use of Proverbs* in 1934. A return to the subject seems timely, given the confluence of three currents of scholarship today. First, a focus in recent decades on the many continuities between medieval and early modern intellectual life in England has helped to lower the once rigid boundary between the two eras, a bright line first imposed by "Renaissance" writers who saw themselves as participating in a rebirth of learning after a time of dark "medieval" ignorance.[10] Brian Stock makes the point aphoristically: "The Renaissance invented the Middle Ages in order to define itself."[11] The training of modern scholars has long reinforced this division by encouraging research in one or the other "period." I do not see this study as an effort to cross a discernable period divide in order to recover a "Renaissance" reading of Chaucer, newly favorable to proverb-spotting. Rather, I approach proverb-conscious reading as a continuous premodern practice, recommended, for example, by Albertanus's work of 1246, but I focus most of my attention on the timespan between the composition of the *Canterbury Tales* (ca. 1388–1400) and the appearance of Speght's proverb-marked Chaucer edition in 1602. By so doing, I hope to open a more extensive range of contexts for a view of proverbs very different from our own and to show where a proverb-conscious reading of the *Tales* might take us.

With its fresh attention to marginal annotation and other use marks by readers, a second current of scholarly interest connects the material history of the book to the recovery of past reading practices, expanding the available evidence for the transmission and reception of early literature.[12] Proverbs were prime targets for annotation by premodern readers, and my study draws on book history and the history of reading as points of departure for examining the once widespread and now vanished practice of proverb-conscious reading.[13] Finally, from a third development also related to the history of reading practices comes evidence for the idea, apposite to Chaucer's proverb use in the *Canterbury Tales*, that in comparison to the holistic meanings modern readers commonly seek in works of literature, premodern writing often encourages the discovery of meanings local to a particular segment of a long work, a propensity carried over from manuscript culture to early modern printed texts. Because premodern works are so often made up of disparate parts creatively reassembled from preexisting sources, readers were more accustomed to dealing with "starts and stops and bumps and skips," in the words of John Dagenais, and more accustomed to engaging in what Arthur Bahr in *Fragments and Assemblages* calls "compilational reading."[14] Proverbs themselves could cause starts and stops and suggest local meanings distinct from or even in opposition to the drift of the larger whole, as we will see in the *Canterbury Tales* in the course of this book.

With care and historical imagination, we can work back toward a fuller understanding of the position of proverbs in the intellectual world of medieval and early modern Europe and thus share more fully in the cultural products that draw on their powers. In the late fourteenth century, when Chaucer was writing the *Tales*, interest in proverbial wisdom was still growing in intensity toward its zenith in the sixteenth century. Chaucer is justly heralded for literary innovation of many sorts, but his success at catching this particular wave, the surge of interest in proverbs that crested over a century later with the multiple editions of Erasmus's *Adages*, has gone largely uncelebrated because it is hard for us now to imagine that proverbs mattered as much as they once did.

As befits a foundational work, the primary accomplishment of Whiting's 1934 study *Chaucer's Use of Proverbs* was to identify Chaucer's proverbs and link them in his introduction to then-current scholarship on the proverb, to which he was already a significant contributor. The majority of the book consists of a work-by-work list of Chaucer's wisdom expressions, divided into "proverbs" and "sententious remarks," and lightly interspersed with commentary, most often in the form of brief references to the fictional contexts in which they are uttered. Whiting's commentary proceeds primarily proverb by proverb; analysis is relatively sparse and often rudimentary: "Chaucer used proverbs to cap a climax, to emphasize a situation; he used them seriously and he used them humorously."[15] His magisterial contribution to the study of Middle English proverbs came much later in the form of a 1968 index, *Proverbs, Sentences, and Proverbial Phrases from English Writings Mainly Before 1500*. Compiled in collaboration with Helen Wescott Whiting, this volume remains essential to the study of Chaucer's proverbs; it must be the most frequently cited work of scholarship in what is still the standard critical edition, the *Riverside Chaucer*. Letter and number combinations keyed to the Whitings' index appear in abundance throughout its explanatory notes, and I supply these "Whiting numbers" for the proverbs treated in this book. Decades have passed since these tools became available, and yet the poet's proverb use remains surprisingly underexplored.[16] Consider Douglas Gray's apt description of Chaucer as "the medieval English poet who shows the greatest skill in their handling," possessed of "an intimate knowledge of proverbs and an instinctive awareness of their nature and literary possibilities."[17]

An aspirational model for this study is a readable volume by the late art historian Walter S. Gibson, *Figures of Speech: Picturing Proverbs in Renaissance Netherlands*. Readily accessible to nonspecialists with an interest either in proverbs or in premodern Northern European painting, Gibson's book begins with the observation that all of us hear proverbs every day, but we rarely think much about them as a form. He notes that if we use them in serious writing, we tend to apologize for lapsing into "clichés, bromides, and platitudes—the ultimate sins in our search for originality."[18] Tellingly, none of these derogatory terms for the proverb even existed in Chaucer's English; the *Oxford English Dictionary* shows *cliché* derived from modern industrial printing, *bromide* comes from a nineteenth-century sleeping draught, and *platitude* was borrowed from French in the eighteenth century, just as proverbs were becoming déclassé. Gibson's book demonstrates that, contrary to our modern biases, influential premodern Netherlandish painters saw proverbs as fertile ground for creativity, humor, and fresh thought. Many of the features that attracted painters like Bosch and Bruegel to the proverb appealed also to Chaucer and his contemporary audiences. In the chapters that follow, I argue that the special qualities of the proverb and Chaucer's extraordinary skill in wielding them make these tiny expressions not just vital to his dialogue and character drawing but also an underacknowledged asset to his poetic art as a whole.

Chaucer was fond of issuing disclaimers to manage the expectations of his readers, and, before going further, here are mine. Both Chaucer studies and proverb scholarship have long been flourishing fields, accumulating immense bibliographies, and I have been very selective in citing previous scholarship, especially readings of Chaucer. Many excellent companion guides offer accounts of the lively controversies among specialists, including problems of dating, tale order, and establishment of the text, as well as providing well-selected bibliographies.[19] I have attempted to make this book persuasive to Middle English specialists and yet still welcoming to any reader interested either in proverbs or in the *Canterbury Tales*. Much of my argument relies on historically contextualized close reading, and in a practice that may seem to be a deterrent to nonspecialist readers, I quote extensively from Chaucer's poetry, in most cases glossing obsolete words and expressions instead of offering full "translations" into modern English, as is now increasingly the practice even in specialist studies.[20] Chaucer's English is a wonderfully expressive linguistic medium, well worth the effort by those unaccustomed to reading it. If my glossing succeeds, the reader should find that unglossed words mean what they sound like; only the spelling differs.

I conclude this introduction with an outline of the book's structure. Chapter 1 begins with the historical circumstances that fostered the premodern passion for proverbs and then offers a theory of how proverbs work. It examines the goals of the proverb-marking in Speght's 1602 edition and ends with a preview of the special contributions that proverbs make to the *Canterbury Tales*. In chapter 2, a proverb-conscious reading highlights a series of ideological duels between clerics and *cherles* (working men, peasants) in the tales of the Miller, Reeve, Friar, Summoner, and, climactically, the Canon's Yeoman. Although we can know little about the historical realities of peasant speech, the widely shared belief that peasants were adepts in proverb use serves in Chaucer's fiction as a means by which the work's many aggrieved *cherles* challenge the clerical claim to a monopoly on wisdom and assert alternative sources of truth. A subtler dimension of the work's overt anticlericalism emerges when we note that a series of fictional churchmen imply or declare their possession of all the truths and all the knowledge that matters. The unusually broad social vision Chaucer adopts in the *Canterbury Tales* compels the poet, in giving voice to his *cherles*, to imagine what it would be like to be categorically excluded from the culture's highest wisdom. These fictional *cherles* use their proverbs to reveal and to contest their exclusion, championing the value of other forms of knowledge, other wisdoms.

Chapter 3 focuses on the *Wife of Bath's Prologue* and *Tale*, in which Chaucer draws a harrowing portrait of the harmful effects of antifeminist proverbs on women, also largely excluded from Latinate culture and clerical wisdom. The chapter offers something largely absent from the vast scholarship on the Wife's performance: consideration of its antifeminist proverbs *as proverbs*. The special powers of the proverb—its ready familiarity, apparent communal acceptance, and ability to name and transform situations—make it an ideally efficient instrument for asserting masculine superiority and containing the threat posed by recalcitrant women. But proverbs also provide strategies for challenging and resisting antifeminist *auctoritees*. Like Chaucer's younger contemporary, Christine de Pizan (1364–ca. 1430), the fictional Wife reinterprets antifeminist proverbs, reappropriates their abuse as praise, and wields proverbs of her own. Offering a fresh perspective on the tale that follows, I argue that the *Wife of Bath's Tale* features a feminine wisdom figure who models a healthier, less invidious form of proverb use than is practiced either by the battered Wife herself or by the clerks whose proverbs have demoralized her so deeply.

Chapter 4 addresses the *Tale of Melibee* and the intriguing question of why, in a fictional setting in which travelers on a pilgrimage entertain one another with stories, Chaucer includes this enormous proverb collection, closely translated from a French version of a sprawling 1246 Latin work by Albertanus of Brescia. Chaucer explicitly juxtaposes *Sir Thopas*, the only tale with no proverbial wisdom at all, with the *Tale of Melibee*, where over two hundred proverbs, the most of any tale, overrun a slender storyline. Judged as a story, *Melibee* is even more problematic than the parodic *Sir Thopas*, but once it is recognized that its proverbs are the main event and the framing story only secondary, it can be seen to offer instruction in how to use proverbs critically, advocating "free choys" for the reader in adopting or rejecting wise counsels (VII.1083). In the *Tales*, *Melibee* represents the riches of the international proverb tradition, Chaucer's great unsung source (unsung by modern critics but not by premodern readers), a trove of sayings ripe for reapplication elsewhere in the work, both in earnest and in game.

My conclusion addresses larger questions about the role of proverbs in Chaucer's poetic art. It takes up the pairing of the Monk's lugubrious lockstep tragedies with the universally admired *Nun's Priest's Tale*. While proverb use in the former consists largely of harping repeatedly on the same *moralite* about the untrustworthiness of Fortune, in the latter, widely recognized as the closest Chaucer comes to articulating his mature goals for his fiction, readers are famously enjoined, "Taketh the fruyt, and lat the chaf be stille" (VII.3443). From this revealing pairing, the proverb emerges as a potent tool that can provide vital support for an authorial viewpoint. At the same time, however, its capacity to pronounce with devastating brevity on what a story *means* can threaten to narrow and restrict the multiple significations carefully built up within Chaucer's fictions and deprive readers of some of the pleasure of discovering them. But by being given a plethora of contradictory proverbs, readers of the *Nun's Priest's Tale* are provided with the means to plumb a fiction's depths of meaning for themselves, equipped to exercise the "free choys" in proverb use advocated by *Melibee*. Thus, far from banishing "sentences and proverbes" as incompatible with the highest reaches of poetry, the *Nun's Priest's Tale* places them at the center of the liberating possibilities the *Canterbury Tales* extends to its readers.

CHAPTER 1

## PROVERBS AND PREMODERN READING PRACTICES

> [Proverbs] have a kind of magical character:
> they transform the situation.
> —WALTER BENJAMIN, "ON PROVERBS," 1932

Teased by a mischievous poetic speaker about the uselessness of maintaining a stone wall that serves only to separate apple trees from pines, the dour New England neighbor in Robert Frost's 1914 poem "Mending Wall" only says, "Good fences make good neighbors" (27).[1] Frost's speaker tries to trouble his neighbor into thinking about his proverb: "*Why* do they make good neighbors? Isn't it / Where there are cows? But here there are no cows" (30–31, emphasis in original). For the neighbor, however, the proverb is not something to think about, let alone think *with*, but rather an escape from thought:

> He moves in darkness as it seems to me,
> Not of woods only and the shade of trees.
> He will not go behind his father's saying,
> And he likes having thought of it so well
> He says again, "Good fences make good neighbors."
> (41–45)

His intellectual "darkness" is revealed not by his recollection of his father's saying but by his refusal to "go behind" it. Yet like the imagined neighbor, the poet, too, finds the proverb worth quoting twice. Frost was sympathetic to rural speech, and perhaps he was attracted by its rhythm and its simple but satisfying parallel construction. Nevertheless, its status as a prefabricated formula meant to substitute for thought and cut off discussion is clear. Thus, it illustrates one end of what was once a broad spectrum that extended from reductive truisms repeated by the unreflective to the distilled wisdom of the culture's most venerated writers and thinkers.

This chapter begins with the honorific end of this spectrum, the high value premodern audiences placed on proverbs and the circumstances that fostered their interest, followed by an explanation of the terminology adopted in this study. I then offer a theory of the work that proverbs were, and to a surprising degree still are, capable of performing. Drawing on Erasmus and some generative modern theoretical pieces—a relatively little-known but brilliant late essay by Mikhail Bakhtin, "The Problem of Speech Genres"; an equally brilliant aphoristic fragment, "On Proverbs," by Walter Benjamin; and some compatible thoughts on the proverb from a well-known essay by Kenneth Burke—I argue that, in Benjamin's words, the "magical character" of the proverb lies in its ability to "transform the situation."[2] Following a closer look at the goals of Thomas Speght's marking of "sentences and proverbes" in his 1602 edition of Chaucer's works, a final section previews the special contribution proverbs make to the celebrated generic variety and multivocality of the *Canterbury Tales*.

THE PREMODERN PASSION FOR PROVERBS

The cultural changes that led to the present jaded attitude toward proverbs began with a growing sense over the course of the eighteenth century that they were socially and stylistically "low," rather than, as had been held since classical antiquity, adaptable to all stylistic registers from lowest to highest. With its exaltation of individual creativity, the Romantic movement further eroded the proverb's status, as did the literary modernism of the early to mid-twentieth century, with its horror of cliché.[3] Along with our greatly increased literacy, the vast expansion of media resources now provides ready access to complete texts of whatever surviving works from the past we might like to consult, making individual readers less prone to spotting and storing up snippets of past wisdom. Print and electronic media stand ready to advise on everything from weather prediction to the raising of children. As a result, aside from rustic dialogue and ironic uses, proverbs are now rare in serious literary writing; they have migrated to advertising, journalism, social media, and ordinary speech, where they continue to flourish.[4]

Proverbs proliferated in a vanished world in which books were scarce and localized resources and a trained memory still served as an important means of retaining one's knowledge. Their sources were multiple. Ordinary people would have picked up vernacular proverbs from the spoken language, along with colloquialisms and idioms (with which proverbs sometimes overlap), proverbial phrases ("as meek as a lamb," "to roar like a lion"), and other features of their mother tongue. In addition, from antiquity onward, scholars carefully conserved fragments of prestigious texts, small but dense with meaning, for contemplation and reuse. These expressions of diverse origin served as the basis for early literacy training in Europe. Medieval and early modern children were taught to read Latin using proverb-centered works such as the *Distichs of Cato* and the *Liber parabolarum*; they spent much of their elementary school day translating Latin proverbs into the European vernaculars and translating vernacular proverbs into Latin. These bits of learning memorized and translated in the schoolroom joined anonymous expressions circulating orally and proverbs gleaned from Latin and vernacular literary sources to form the renewable corpus of shared wisdom that Chaucer's readers knew as *sentences* and *proverbes*; I address these terms in the next section.[5]

English schoolmasters varied the severely didactic sententiae derived from Latin works like Cato's *Distichs* with racier proverbs of the type also preserved in Chaucer's verse: "As the cok craws, the chikyn *herys* ['hears']"; "Bornt hand *fyr dreydis* ['fears the fire']"; "Far from the *ee* ['eye'], far from the hart"; "*Betwyx two stolys* ['between two stools'] *fals the ars down* ['the arse falls down']."[6] Premodern readers and writers imbibed large numbers of proverbs at an age when their ideas about literature were still in formation; small wonder that these expressions continued to play a significant role in their mature literary experiences. By studying fables paired with explicit morals, often couched in the form of proverbs, students were also trained to explore possible relationships between abstract statements of moral wisdom and fictional narratives that unfold over time, an experience certain to leave its mark on a future writer of poetic fiction.[7] In medieval England, where French was also a spoken vernacular, proverbs often had trilingual equivalents, and French poetry and French translations of Latin works helped to supply Chaucer with his generous stock of English proverbs.[8]

As we would expect given the proverb's centrality to premodern literary culture, what little direct commentary survives from Chaucer's early readers includes special praise for his proverb use. From the beginning, Chaucer's works were regarded as a valuable source of proverbial wisdom, and the surviving comments attest to the proverb-conscious reading practice implied by Speght's marking of proverbs. Chaucer's fellow poet John Lydgate admired his skill in amplifying his works "with many proverbe *divers and vnkouth* ['various and novel']"; another early disciple, John Metham, commended Chaucer in a mid-fifteenth century poem, "Amoryus and Cleopes," for writing "profoundely / Wyth many proverbys."[9] In his "Prohemye" to the *Canterbury Tales*, England's first printer, William Caxton, praised Chaucer's "short quyck and hye sentences," playing on the description in the *General Prologue* of the Oxford Clerk's speech as "short and quyk and ful of *hy sentence* ['elevated meaning']" (I.306). Caxton's praise also plays on the multiple meanings of Middle English *sentence*, which include reference to an individual wisdom expression, as in Speght's decision to mark "sentences and proverbes." Richard Brathwait wrote in 1665 an appreciative prose explication of the *Miller's Tale* and the *Wife of Bath's Tale* in which he makes a connection between Chaucer's sententiae and those in Erasmus's collection.[10] In an essay aptly titled "Proverbial Chaucer and the Chaucer Canon," Julia Boffey cites further evidence for the contemporary tendency to regard Chaucer's works as rich sources of proverbial wisdom.[11] In light of the many excellences of his poetry, singling out his proverbs for praise in this way seems simply benighted unless we ask what these readers saw in Chaucer's proverb use.

An invaluable resource for understanding the pleasure his readers once took in Chaucer's proverbs is Erasmus's 1508 introduction to the *Adages*. A recent editor describes this compelling essay as "a major theoretical statement, one of the most thorough discussions of the proverb up to that time in Western literature, even including those surviving from the ancients."[12] Despite the political and religious upheavals that mark the century between them, in regard to the proverb, Erasmus's thought world is close enough to Chaucer's to illuminate the poet's proverb use. Erasmus's understanding of the proverb was shaped by texts from classical antiquity, some of the most important also familiar to Chaucer, including the works of Virgil and Ovid and Horace's influential *Ars Poetica*. The deliberate daily mixing of Latin and vernacular proverbs in the premodern schoolroom meant that pupils from well before Chaucer's day through the time of Erasmus and beyond became familiar with both, and the interchange went in both directions, vernacular to Latin as well as Latin to vernacular.[13]

Many of the Latin proverbs Erasmus collected had—and still have—well-known vernacular equivalents, some with a surprisingly folksy sound in English: "to have one foot in the grave" (II.i.52), "to be in the same boat" (II.i.10), "to put the cart before the horse" (I.vii.28), "one swallow does not make a summer" (I.vii.94), "to be afraid of your shadow" (I.v.65), "blind leading the blind" (I.viii.40), "like father like son" (I.vi.33), "to look a gift horse in the mouth" (IV.v.24), "to teach an old dog new tricks" (I.ii.61), and, all too familiar to my own son, "many hands make light work" (II.ii.95).[14] A direct conduit into English from Erasmus's Latin was the much abridged and rearranged translation of the *Adages* by Richard Taverner that appeared around 1539. Compilations by John Heywood, *A Dialogue Conteinying . . . All the Proverbes in the English Tongue* (ca. 1549), and John Ray, *A Collection of English Proverbs* (1670, revised and expanded 1678), also helped to naturalize Latin proverbs in English.[15]

Erasmus's introduction to the *Adages* celebrates the proverb in ways that help us to understand why premodern writers prized it so highly. In contrast with our preconceptions about platitudes, he presents the proverb as an incisive intellectual tool: "An idea launched like a javelin in proverbial form strikes with sharper point on the hearer's mind and leaves implanted barbs for meditation" (16).[16] Among the ancients, he argues, "it was the most learned and eloquent who sprinkled their books most freely with adages" (11), mentioning Aristotle, Plato, Plutarch, and the wisdom books of the Hebrew Bible, among many other distinguished sources. Of the first proverb in his collection he writes, "Anyone who deeply and diligently considers that remark of Pythagoras 'Between friends all is common' [*Amicorum communia omnia* (I.i.1)] will certainly find the whole of human happiness included in this brief saying." These few words, he continues, encapsulate in memorable and readily reusable form the fruits of many volumes of Plato's philosophical writings; if humankind could truly be persuaded of this proverb's import, "war, envy, and fraud would at once vanish from our midst" (13). Another striking claim for the same expression: "Nothing was ever said by a pagan philosopher which comes closer to the mind of Christ" (29). As a result, "an ocean of philosophy, or rather of theology, is opened up to us by this tiny proverb" (14).

Hyperbole numbers among Erasmus's favored tropes, but the massive labor he invested in collecting proverbs and expounding on their meanings testifies that, while the language of his claims can be extravagant, they are made in earnest. Compiling, revising, and explicating the sayings in the multiple editions of the *Adages* consumed a substantial part of his career.[17] The result was a huge and much-pirated success, and its wide-ranging meditations on proverbs such as "Know thyself" (I.vi.95), "Make haste slowly" (II.i.1), and "War is sweet for those who have not tried it" (IV.i.1) show Erasmus acting on his insistence that proverbs must be pondered "deeply and diligently" if they are to yield their wisdom.[18] As we will see in chapter 4, in the thirteenth-century work that served as the model for Chaucer's *Melibee*, Albertanus of Brescia urges deep and studious reflection upon his own collected proverbs, and his Prudentia instructs Melibeus in how to go about it. Centuries later in the *Adages*, Erasmus presents the proverb as a compact yet vigorously expansive literary powerhouse: a sharp argumentative weapon, a spur to contemplation, the bearer of an "ocean" of philosophy and theology, a bridge from pagan antiquity to the mind of Christ, a source of stylistic fluency, and a key to winning the admiration and assent of ordinary people.

Like the best literature, Erasmus writes, the best proverbs are those that "equally give pleasure by their figurative colouring and profit by the value of their ideas."[19] He thus extends to the proverb the functions that Horace assigns to poetry; the idea that its purpose was to provide profit and pleasure gained widespread currency through a famous passage from the *Ars Poetica*.[20] That proverbs were seen as offering profit in the form of moral instruction comes as no surprise, but Erasmus also emphasizes the aesthetic pleasure they provide, especially through their unexpectedly deft use of metaphor, a capacity he calls *festivitas*.[21] Proverbs thus combine the concentrated essence of the two qualities specified by Chaucer's Host when he speaks of rewarding the teller of "tales of best sentence and moost solaas" (I.798). The primary meaning of *solaas* in Middle English was 'joy, pleasure, happiness'; its present primary meaning, 'consolation', also existed but was less common (*MED*, s.v. "solas"). With this echo of Horace's dictum that the purpose of poetry is to afford profit and pleasure, Chaucer announces his ambition to produce more than the diverting entertainment repeatedly demanded by the unreflective Host, aiming also for the deeper intellectual pleasures that Horace sought in poetry and Erasmus claims for the proverb.

Premodern readers left evidence of their passion for proverbs by marking them in books, compiling them into collections, and adding them to the eclectic gatherings of literary extracts, known first as *florilegia* and later as commonplace books, the height of whose popularity extended from the sixteenth to the late seventeenth centuries.[22] Angus Vine emphasizes that we should think of this premodern activity not as a simple mechanical process but rather as an active form of knowledge making: "Transcription was perceived at this time not only as a process of copying, but also as a means of organizing, reorganizing, and thereby improving knowledge and information."[23] Participating in a textual practice that went back to classical antiquity, Erasmus annotated proverbs in his own books as preparation for transcribing them into his collection. One of his marked-up volumes, a work by Athenaeus, is now in the Bodleian Library.[24] An anecdote from the *Adages* provides an entertaining and instructive glimpse into one of the motives that animated the premodern search for proverbs. Erasmus reports that he caught sight of a friend's copy of an immense Greek lexicon, an anonymous work called the *Suda*, "which had the proverbs marked in the margins." He begs to borrow it, if only for a few hours, so that a servant can annotate Erasmus's own copy. Surprised when his friend denies him a simple favor that would save him many days of work, Erasmus persists until, "like a man who confesses under torture," the friend finally explains: "Everything is now becoming public property from which scholars hitherto had been able to secure the admiration of the common people."[25] The friend's fears reveal not just his concern about losing his monopoly on a fertile source of proverbial wisdom for use in his own speech and writing but also his belief that proverbs provide a common ground between a man of letters like himself and the ordinary people he hopes to impress and persuade.

Erasmus's high regard for proverbs as sources of profit and pleasure was by no means an eccentric personal mania. So strong was the fervor for proverbs in late medieval and early modern culture that they escaped from the pages of literary works and proverb collections to become a form of interior decoration, appearing on walls, tapestries, plates, knives, sundials, and other varied and surprising surfaces.[26] In the fifteenth century, the walls of the Percy family homes at Leconfield and Wressle in Yorkshire were inscribed with elaborate programs of English proverbs and other brief texts. The manuscript that records these sayings and their former locations testifies that they were spread decoratively throughout the two houses and their garden structures.[27] Between 1563 and 1568, Sir Nicholas Bacon had the walls of the largest and most public room of his great house, Gorhambury, painted with Latin *sententiae*; these too have been preserved in a manuscript that offers some clues to their arrangement on the walls.[28]

Such décor doubtless served to proclaim to visitors the erudition and rectitude of the household. But in receptive minds, strategically placed proverbs could also promote the immersion prescribed by Erasmus, who recommended that a pupil being trained as an adviser to princes should frequently encounter maxims "carved on rings, painted in pictures, inscribed on prizes, and presented in any other way that a child of his age enjoys, so that they are always before his mind even when he is doing something else."[29] Indoctrination by means of even the most morally improving proverbs has its sinister side, as we learn in the *Canterbury Tales*, but their *festivitas*, their lighter role in amusement and play, is reflected in their voluntary inscription on rings and other personal items. Pictorially represented on a Flemish tapestry from around 1500 now in Boston's Isabella Stewart Gardner Museum is the proverb "Between two stools, the arse falls down."[30] Rather than admonishing its viewer to moral reflection or right action, this whimsical representation acknowledges human fallibility by showing a man who, unsuccessful at occupying two mutually exclusive positions at once, sprawls on his behind.

## WHAT WAS A *PROVERBE*?

Today we think of a proverb as an anonymous, familiar saying such as "Don't count your chickens before they hatch" or "The grass is always greener on the other side of the fence," but the medieval and early modern word *proverbe* had a broader frame of reference. Many modern scholars, especially those studying living traditions of proverb use, have sought a rigorous definition that would separate the proverb from all other verbal forms, but as Mark Meadow writes, "The distinction drawn today between proverbs proper and proverbial expressions, or indeed other linguistic figures, is not one supported by the original sources, and should be, if not dismissed altogether, at least set aside when considering pre-modern materials."[31] In dealing with premodern texts, an historicist approach guided by the judgments of contemporary witnesses seems to me more practical than an effort to arrive retroactively at an airtight formal definition. For the works of Chaucer, we have the manicules with which Speght marked "sentences and proverbes," designations often supported by Chaucer's own labeling of his proverbs and by inclusion in the Whitings' 1968 index, when accompanied by other instances of the same expression.[32] Speght is my premodern witness: with only a very few noted exceptions, the *proverbes* treated in this book are marked in his revised edition. I reproduce his manicules only in block quotations, and I sometimes specify that an expression is "Speght-marked" if its status as a "sentence" or "proverbe" seems questionable to modern readers, but unless explicitly noted, all *proverbes* treated here are "Speght-marked."

By describing the marked expressions in his 1602 edition as "sentences and proverbes," Speght acknowledges a difference between the two, but it is telling that he made no effort to sort one from the other. He uses the same pointing hands for all, clear evidence that he anticipated no need for Chaucer's readers to distinguish his "sentences" from his "proverbes" in their reception of his works. At their extremes, the two seem easily separable. What most moderns would recognize as a proverb, an unattributed, pithy expression still in oral circulation in English, such as Chaucer's "bet than nevere is late" (VIII.1410, L89), is not hard to distinguish from a "sentence," or "sententious remark," often a lengthy, florid quotation attributed to a well-known author. But between these extremes lie many examples harder to categorize, and premodern writers observe no consistent distinction between the two. For Chaucer, *sentence* is generally the more restricted term, often (but far from uniformly) applied to an expression from a named authority, such as Seneca, Cato, or the biblical wisdom books, as in the "sentence" cited by the Man of Law from Proverbs 15:15, "Yet of the wise man take this sentence: / 'Alle the dayes of povre men been *wikke* ['cursed']'" (II.117–18, D32).[33] *Proverbe* tends to be Chaucer's overarching category, equally applicable to an elaborate literary *sentence* or a pithy anonymous saying in wide circulation. The *Wife of Bath's Prologue* twice describes as a *proverbe* a saying attributed to Ptolemy's *Almageste*, a work whose textual status the speaker emphasizes (III.324–25, 328, cf. 182–83). That a *sentence* is also a *proverbe* in Chaucer's lexicon is neatly illustrated in the *Parson's Tale*, where one saying from the biblical book of Proverbs is called "the sentence of Salomon" (X.127) and another "the proverbe of Salomon" (155).[34] In Chaucer's usage, then, *proverbe* encompasses the often more restricted field denoted by *sentence* and extends over a much wider territory as well. Attempts to draw a bright line around the "proverb proper" move us away from premodern usage.

Reflecting the views of his day, however, Whiting's 1934 study sought to separate Chaucer's "popular" proverbs from his "learned" sententious remarks. Acknowledging that "it is sometimes very hard to distinguish between a proverb and a sententious remark, and I can scarcely hope that all readers will agree with all my decisions," he based his binary division on an expression's apparent origin, with its use raised only as a secondary possibility: "I consider as proverbs sayings which are, or appear to be, popular in origin, or which have become thoroughly popular in use, while sententious remarks show clearly their learned origin."[35] His desire for such a distinction shows the influence of nineteenth-century ideas about the proverb as the unschooled expression of a romanticized folk. In an article published shortly before *Chaucer's Use of Proverbs*, he writes that the proverb, "owing its birth to the people, testifies to its origin in form and phrase."[36] In the book itself he holds that the poet "loved and appreciated the rich pawky wisdom of the folk."[37] A scholar writing today would be wary of a distinction based so heavily on origins, especially when dealing with an ancient form like the proverb, subject to wide circulation in multiple languages, with and without attribution.

It is instructive in hindsight to see how Whiting's preconceptions about proverbs as the "wisdom of the folk" conflicted with his actual experience of Chaucer's *proverbes*, which appear in the poet's most stylistically elevated works and in dialogue written for his highest-ranking and best-educated fictional characters. To explain this contradiction Whiting wrote, "Chaucer's usage disproves the appealing but fallacious belief that because proverbs spring from the folk they are common in literature close to the folk and uncommon in more artistic flights."[38] The position that proverbs "spring from the folk" shows considerable strain when he points out that medieval rhetoricians such as Matthew of Vendôme and Geoffrey of Vinsauf "recommend the proverb highly as a fitting and artistic beginning or end for a literary work." At the end of his discussion of *Troilus*, he seems to abandon the folk altogether: "Neither here nor elsewhere does Chaucer regard proverbs as fitting wisdom for peasants and rustics. He feels that they add *ton* and a touch of sophistication to the characters who use them."[39] Whiting could not hold consistently to his theoretical distinction between expressions of "popular" and "learned" origin because all his data was telling him that no such line could be drawn in practice.

Shortly before the publication of *Chaucer's Use of Proverbs*, another foundational work, Archer Taylor's 1931 study *The Proverb*, had flatly declared that, as applied to the proverb, "obviously the distinction between 'learned' and 'popular' is meaningless." In support, he points out that Saint Jerome cites as a "common proverb" the expression "Don't look a gift horse in the mouth." But, he continues, "we cannot hope to discover whether the modern proverb owes its vitality to St. Jerome or to the vernacular tradition on which he was drawing."[40] To press Taylor's point a bit further, even if we could be absolutely certain that today's proverb "owes its vitality" to the writings of Jerome, if Jerome himself encountered "Don't look a gift horse in the mouth" as, say, an illiterate fruit seller's retort to a complaint about the bruises on a freely given pear, what does the label "learned" tell us about the expression's *origin*, despite its appearance in the writings of one of the greatest scholars of late antiquity?

As Taylor rightly saw, attempts to separate popular from learned expressions are doomed to frustration. One might guess that the folksy-sounding and still widely circulating phrase "to call a spade a spade" originated with a plainspoken working person, perhaps a habitual user of the implement in question. It happens, however, to be traceable to the classical scholarship of Erasmus, who erroneously took the Latin word *scapha*, a skiff or small dugout boat (from Greek *skaphê*), to refer to the digging tool in an expression along the lines of "calling figs figs, a skiff a skiff." In his edition of 1515, Erasmus changed *scapha* to the more familiar Latin word *ligo*, 'a spade'. Thanks to the enormous influence of the *Adages*, the proverb was adopted into English in the form we know it. Erasmus was also responsible for the switch from Pandora's *pithos* or jar, as the ancients had it, to the box, *pyxis*, we hear about today.[41] Whatever their origins, proverbs pass easily over boundaries of social class and educational level; in speech and in writing, they travel as readily as the prickly seed burs that stick to any passing fur or cloth and resow the original plant in unexpected new locations.

As Whiting's work with the proverb continued, he came to recognize that his attempted division between expressions of popular and learned origin could not be sustained in practice. In the introduction to the index, *Proverbs, Sentences, and Proverbial Phrases Mainly Before 1500*, that he and Helen Wescott Whiting published over three decades later in 1968, he dismisses with wry good humor the now-abandoned task of sorting "popular" proverbs from "learned" sententious remarks. In so doing, he also provides a brief but amusing glimpse of another foundational Chaucer scholar, George Lyman Kittredge: "In the field of popular and sententious wisdom, definitions and generalizations are harmless exercises in ingenuity and fallibility, but they belong, if anywhere, in an introduction and should not be permitted to limit the scope and usefulness of a collection. Mr. Kittredge was fond of quoting from a freshman of long ago who wrote, 'This casts a dark light on the subject,' and that remark is an appropriate epigraph for this and most similar discussions."[42] The cultural historian Roger Chartier warns persuasively against just this kind of fruitless quest for what he calls "the always illusory correspondence between a series of cultural artifacts and a specific socio-cultural level."[43] The "popular" proverb is elusive because the distribution of cultural products "is always more complex than it might seem at first glance, as are their uses by groups or individuals.... The 'popular' cannot be found ready-made in a set of texts or habits that merely need to be identified, listed, and described." Rather than pursue an illusory one-to-one correspondence between a cultural product and a user's social class or educational attainment, Chartier proposes that scholars instead study "differentiated practices and contrasted uses of the same texts, codes, or models."[44] The *uses* to which Chaucer puts his proverbs can be examined more profitably than their origins, and the chapters that follow explore these uses.

One further obstacle to the study of premodern proverbs also relates to overly limiting definitions and the illusory search for origins: the stipulation still current among some proverb scholars that to qualify as a proverb, an utterance must be "traditional" or "in circulation."[45] From the point of view of reception, however, an intrinsic problem with such definitions is that an individual who encounters a proverb for the first time is rarely if ever in a position to judge its prior circulation. Yet hearers and readers recognize and know what to do with newly encountered proverbs. Shirley Arora, an anthropologist who studied a living tradition of proverb use, posits that the "perception of proverbiality" is more important in shaping reception than an expression's actual prior history. On the basis of her fieldwork with Spanish-speaking residents of Los Angeles, Arora concludes that an expression, whether "traditional, or not—will function as a proverb, with all the accompanying weight of authority or community acceptance that the concept implies, as a direct result of the listener's perception, right or wrong, of its 'proverbiality.'"[46] Arora's fieldwork helps to explain the explicit verbal marking that premodern writers so often give their proverbs ("as the proverbe seith," "thus men sayth"), so useful in creating the "perception of proverbiality." Tom Shippey, a scholar of premodern literature, has coined a similar term, "proverbiousness," to describe a saying "which sounds like a proverb but which may arise from a particular occasion and have a known individual originator."[47]

Cognitive scientist Richard P. Honeck arrives by experimental means at a conclusion that supports Arora's fieldwork: when his researchers confronted subjects with made-up proverbs such as "Not every oyster holds a pearl," or "A net with a hole in it won't catch any fish," the subjects recognized the genre and, as a result, they knew how to interpret the expression; they did not, for example, look around for the oysters or damaged nets ostensibly under discussion. The language centers of our brains, Honeck argues, recognize and make sense of unfamiliar proverbs just as they make sense of other nonliteral utterances, including metaphors.[48] Our ability to recognize new proverbs may also stem from special intonation by their speaker. Proverbs are quoted or performed, not just spoken, and John Miles Foley describes the signals and cues that announce a speaker's entry into the "performance arena," an effect that carries over into written communication.[49] In keeping with Arora's and Honeck's evidence that an expression need not be "in common use" to be understood as a proverb, Shippey's coinage, "proverbiousness," also allows for expressions freshly minted by their speakers or newly excerpted from the flow of a longer written text. A portion of a longer text can become a proverb by virtue of this process of excerpting, especially when it is inscribed in a collection under a general heading such as "integrity" or "fortitude." Describing the "commonplace," a largely postmedieval term that falls under the wide umbrella of the *proverbe*, Jeff Dolven writes, "By virtue of having been picked out and recorded, those particular words can themselves now be recognized as a general case within which some aspect of our experience might fit—a place where that experience can be put."[50] Many proverbs possess formal features such as rhyme, alliteration, repetition, and parallel construction that help to make them memorable,[51] but equally or more important is the use to which a saying is put, and the hearer's or reader's recognition of that use. Once perceived as a proverb (or a sentence, adage, maxim, or commonplace), an expression can *function* as such, whether excerpted from a prestigious written text, in oral circulation for generations, or invented on the spot.

### WHAT PROVERBS (STILL SOMETIMES) DO

A measure of the proverb's hardiness as a verbal form is its survival into our own day despite our changed attitude toward formulaic language and our vastly increased access to knowledge, advice, and varieties of moral reasoning. Despite their decline in prestige, proverbs are still sometimes capable of powerful effects, even among sophisticated thinkers. They have persisted from the distant past into modernity in part because of the help they offer in transforming the dizzying variety of human daily experience into recognizable patterns so that individuals can act with more confidence or accept that a response would be futile. In texts of great antiquity such as the Hebrew scriptures, proverbs represent some of the first recorded attempts to impose order on human knowledge and experience. The numerical sayings in the Hebrew Bible exemplify these early efforts, "There are three things that never are satisfied, and the fourth never saith: It is enough"; "Three things are hard to me, and the fourth I am utterly ignorant of"; "By three things the earth is disturbed, and the fourth it cannot bear" (Proverbs 30:15, 18, 21).[52]

One of the most astute of modern thinkers at mediating the gap between the rhetorical culture inherited from antiquity and post-Romantic ideas about literature as individual self-expression is Kenneth Burke, who argues that not only do proverbs help to order and codify raw experience but like literature itself, they perform a variety of other significant actions, including consolation, vengeance, admonition, exhortation, instruction, and foretelling. Unworried by their lack of originality or their apparent verbal simplicity, Burke emphasizes the ability of proverbs to make things happen: "What I want is categories that suggest their active nature." He describes proverbs as "*strategies* for dealing with *situations*," and, as strategies, they support the attempts of a user to "*size things up* properly" or, if need be, to "change the rules of the game until they fit his own necessities" (emphases in original).[53]

For those without benefit of Burke's deep immersion in premodern rhetorical thought, the proverb's powers may need to be rediscovered experientially, perhaps through contact with a culture of active proverb users, as happened to the French literary critic Jean Paulhan in the early twentieth century. In an essay called "The Experience of the Proverb" written in 1913 and published in 1925, Paulhan expresses frustration that, although confident in his fluency in the local language after several years of living with a Malagasy family in colonial Madagascar, he nevertheless still struggles to master proverb use, a practice critical to credibility in speech and argument in Malagasy culture. He has come to recognize that proverbs represent a "special language" distinct from ordinary speech, and he has learned many proverbs, but when he tries to apply them, they seem "complex, manifold, difficult to boil down."[54] Most of the proverbs he cites in French translation appear straightforward in their wording, and their imagery is often drawn from universals of daily life. He finds them "complex" nevertheless, in the sense that they carry "too many unexpected meanings": "A piece of stone is stone"; "The cicada's voice is heard above the fields, but its body can be held in one hand."[55] The central mystery of the proverb for Paulhan is that, despite the unsettling multiplicity of possible meanings in advance of application, once an adept from the culture links a proverb to a particular situation, it instantly appears "natural, self-evident"; "The proverb's success depends upon this movement."[56] He ends the essay with the acknowledgment that he has succeeded only in describing the mystery, not in solving it.

In a brief but characteristically insightful journal fragment written around 1932, Walter Benjamin responds to the challenge posed by Paulhan's essay. In his own writings, Benjamin was drawn to proverbs and fables by their metaphor-like ability to give material form to abstractions.[57] He approaches Paulhan's problem by redefining it. Claiming that "proverbs cannot be applied to situations," Benjamin suggests that instead, "they have a kind of magical character: they transform the situation."[58] Paulhan's mistake was in trying to "apply" a proverb only in the very limited sense of matching it to a situation, and he was disappointed when no one from within the culture was impressed by what seemed to him perfectly successful matches. As Benjamin saw, Paulhan's Malagasy interlocutors give him no credit for a proverb that merely suits or describes a situation; the challenge is to find one that transforms it in some illuminating way, just as a well-chosen metaphor can alter our perception. Ideally, from a welter of expressions whose possible meanings seemed to Paulhan "manifold" and "difficult to boil down," a skilled proverb user chooses or invents one capable of transforming the situation in a way that rings true for adepts, one that not only inspires confidence that the situation has been correctly "sized up" (to return to Burke's language) but also enables an appropriate response.

Aphoristic in its compression, Benjamin's fragment asserts that a proverb "proclaims its ability to transform experience into tradition."[59] Cumulative human experience for Benjamin is a precious resource, access to which is endangered by the ruptures of modernity. His influential essay "The Storyteller," written a few years later, begins with the premise that with the decline of the traditional tale, a longstanding human capacity is now in jeopardy: "the ability to share experiences." The essay ends by asking whether "the storyteller's role does not consist precisely in reworking the raw material of experience." This question leads him once again to the proverb, the verbal form which perhaps "offers the best idea of this procedure." It, too, is diminished by modernity (a "ruin"), but like a traditional tale, the narrative it implies and the moral stance it encodes can rework a bewildering variety of "raw" experiences into shareable and enduring form: "A proverb, one could say, is the ruin that stands on the site of ancient stories and in it a moral winds around an attitude like ivy on a wall."[60] The power "to transform experience into tradition" may be as concise a description as possible of the most significant work that the proverb does: it transforms human experiences into a compact and communicable form that, by virtue of its recognizable genre rather than any prior history of use, wields the considerable authority of tradition.

Whatever the validity of Paulhan's report on Malagasy proverb use, it led Benjamin to offer an observation consistent in important ways with the more recent experimental findings of Honeck, the psycholinguist cited earlier. Benjamin's belief that the proverb "proclaims" or "declares" its own transformational ability speaks to its capacity for generic self-identification, the property that allows us to recognize a proverb when we hear or read one, even one newly coined or new to us. An imagistic or metaphorical proverb such as "One bad apple spoils the whole barrel" makes use of what Honeck calls its "vehicle," a realm of knowledge familiar to its user, often from personal experience, such as the effect that an overripe piece of fruit has on the fruit around it if not promptly removed. Familiarity with this concrete everyday reality enables the user to reason about what Honeck calls the proverb's "topic," often something much more elusive and abstract, such as fate, time, the vanity of human wishes, or, as the "bad apple" expression is customarily used, the potential for one misbehaving member to demoralize a whole group.[61]

Different as they are, the theorists cited here agree in locating a proverb's power in its capacity to connect an individual situation to an established image or pattern, producing a new level of confident understanding (Benjamin's "transformation" of the situation) that enables decisive action, cautious restraint, acceptance of what is, or some other fitting response. Thus, as Honeck posits, proverbs function as miniature theories, and as such, they are generative: they can be applied to an infinite number of new situations, and, once applied, they transform those situations. The "situations" can be as straightforward as observing a red sky at morning and taking precautions against bad weather or as complex as the moral decisions Burke envisions in claiming that proverbs serve the same functions as literature by providing "equipment for living." As Anne W. Stewart writes of the ancient sayings in the biblical book of Proverbs, "They prompt the student to engage moral complexity and acquire the capacity to negotiate the way of wisdom in everyday contexts."[62]

When proverbs move into fiction from speech in the world or from didactic writings, new questions arise, and I address some of these in the final section of this chapter. For the moment, a quick look at Chaucer's *Cook's Tale* will provide a stylized fictional representation of the process we have been discussing, in which a proverb transforms a troubling situation and enables confident action.[63] Chaucer represents the tale's master victualer as increasingly exasperated by the riotous behavior of his apprentice, Perkyn Revelour, until "atte laste," he thinks of a proverb that enables him to act:

| | |
|---|---|
| But atte laste his maister *hym bithoghte*, | thought |
| Upon a day, whan he his *papir* soghte, | apprenticeship document |
| Of a proverbe that seith this same word: | |
| ☞ "Wel bet is roten appul out of hoord | |
| Than that it rotie al the remenaunt." | |
| So fareth it by a riotous servaunt; | |
| It is ful lasse harm to lete hym pace, | |
| Than he *shende* alle the servantz in the place. | ruin |
| (I.4403–10, A167)[64] | |

As the application of the proverb in the last three lines indicates, the saying—another of Chaucer's proverbs still in use today—has transformed the situation to the satisfaction of the fictional master. By calling up his experience of rotting apples that threaten the remaining sound fruit, the proverb prompts him to dismiss his rowdy apprentice.

Incitement to action seems to be one of the perennial functions of the proverb. "Nothing ventured, nothing gained," is still heard today, and earlier versions of this saying abound in Chaucerian texts. In *Troilus and Criseyde*, Pandarus urges Troilus to venture with a version for lovers, "Unknowe, unkist" (1.809, U5). With this two-word saying—surely the minimum length for a proverb—Pandarus persuades the prostrated lover to stop lamenting over a woman who doesn't know of his passion and take the necessary action that could win him her kiss. After long and self-tormenting deliberation about the possible results of accepting Troilus as a lover, Criseyde's thoughts finally clear, and she arrives at a proverb closer to our modern version, "He which that nothing undertaketh, / Nothyng n'acheveth" (2.807–8, N146), and she resolves to take the risk. In his turn, her aggressive new suitor Diomede deliberates on how best and most efficiently to set his "hook and lyne" to "fisshen" Criseyde "into his net" (5.772–77). Like Troilus and then Criseyde, after a period in which he "goth now withinne hymself ay arguynge," that is, after his own period of internal debate, Diomede too finds his formula for action in yet another version of the same proverb, "he that *naught n'asaieth* ['attempts nothing'] naught n'acheveth" (5.772, 784).

In *Troilus*, versions of this proverb not only move its characters from internal debate to action but also raise questions about the poem's larger meanings. The last to see where events are headed, Pandarus in Book Four offers Troilus a version of a related proverb, "Fortune favors the bold" (or the brave, or hardy, F519): "Fortune . . . / Helpeth hardy man unto his enprise" (4.600–601). Versions of "nothing ventured, nothing gained" and "Fortune favors the bold" proliferate in *Troilus* because the poem ultimately asks its reader to question what of value can be gained by venturing, in love or in any human endeavor, when all is subject to betrayal by this "false worldes *brotelnesse* ['instability']" (5.1832).[65] In the *Canterbury Tales*, where the Reeve's fabliau recasts the tragic love triangles of *Troilus* and the *Knight's Tale* as darkly comic triangles of vengeful bedhopping, the student John is moved to action by yet another variant of our expression. Justifiably concerned that he will be the butt of a future comic anecdote if he fails to take bold action, John reminds himself that "'Unhardy is unseely,' thus men sayth" (I.4210, U3)—that is, "The 'unhardy' individual is unhappy (or unsuccessful)." Represented as urged on by the proverb, the character arises from his bed and takes the less-than-heroic risk of secretly moving a cradle so that his host's wife is misled to his bed. In these Chaucerian fictions, versions of "Nothing ventured, nothing gained" and "Fortune favors the bold" transform situations into choices between the possibility of reward and the near certainty of frustrated desire ("Unknowe, unkist"), moving their imagined users to act.

Another striking textual representation of the premodern proverb's transformational power comes from a near-contemporary of the *Canterbury Tales*, *The Book of Margery Kempe*, in which the protagonist expresses anxiety about a newly coined "proverbe" that threatens to redefine her identity in what seems to her an irrevocable, negative, and unjust way. Not long after converting to a strenuously Christian and self-denying way of life, Kempe dines at a house in her neighborhood and is later accused of having said at table, "A, thu fals flesch, thu woldist now etyn reed heryng, but thu schalt not han thi wille!"⁶⁶ That is, her neighbors charge that she rebuked her own body with the words, "Ah, you false flesh," accusing it of a desire to eat red herring, and then, they claim, she sanctimoniously denied herself even that ("you shall not have your will!"), even though this simple fare would have been permissible on a fasting day. They took her alleged speech of self-denial as hypocritical posturing, claiming that, while abstaining from herring, she showed herself perfectly willing to eat a better fish, "good pike." To her consternation, they continue to taunt her with the saying "Fals flesch, thu schalt ete non heryng," until with repetition, "it sprong into a maner of proverbe" against her.

Margery Kempe's fear is that, as a kind of *proverbe*, the taunt has the power to transform her devout observances into hypocritical posturing. She resists, not only with vehement denials that she ever spoke the words but also through the time-honored practice of fighting back with a counter-proverb of her own. She reports telling her detractors, "Ye awt to seyn no wers than ye knowyn, and yet not so evyl as ye knowyn" ['You ought to say no worse than you know, and not even as evil as you know'], thus generating her own "maner of proverbe" recommending generosity and benefit of the doubt in judging others. In narrating this portion of her book more than forty years later, the speaker remembers the mocking expression vividly and takes pains to discredit it in the minds of readers. As Rebecca Krug observes of this scene, "The *Book* takes the opportunity to reclaim the upper hand in relation to the power of proverbial language," and in so doing, its author "reclaims her right to define herself."⁶⁷

Two examples from our own day testify to the proverb's ability to transform a situation by placing it within a new set of parameters. The first involves an academic search, many decades ago, that yielded two finalists, one a fiery young woman whose obvious brilliance was matched by her rage at what she saw as unwarranted resistance in the academy to the kind of experimental work she did. The other was a steady candidate with all the right credentials and a book in hand from a prestigious press, a book that seemed to some in the hiring unit to lack an argument. The supporters of the "safer" candidate looked set to carry the day until someone cited a proverb, not from anonymous tradition but from William Blake's "Proverbs of Hell": "The tygers of wrath are wiser than the horses of instruction."[68] Although neither candidate ultimately assumed the position, once Blake's proverb was uttered, for the majority there was reportedly no going back to the previous view of the situation, no reviving the case for the "safer" candidate, even though the wrathful tyger-candidate still posed the same alleged risk.

A second example involves a public outcry aimed directly at a proverb's power to transform situations. It would be hard to think of a linguistically simpler construction than this near-tautology in words of one syllable, and yet the titles of the following journalistic pieces, posted between 2014 and 2016, speak for themselves: from the *Huffington Post*, "Stop Saying 'Boys Will Be Boys'"; from *Psychology Today*'s online site, "The Danger of 'Boys Will Be Boys': Why This Phrase Should Be Banned from Our Vocabulary"; and from the *Washington Post*, "Why We Must Stop Saying, 'Boys Will Be Boys.'" Writing in the *Observer* in 2016, Selena Strandberg warns that this proverb "carries with it significant, unacknowledged weight"; it "captures the root of gender inequality."[69] In the minds of those who seek to boycott or ban it, this proverb works to transform an instance of harmful masculine behavior into something excusable, or even somewhat loveable—it is just what boys do. Despite the decline in the cultural prestige of proverbs since the time of Margery Kempe, the expression's opponents share her view that its transformative power poses a threat. Erasmus would have understood the capacity these modern writers attribute to the proverb: "What could be more convincing, I ask you, than what is said by everyone? What is more likely to be true than what has been approved by the consensus, the unanimous vote, as it were, of so many epochs and so many peoples?"[70] If, despite its attenuated reputation, the proverb can still work its transformative magic for good and for ill in our day, we should not be surprised by the many ways an author could put it to work in texts created during its premodern literary prime.

## THOMAS SPEGHT, CURATOR OF CHAUCER'S PROVERBS

Schoolmaster and Chaucer editor, Thomas Speght merits our attention here for his stated belief that, if his wisdom expressions were left unmarked, readers of Chaucer would be left to search them out for themselves, and for his subsequent move to spare them that effort by flagging many hundreds of "sentences and proverbs" in his 1602 revised edition. Far less illustrious than Erasmus but sharing the great scholar's devotion to searching out proverbs in literary texts, Speght is best known to Chaucerians for initiating the practice of including a glossary of unfamiliar words in editions of the poet's works and for his authorship of "the most exasperating note ever written on Chaucer," in which he declines to explain the poet's allusions to the now-lost story of Wade and his boat on the grounds that "the matter is long and fabulous."[71] A subsequent impression of his revised edition was printed in 1687, in which asterisks at the heads of lines replace the marginal manicules of 1602. Contemporary scholars in university positions questioned a schoolmaster's qualifications for editing a great poet, but nevertheless, taken together, Speght's works remained the definitive edition of Chaucer for well over a hundred years.[72]

Despite letting down posterity by neglecting to tell the story of Wade and his boat, Speght remains a valuable witness to premodern engagement with Chaucer's proverbs. As Derek Pearsall writes, Speght was "intimate with Chaucer's poetry in a way that we, across many more centuries, can never be."[73] As an example of this proximity, Pearsall mentions the favorable account Speght provides of recent improvements at the Tabard Inn (Chaucer borrowed for his fiction the names of an existing Southwark inn and its innkeeper); according to the entry for "Tabard" in Speght's 1602 glossary, prior to these renovations, the Tabard of his day had fallen into a sad state of disrepair.[74] A prefatory letter to the 1598 edition by Francis Beaumont (a relative of the dramatist of that name) traces his and Speght's devotion to Chaucer back to their student days at Peterhouse, Cambridge, thirty years earlier, when a company of "aunceint learned men of our time ... did first bring you and mee in love with him." Another of Chaucer's great admirers, Edmund Spenser, was also in residence at Cambridge during these years. It would be fascinating to know more about how these "aunceint learned men" of the late 1560s and early 1570s kindled such ardor for Chaucer's poetry in a younger generation of scholars and writers.[75]

Scholars who comment on Speght's proverb marking associate it with other early modern efforts to emphasize Chaucer's erudition as evidence of the English poet's worthiness to succeed the great writers of antiquity.[76] The title of Speght's volume, *The Workes of Our Antient and Lerned English Poet, Geffrey Chaucer ...*, and its provision of a list of illustrious authors quoted by Chaucer both testify to this effort. Beaumont's 1598 prefatory letter defends what he calls Chaucer's "incivilitie" by citing racy passages from the works of the ancients, lest the medieval poet's bawdiness be thought an obstacle to the status of learned greatness.[77] Speght's highlighting of such high-minded lines in the *Miller's Tale* as, "For thus seith Salomon, that was ful trewe: / 'Werk al by *conseil* ['counsel, wise advice'], and thou shalt nat rewe'" (I.3529–30), might seem to us ineffectual as a distraction from other lines in the same tale, such as "at the wyndow out she putte hir hole" (3732) or "with his mouth he kiste hir naked ers / Ful savourly" (3734–35). But by reinforcing the attention that Chaucer draws to his *proverbes*, however ironic in context, Speght's annotations encouraged readers of Chaucer's fabliaux to notice the *sentence* to be found amid the scandal and the laughter. So firmly did Erasmus trust in the efficacy of marking proverbs as a means of directing reader response that he thought schoolboys could safely be given an unexpurgated text of Virgil's homoerotic *Second Eclogue*, so long as they were set the task of searching out its proverbs and sorting them into edifying categories.[78]

While many of Speght's pointing hands indicate learned quotations useful in building Chaucer's reputation for probity and erudition, examination of his choices reveals that this prevailing explanation of their function is only partial. Chaucer also drew upon the spoken language for his proverbs, and Speght marks many expressions with no claim to emanate from those prestigious *auctoritees* who could elevate Chaucer's reputation for learning. As an example, he marks the boast by the thieving summoner in the *Friar's Tale*, "I spare nat to taken, God it woot, / But if it be to hevy or to hoot ['I don't refrain from stealing, God knows, unless it is too heavy or too hot']" (III.1435–36, H316), a livelier version of today's expression about making off with everything that is not tied (or nailed) down. In the *Wife's Prologue*, along with many attributed *sententiae*, Speght marks expressions that work toward constructing the fictional speaker's rebellious spirit and contribute to the illusion of idiomatic speech, but do little to elevate Chaucer as a learned poet: "Yet koude I *make his berd* ['get the better of him']"; "as an hors I koude byte and whyne"; "in his owene grece I made hym frye."[79] The idiom "a twenty devel wey ['in the name of twenty devils']" also caught his eye (I.3713, 4257). Along with "sentences and proverbes" that reveal Chaucer's considerable learning, he also highlighted anonymous sayings notable for their metaphorical impact, or because they had become unusual by his day, or just for their interesting turns of thought or language. Like Chaucer's learned quotations, these expressions too can enlighten, but in ways that are entertaining and widely accessible. Committed as Speght was to elevating Chaucer's status, his markings also reveal that he was interested in proverbs for their own sake.

Detailed analysis of the placement of Speght's manicules has been sparse, but Pearsall and Clare R. Kinney both rightly judge that it reveals little selectivity on the editor's part. Pearsall writes that the placement of manicules in the *Nun's Priest's Tale* involves "no great sophistication," Kinney that the markings in *Troilus* ultimately fail as "an interpretive digest of the poem."[80] Kinney notes that Speght's markings take no account of Chaucer's ironic subversion of proverbial wisdom nor of the credibility of the character who cites it: he marks more proverbs spoken by the comic figure Pandarus than by the poet-narrator, for example. Further, some of the marked proverbs contradict one another, and Speght's annotation neglects the Christian turn away from the pursuits of this world at the poem's end. In noting the lack of sophistication and critical insight in the placement of Speght's manicules, however, both Pearsall and Kinney assume that his aim would have been to select critically those sententiae that support a holistic interpretation of the work in question, when his goal seems to have been simple inclusion. What Speght delivers is what is promised on the 1602 title page, "Sentences and Prouerbes noted." In a letter rededicating his revised Chaucer edition to Elizabeth I's minister Robert Cecil, he states more precisely that he has annotated "most of his Sentences and Proverbes." By allowing that he may have missed a few, he implies that completeness rather than selectivity was his goal.

While it seems reasonable now to assume that expressions singled out for the reader's attention must or should contribute to a coherent interpretation of the whole, this assumption stems from modern expectations about how meaning is built up in a literary text. Because premodern writers were taught to read and write with Latin proverbs, fables, exempla, and other forms that were often excerpted from longer texts and recombined, schoolchildren first experienced Latin literature as "an assemblage of separable quotations which were authoritative, morally loaded, and available for extraction and placing in appropriate contexts."[81] These initial experiences with literature treated as material for creative compilation would also color a reader's expectations of vernacular texts, as Kinney acknowledges in an apt description of Speght's proverb marking as an application to a vernacular work of "the ubiquitous humanist interest in quarrying the classical authors for fragments of detachable wisdom."[82]

With the acquisitiveness of a collector rather than the discretion of a modern literary critic or the single-mindedness of a publicist for Chaucer's extensive learning, Speght marked a variety of expressions potentially worth pausing over, pondering, or remembering, and he marked them as they came along, whoever the speaker and whatever the expression's consistency or credibility in context. A striking example is a proverb paraphrased by Whiting as "A Man may (not) sin with his wife and (nor) hurt himself with his own knife" (M154). In the *Parson's Tale*, minus the "not" and "nor," a version of the saying warns against the sin of lechery within marriage (X.859). In the *Merchant's Tale*, however, the self-serving January adds the negatives, twisting the proverb into the anti-doctrinal claim that lechery in marriage is no sin and the obviously counterfactual assertion that a man cannot hurt himself with his own knife (IV.1839–40). Direct opposites in their import, each is a version of a proverb, and from Speght, each receives its own impartial manicule.

One area in which Speght may possibly show some restraint, if it is at all intentional, is in marking antifeminist proverbs in the *Wife of Bath's Prologue*. They occur in long strings, and his method seems to be to acknowledge many but not all. Perhaps it is wishful thinking to imagine that encouraging the reader's careful attention to each and every scurrilous attack on women might have seemed a dispiriting prospect, even at the time. It is tempting to speculate that if, as it appears, Rachel Speght (1597–1661) was Thomas Speght's niece, he may have belonged to a relatively enlightened family. In 1617 Rachel Speght made common cause with Chaucer's Wife of Bath "and al hire secte" (IV.1171) by writing *A Muzzle for Melastomus*, a work that defends women from antifeminist attacks.[83] Another place where Speght leaves an occasional proverb unmarked is *Melibee*, where they occur so abundantly that every text column could be studded with manicules, defeating the purpose of singling out "sentences and proverbes" for special attention. But overall, in marking proverbs in the *Canterbury Tales*, he lives up to the promise on his 1602 title page that readers will find "Sentences and Prouerbes noted"—not critically selected but consistently noted.

Before we leave Speght and his pointing hands, I want to look briefly at the surviving evidence in support of his conviction that some appreciable portion of Chaucer's premodern readers would search out his proverbs for themselves in the absence of editorial annotation. In an illuminating study of readers' marks in sixteenth- and seventeenth-century folio editions of

Chaucer, Alison Wiggins describes Speght's proverb marking as evidence of a "thirst for Chaucerian *sententiae*" that began with reader preferences already present in fifteenth-century manuscripts and gained momentum in the sixteenth century, as the enthusiasm for commonplace books increased. She reports her findings: "Of the thirty-seven copies of folio *Works* of Chaucer examined for this study, nineteen have sententious or proverbial lines marked in some way, normally as part of a systematic programme in which an annotator has scrupulously worked through a section of the volume, marking selected lines with a particular symbol (such as a cross, a short vertical line, a three-leafed clover, or a stylized three-leafed clover in the form of a triangle of three dots)." Wiggins finds that, in particular, the *Wife of Bath's Prologue* and the *Tale of Melibee* (focal points also for earlier annotators of Chaucer manuscripts) were "highly valued as dense repositories of *sententiae*, proverbs, and memorable phrases," and both were "regularly annotated with dots, ticks, manicules, or clover leaves to indicate notable lines."[84] To these survivals, Betsy Bowden adds that she found proverbs marked by hand in a 1498 Wynkyn de Worde Chaucer in the Folger Library and in a 1526 Pynson and a 1542 Thynne edition, both at the Beinecke Library at Yale.[85]

Whether these annotators also copied their chosen extracts into handwritten proverb collections of their own is harder to answer since such early personal compilations rarely survive, unlike the large and costly printed Chaucer editions examined by Wiggins. One collection with extracts from Chaucer and other authors was compiled at the turn of the seventeenth century by Anne Bowyer, mother of Elias Ashmole, whose collection formed the basis for the Ashmolean Museum at Oxford. It isn't clear which Chaucer edition she read: the likeliest for her use circa 1600–1610 were Speght 1598 or 1602 or John Stow's edition of 1561. According to Victoria E. Burke, the expressions Bowyer transcribed overlap somewhat but not completely with those marked in Speght's 1602 edition.[86] As another form of premodern attention to Chaucer's proverbs, I mention here also William Painter's punningly titled *Chaucer New Painted* (1623), a versified collection of proverbs, very few of them from Chaucer, but set in a brief narrative frame in imitation of the *Canterbury Tales*.[87] Of Painter's appropriation of Chaucer's name for his collection, Louis B. Wright remarks, "The zest for reading proverbs out of Chaucer seems to have grown in the late sixteenth and early seventeenth centuries with the increase in popularity of all types of aphoristic learning."[88] "Zest" is a well-chosen word.

If the search for wisdom expressions on the part of premodern readers strikes us as a somewhat ruthless and reductive form of reading, perhaps for readers accustomed to seeking local, "compilational" meanings in the often meandering, episodic byways characteristic of much premodern literature, it would be the modern pursuit of a unified meaning across a whole work that seems ruthless.[89] The many proverbs that Chaucer repurposes from his own favored authors reveal that he too was a proverb-conscious reader, creatively ransacking earlier works for extractable wisdom and striking uses of language.[90] By systematically highlighting Chaucer's proverbs, however disparate or contradictory, Speght honors by default Chaucer's own practice of tossing out proverbs and leaving it to the reader to weigh them against his narratives, deciding whether they are ironic, conflicting, playfully misleading, or an effective shortcut to the heart of the matter at hand. By failing to guide readers toward a holistic interpretation of his own, Speght's indiscriminate markings leave readers free to choose for themselves, in keeping with the famous injunction at the end of the *Nun's Priest's Tale*, "Taketh the fruyt, and lat the chaf be stille" (VII.3443).

## THE PROVERB AS EMBEDDED MICROGENRE IN THE *CANTERBURY TALES*

The proverb is the smallest but also the most profusely represented of the many verbal forms that contribute to the celebrated generic variety of the *Canterbury Tales*. This chapter's final section takes a closer look at some ways in which proverbs support the work's complexity and multi-vocality. The proverb is a prime example of what I have elsewhere called embedded microgenres: that is, recognizable verbal forms capable of circulating on their own and yet short enough to appear in their entirety (or very nearly so) within the compass of longer works.[91] A comprehensive study of the microgenres in the *Canterbury Tales* might include charms, popular songs, elegies, orations, letters, and the many brief anecdotes and exempla embedded in its longer narratives, but none is as omnipresent as the proverb. The effects that Chaucer's proverbs achieve, they achieve by means of their recognizable genre, hence the importance of the "perception of proverbiality" discussed earlier. Chaucer's imagined storytellers and the speakers within their fictions often draw special attention to their proverbs, overtly framing them and explicitly identifying their genre: "Lat this proverbe a loore unto yow be," advises Pandarus (*Troilus* 2.397); "Therfore I wol seye a proverbe," announces the narrator of *The House of Fame* (1.289); the master victualer we saw in the *Cook's Tale* is stymied until "hym bithoghte, / ... Of a proverbe that seith this same word" (I.4403–5). "Wel may that be a proverbe of a shrewe!" exclaims the Wife of Bath in response to a misogynist expression (III.284). The Monk guarantees an expression's *bona fides*: "This proverbe is ful sooth and ful commune" (VII.2246). "Remembreth yow of the proverbe of Salomon," the Parson intones (X.155).

A particularly elaborate act of framing suspends the action of the otherwise briskly moving *Miller's Tale* as the Miller offers a *proverbe* to explain Alison's preference for the actively scheming Nicholas over the limply pining Absolon:

| | |
|---|---|
| But what availleth hym as in this cas? | |
| She loveth so this *hende* Nicholas | *courtly, possible play on 'handy'* |
| ☞ That Absolon may blowe the *bukkes* horn; | *buck's* |
| He *ne hadde* for his labour but a scorn. | *had nothing* |
| And thus she maketh Absolon hire ape, | |
| And al his ernest turneth til a *jape*. | *joke* |
| Ful sooth is this proverbe, it is no lye, | |
| ☞ Men *seyn* right thus: "Alwey the *nye slye* | *People say; nearby sly one* |
| Maketh the *ferre* leeve to be *looth*." | *Makes the faraway lover disliked* |
| For though that Absolon be *wood or wrooth*, | *crazed or angry* |
| By cause that he fer was from hire sight, | |
| This *nye* Nicholas stood in his light. | *nearby* |
| (I.3385–96) | |

After the first six quoted lines, which sum up the relative standings of the two aspiring lovers, Chaucer's fictional speaker devotes a full line to identifying the proverb's genre and affirming its truth: "Ful sooth is this proverbe, it is no lye." The next line adds the common Middle English proverb marker "Men seyn," ('people say'; a modern equivalent is "as they say") and guarantees accurate transmission by adding "right thus." The last three quoted lines walk the listener or reader through the proverb's application to the two rival suitors, the relatively distant Absolon and the live-in lodger Nicholas.

In this case, to borrow the words of Hans Robert Jauss, the proverb's primary function is to provide "retrospective insight into the unavoidable course of things"; its mode is "resignation or irony."[92] The proverb offers Absolon and others in his plight the consolation of popular philosophy: whatever his level of frustration (be he crazed or merely angry), experience shows that his losing out is simply how the world goes.

Although the teller assures us that "Men seyn right thus," we may of course question whether the Miller's *proverbe* actually circulated in this form. Consistently playful about his sources, Chaucer very likely made up some of the expressions he solemnly labels as old, wise, or common. In *Troilus*, he attributes the proverb, "The newe love out chaceth ofte the olde," to an otherwise unknown Zanzis "that was ful wys" (4.414–15). The Whitings' index locates two instances prior to 1500 of the Miller's expression about the advantage enjoyed by the lover who is nearer (S395): one in the passage in question and the other shortly thereafter in the *Confessio Amantis* (2.1899–902), the work of Chaucer's known reader and friend John Gower. Gower calls the expression an "old sawe," a term one sometimes hears used pejoratively today, as if it equates a proverb with a rusty old hand tool, but in Middle English it simply means 'an old saying'. As is so often the case, we cannot know whether Gower's use of Chaucer's expression offers independent testimony to its wider circulation, or whether he accepts it as a *proverbe* because Chaucer says it is. Whether Chaucer found or created this version of the widespread expression, "Far from Eye, far from heart" (E213, cf. E216), the effect is the same: the "perception of proverbiality," not the expression's often unknowable origins, confers its status as usable wisdom.

Three properties in particular make the proverb an especially valuable microgenre for embedding in longer literary texts: exceptional brevity, well-defined yet voice-permeable boundaries, and a self-contained completeness of meaning, the last a key property for opening up the text it inhabits to new perspectives and alternative worldviews. In her classic study of genre theory in the time of Erasmus, Rosalie Colie captures the central importance of the proverb's brevity: it "sums up a mass of experience in one charged phrase, demonstrating the community of human experience"; it "compresses much experience into a very small space; and *by that very smallness* makes its wisdom so communicable" (my emphasis). Its brevity and compression enable the proverb to offer in just a few words a miniature worldview, or what Colie calls "a 'set' on the world."[93] Using two modern proverbs to illustrate this capacity, Paul Hernadi observes that the saying

"Where there is a will, there is a way" implies a world "totally susceptible to human desires," whereas, in four words, the expression "Man proposes, God disposes" compresses an opposing worldview.[94]

In Chaucer's works, we have seen that Pandarus's "Unknowe, unkist" completes its reasoning and offers its incentive in just two words. As the fictional pilgrims approach Canterbury on a journey that Chaucer will soon begin to compare more openly to the journey of life, the Yeoman-narrator's proverb "Bet than nevere is late" (VIII.1410, L89) encapsulates in small a theology in which sincere repentance, accompanied by appropriate rituals, can open the path to salvation even in the believer's last moments. As Middle English proverbs go, two- to five-word expressions such as these are on the shorter side; sayings labeled as *proverbes* by their users in this period seem to have averaged somewhere between eight and twelve words long.[95] But even a *proverbe* of a dozen words is a very compact conveyance for what Erasmus calls an "ocean" of meaning and Colie "a 'set' on the world."

Those proverbs that achieve oral and written circulation in more or less the same form are able to hold their shape because their wording is brief and memorable but also thanks to a less obvious property, the well-defined and yet voice-permeable boundaries that separate them from the speech or writing around them. As part of the ambitious program outlined in "The Problem of Speech Genres," Bakhtin sought to expand genre theory to encompass the whole of human speech, oral and written, including "all literary genres (from the proverb to the multivolume novel)." I will pull only a few threads here from a complex work in progress that I have discussed elsewhere, but for our purposes, Bakhtin's essay offers the helpful concept of the "utterance," a speech act of any length, spoken or written, either freestanding or, when nested in a longer work, preceded and followed by a change of speaker.[96] It is easy for modern editors of literary texts to put quotation marks around a proverb because it is almost always perfectly clear where the quoted utterance begins and ends. Not only is it the real or imagined work of a different "author," the proverb also speaks in a different voice, distinct from the speech or writing that surrounds it. When a proverb is embedded in a longer written text, its fixed boundaries act almost as a tough shell, conferring on it the object-like quality that has stirred the acquisitiveness of collectors from antiquity to the present. Erasmus likens the difficulty of placing an adage well to the skill required "to set a jewel deftly in a ring." Concerning the proverb's value relative to its size, he asks, "What man of sane mind would not prefer gems, however small, to immense rocks?"[97] Their durable boundaries allow proverbs to circulate on their own, become embedded in longer written works, and then be mined back out again, often intact, by collectors, speakers, and writers.

Most proverbs possess firmly defined borders, and yet, as Bakhtin points out, when a proverb or other completed utterance is "absorbed" into a larger utterance, written or spoken, its "clearly delimited" boundaries remain in place but become porous and allow voices to flow through as if by a kind of osmosis.[98] For an example, we may return briefly to the proverb used by the narrating Miller to explain the respective success and failure of Alison's two lovers. How we hear the proverb "Alwey the nye slye / Maketh the ferre leeve to be looth" (I.3392–93) will depend in part on how we hear the narrating voice that cites it. How much irony leaks from the Miller's voice through the porous boundaries of the proverb, which purports to be a piece of timeless wisdom capable of explaining why one lover succeeds and the other is left to "blowe the bukkes horn"? Despite the totalizing explanation offered by the proverb ("*Always* the nearby sly one makes the faraway lover disliked"), the tale suggests something rather different. Nicholas's proximity is far from his only superior asset in Alison's eyes, and living outside his beloved's house is hardly the worst of Absolon's liabilities; the reader assumes he would fare little better even if the living arrangements were reversed. The voice of the narrating Miller flows through the proverb's boundaries and infuses it with irony, not just at the expense of Absolon, for whom its retrospective consolation could work only in concert with a large gap in self-knowledge about his charms as a lover, but also at the expense of the proverb's portentous dispensing of definitive wisdom ("Always"). The narrating Miller's send-up of the proverb reenacts in miniature his send-up of received authority in his response to the *Knight's Tale*.

The voicing of proverbs in the *Canterbury Tales* becomes even more complex when their users are speakers within the tales narrated by Chaucer's fictional pilgrims. "The worste" of the three riotous youths in the *Pardoner's Tale* cites a forerunner of today's expression, "Easy come, easy go," as a way of justifying his plan to squander the bushels of coins found under a tree: "lightly as it comth, so wol we spende" (VI.781, C384). The primary meaning of Middle English *lightly* in this context is 'easily' or 'readily', but the word can also connote a lack of moral seriousness, and the belligerent, swaggering voice of this "riotour" inflects how the reader hears the words of his proverb. In the mouth of a reputable speaker cheerfully resolving to spend an unexpected windfall in some generous, open-handed way, the import of the same proverb would be entirely different. In a multilayered fiction like the *Canterbury Tales*, the narrating voice of the Pardoner also permeates the boundaries of the rioter's proverb, "re-accentuating" it, to borrow another useful term from Bakhtin, with the Pardoner's own cynical voice.[99] This triple-voicing, involving the quoted proverb, the riotous youth, and the Pardoner-narrator, reminds the reader that, in addition to the youth's own negative qualities, the Pardoner's relationship to the choice between freely spending or hoarding money is wholly compromised by his vaunted practice of—while profitably preaching against—avarice.

The proverb's fixed boundaries contribute to a third key property: its self-contained completeness or finality, what is sometimes called its "stop the world" quality. The proverb is the example *par excellence* of what Bakhtin calls the "finalized wholeness" or the "special semantic fullness of value" of the completed utterance. If nested within a larger discourse in speech or writing, once an utterance is completed, when it has said everything it has to say, it "relinquish[es] the floor to another," enabling a response such as assent, demurral, silent reflection, or initiation of action in the world.[100] In his theoretical sophistication, Erasmus, too, recognizes this quality, citing it as one of the challenges of deft proverb use: "For every proverb stands by itself and for that reason must anyway be followed by a new beginning."[101] Cited above for its brevity, the Canon's Yeoman's expression "Bet than nevere is late" also exemplifies this related quality, a proverb's "finalized wholeness" or "special semantic fullness of value" (VIII.1410). The speaker uses it in an apostrophe to those who practice alchemy, urging them to give it up while body and soul are still intact. As a recognizable utterance imported from outside the fictional speaker's own discourse, the proverb has also accumulated meanings of its own, and its special "fullness of value" provides a kind of surplus that can be activated in the minds of hearers and readers. Especially given the late positioning of the Canon's Yeoman's performance in the fictional pilgrimage as its travelers near Canterbury, the proverb's five words serve not only to caution as yet unrepentant alchemists but also to offer the possibility of conversion and salvation to Christian readers contemplating the end of life's journey.

As a further illustration of the proverb's "fullness of value," we may take a short but proverb-dense passage from the *Knight's Tale* in which the Knight-speaker comments on the coincidence by which Arcite is overheard by his rival Palamon as he hides in the bushes and laments his unrequited love for Emelye:

> But *sooth* is seyd, *go sithen many yeres*,   truth; since many
>                                                years ago
> ☞ That "feeld hath eyen and the wode hath eres."
> ☞ It is ful fair a man *to bere hym evene*,    who can keep his
>                                                composure
> For al day meeteth men at *unset stevene*.     unarranged
>                                                appointments
>
> *Ful little woot Arcite* of his felawe         Very little does Arcite
>                                                know
> That was so *ny* to *herknen* al his *sawe*,   near; hear; speech
> For in the bussh he sitteth now ful stille.
> (I.1521–24, F127, M210)

The opening line ensures the "perception of proverbiality" through the assertion that we are about to hear a truth spoken over many years. The first proverb, "feeld hath eyen and the wode hath eres," is an outdoor version of the modern expression "the walls have ears"; it sets the stage for the proverb that follows by implying an inhospitable world in which spies watch the unsuspecting in open fields and eavesdroppers overhear them if they take cover in the woods.

In context, the second proverb, which concludes "al day meeteth men at unset stevene," conceives of mortals as involuntarily keeping appointments about which they have no knowledge. The *Knight's Tale* contrasts humanity's tragic ignorance with the knowledge possessed by indifferent pagan gods, and thus the proverb's "special semantic fullness of value" enables it to transcend its immediate context and contribute to the possible meanings of this long and complex tale. Given our modern preconceptions about what proverbs do, it is worth noting also that, like many of those we will encounter in this book, "al day meeteth men at unset stevene" is neither a stricture meant to regulate behavior nor a conventional piece of advice. Its philosophical pessimism makes it anything but a trite truism for Christian readers taught to believe in a divinely ordered, benevolent universe. It has the potential to halt this long narrative midstream and in seven words put forward a potentially destabilizing 'set' on the world, a proposition or miniature theory about the insignificance of human volition in the cosmos.[102]

In the chapters that follow, I hope to show that reading proverbially leads to the discovery of new patterns and emphases in the *Canterbury Tales* and raises significant questions about how *proverbe* relates to story, how it affects the multiple meanings layered within Chaucerian fictions. The special qualities of the proverb outlined in this chapter and Chaucer's skill in wielding it render this tiny microgenre potent, disruptive, and sometimes even incendiary.

CHAPTER 2

## THE RIVAL WISDOMS OF CLERKS AND *CHERLES*

The gretteste clerkes been noght wisest men.
—*Reeve's Tale*, 1.4054

If, as I argue in the previous chapter, premodern readers and writers engaged far more actively with proverbs than readers of our own day, then Chaucer's uses of these miniature verbal forms should repay closer attention than they have yet received. This chapter traces one pattern that emerges from a proverb-conscious reading of the *Canterbury Tales*: a rivalry between the condescending or even predatory wisdom of churchmen and the experiential knowledge of a series of aggrieved *cherles*, or ordinary working people, in the tales of the Miller, Reeve, Friar, Summoner, and, climactically, the Canon's Yeoman. I begin with a proverb central to this thread: "The gretteste clerkes *been noght* ['are not'] wisest men" (I.4054, C291).[1] The range of meaning of Middle English *clerk* extends from members of the Christian clergy and university students in training for positions in the Church to authoritative writers and well-educated persons in general, including even non-Christians such as Virgil or Cicero.[2] The lengthy, vehement refutation these seven words provoke from Bishop Reginald Pecock (ca. 1392–1460) testifies to the power premodern proverbs derived from their compression, memorable wording, capacity for transforming situations, and apparent communal sanction.

A look at the forcefulness with which Pecock attacks the users of this proverb will lay the groundwork for this chapter's central argument: as in Pecock's tract, in the *Canterbury Tales* proverbs fuel a high-stakes competition between two contrastive forms of wisdom, a rivalry in which more than a supper is at stake. In a rigidly hierarchical society in which advanced literacy education was limited primarily to its uppermost ranks, the proverb that incurs Pecock's ire makes what he calls the "presumptuous" suggestion that the wisdom possessed by clerks may not be the only, or even the highest, form of human wisdom.[3] Uttered by one of the least personable *cherles* in Chaucer's fiction, the irate and thieving miller Symkyn in the *Reeve's Tale*, the same proverb raises the same disruptive possibility: perhaps clerks do not possess the monopoly on wisdom to which they lay claim. Useful in persuasion and dispute, proverbs were also one of very few verbal forms important to clerical and court culture and yet also widely accessible to the large sector of the population with limited or no formal education. Proverbs in wide oral circulation could be acquired by anyone whose attention they caught. By means of orally delivered vernacular media such as preaching and forms of oratory, the learned transmitted proverbs from scholarly sources to the ears of those unable to read them. In the anecdote from the *Adages* related in the previous chapter, Erasmus's friend testifies that he impressed ordinary people with proverbs mined from a Byzantine lexicon in Greek. Given their accessibility to all disputants, proverbs could help to mediate relations among the different sectors of a hierarchical society. Almost since the time of the work's composition, Chaucer's readers have acknowledged the searching critique of the clergy mounted in the *Canterbury Tales*, but the key role played by proverbs in the turbulent relations it depicts between clerks and *cherles* has for the most part remained hidden in plain sight.

In the later fourteenth century when Chaucer was writing the *Tales*, representing the thought and speech of fictional *cherles* was still a novel undertaking. Proverbs offered a readily available and plausible means of bolstering the authority of fictional speakers from the politically fragmented assortment of ordinary people that made up the third estate. Originally applied to agricultural laborers in an earlier and economically simpler Europe, by Chaucer's day the "estate" or social order made up of "those who work" came to be defined negatively to include those who belong neither to the clergy nor to the nobility.[4] The proverbs Chaucer assigns to his fictional *cherles* provide their represented speech with a direct and recognizable link to the spoken language, and they contributed to his project of opening up a relatively narrow literary tradition to compelling new voices. People of all ranks and educational levels used proverbs, but they exert a special strength in situations of unequal power. It is a natural impulse to add authority to our speech by claiming that our opinions are widely shared, as when today's student protests that "*everyone* thought the exam was too long." As Pecock's indignant refutation reveals, proverbs perceived as coming up from the disorderly third order proved surprisingly threatening to members of the more established and stable orders above them.

## CONTESTING A PROVERB: *ARE* THE GREATEST CLERKS THE WISEST MEN?

The expression attacked by Pecock, "the greatest clerks are not the wisest men," may seem to us to lack the verbal novelty or mnemonic qualities that often separate proverbs from ordinary speech. But because clerical wisdom, broadly defined, was so nearly synonymous with wisdom itself, for medieval listeners and readers it would have registered more intriguingly as a near-oxymoron. If not the most learned, who then would be the wisest men? Readily dismissible if spoken by a lone voice from the third estate, this impugning of clerical wisdom is more arresting when pitched in communally validated words capable of wide circulation. Erasmus's rhetorical question bears repeating, "What could be more convincing, I ask you, than what is said by everyone?"[5] Attempts to dispute proverbs are vanishingly rare in serious modern writing. But in premodern controversy, arguing against a proverb provided an efficient means of contesting a deeply held cultural assumption, as we will see again in the next chapter when Christine de Pizan refutes an antifeminist proverb also cited by Chaucer in the *Wife of Bath's Prologue*.

Modern readers are understandably skeptical of the proverb's ability to encode significant cultural and political ideas; it arose from a way of thinking, reading, and remembering now largely lost to us. Because premodern textual practices put so much emphasis on retaining in memory the best fruits of one's reading, writers habitually drew upon "sentences and proverbes" as a means of preservation. "Trained memory," Mary Carruthers writes, "is a storehouse, a treasure-chest, a vessel, into which the jewels, coins, fruits, and flowers of texts are placed."[6] Erasmus has no qualms about arguing that the *Iliad*'s best wisdom about leadership is captured in memorable form by the two-word Latin proverb, "Festina lente" ('Make haste slowly'), an expression that appears twice in Chaucer, "The proverbe seith, 'He hasteth wel that wisely kan abyde.'"[7] Like the "greatest clerks" proverb, its verbal interest arises from apparent paradox. Erasmus finds in it "an agreeable touch of the riddle . . . made up as it is of contradictory words." "Festina," he explains, captures the active, courageous qualities of Achilles, who nevertheless proves himself too rash and headstrong to exemplify the good leader; "lente" signifies Agamemnon's more deliberative but overly cautious and unheroic leadership. The ideal, this playful essay suggests, lies in the mean between these extremes. Its tone is light, but it nevertheless reveals that in Erasmus's intellectual world, putting "Festina lente" to use as mnemonic shorthand for an important aspect of a venerated work does not demean the *Iliad*, nor does it overinflate the wisdom of a two-word proverb.

Around 1454, in a work of instruction called *The Folewer to the Donet*, Reginald Pecock, Oxford-educated Bishop of Saint Asaph, Wales, and then of Chichester, mounted a resounding attack on the proverbial claim that the "grettist clerkis ben not wisist men" (57.29).[8] Pecock intended the *Folewer* ("Follower," or sequel) for lay readers who had mastered the more elementary *Donet* (a grammar that takes its name from Donatus, author of a fourth-century Latin textbook). Pecock wrote the *Folewer* in English, for "lay men in *her owen* ['their own'] lay tunge," but he held that even books for laymen should be challenging, lest they become vain of their own understanding of the matters therein, and for the most part his argumentation follows the customary methods of scholastic disputation (7.32–8.21). Pecock's decision to air theological arguments in English was to prove disastrous in a climate in which vernacular theology was liable to charges of heresy; had he written in Latin, he might not have been forced to choose recantation, destruction of his works, and loss of his bishopric over execution.[9] He begins his attack on the offending English proverb by polarizing the debate, promising to use its rash speaker's own words to prove him "no wise man" but rather a "fool":

> Wherfore if I schulde here eny man seie that "grettist clerkis ben not wisist men" if perchaunce thei [the clerks] ben not prudentist men in tho gouernauncis whervpon goon . . . lawis of men, or thei ben not kunnyngist to wynne bi marchaundisyng, I kepte here

noon bettir thing of his mouth forto proue him no wise man but to be a fool, eer I schulde passe fro him if he wolde abide. (57.28–35)

[Wherefore if I should hear any man say that "greatest clerks are not wisest men" if by chance they [the clerks] are not the most prudent of men in administering . . . the laws of men, or they are not the cleverest at profiting by selling goods—I desire to hear nothing better from that man's mouth in order to prove him no wise man, but a fool, before I should leave him, if he would stay (to listen).]

As this passage indicates, Pecock considers lawyers and especially merchants among those most likely to subscribe to the objectionable position the proverb voices.

The gist of the bishop's logic is that, while a lawyer knows about law and a merchant about making profits, a clerk's knowledge concerns "highe, worthi, *digne* ['revered'] treuthis," the "methafisik of god and of aungels," to the extent that these divine truths can be known by mortals (55.12–13). Wisdom is hierarchical; he who has "grettist and worthiest wijsdom" is the wisest man (60.14–21), and therefore, *pace* the proverb, the greatest clerks *are* the wisest men. He adds an analogy to drive home the point: assume that three groups of men are rich, the first in precious gems, the second in gold and silver, and the third in sheepskins, leather, wool, and cloth (59.14–60.26). We would not consider the possessors of precious gems to lack wealth because they lack skins and cloth; on the contrary, the group with the most valuable commodity is richest of all, and thus their "highe, worthi, digne treuthis" make clerks richer in wisdom than those with less valuable knowledge. To supplement his formal proofs, Pecock also strikes back at his imagined opponent by a method more familiar to medieval lay audiences: he improvises a counter-proverb of his own, "the wisest merchants are not the wisest men" ("wijsist marchaundis ben not wijsist men," 58.22–23).

Even for the author of an earlier tract entitled *The Repressor of Over Much Blaming of the Clergy* (ca. 1449), the amount of space—roughly three and a half pages of fine print in the EETS edition of the *Folewer*—and the intellectual energy Pecock devotes to refuting this proverb is striking, as is his demeaning of the mental acuity ("kunnyng") of the hypothetical lay speaker: "Therfore if eny man schulde make this chalenge ayens clerkis, lete him be of more kunnyng than this *seier* ['sayer'] is" (59.12–13). Using one of his favored rhetorical figures, *gradatio* or climactic series, Pecock argues that those who presume to use this proverb to make this challenge against the wisdom of clerics

> schulden haue remorce in her conscience that thei euer spake thilk speche, beyng so vnwijs in it silf and beyng a speche so diffamose to her neighboris, and beyng so blasfemose ayens it which is the highest wijsdom of god in erthe, and schal perseuere in heuen into worschip of god, whanne the othire seid wisdomes schulen haue maad her eend here in this lijf. (60.38–61.5)

> [should have remorse in their conscience that they ever spoke that saying, being so unwise in itself and being a saying so defamatory to their neighbors, and being so blasphemous against that which is the highest wisdom of God on earth, which shall persevere in heaven in the worship of God when the other wisdoms mentioned have ended here in this life.]

This climactic series replicates the hierarchy deeply ingrained in Pecock's understanding of "wisdomes": first, the proverb itself lacks wisdom; worse, it slanders other people; and worst of all, it blasphemes God's own eternal wisdom as taught on earth by the clergy. The use of "wisdomes" in the plural in the final clause is revealing, however: it acknowledges more than one kind in this world, if not in heaven. Before wrapping up his lengthy refutation, so disproportionate to the size of the proverb that provokes it, Pecock refers the reader to another of his works, no longer extant, where "more herof is writun" (60.26). He anticipates the objections that he has spoken "*ouyr* ['over'] scharpli in this mater" (60.28) and at too great a length; on the contrary, he replies, he has spoken all too mildly and briefly, especially since he has never heard adequate arguments marshalled "ayens this so greet *defaut* ['offense']" (61.5–9).

Why does Pecock react so strongly? One obvious interpretation of the proverb is that the most accomplished scholars can be impractical in everyday matters. After many years in academic settings, I find this proposition hard to deny, but it is a relatively mild criticism. He first addresses this more benign application, stating firmly that a clerk can have as much "wordli prudence" as the next man (58.27), but he is uncharacteristically brief on this point, relying more on simple assertion than logical proof. If the claim is that all clerks lack this quality, "in greet nombre many *of hem ben and han be* ['of them are and have been'] excellentli prudent" (59.3–4). Defending clerks from the charge that they are impractical in the transactions of daily life is clearly not the site of Pecock's engagement.

Where the learned bishop puts his argumentative energy reveals that what is really at stake is a defense of the value and hierarchical status of the knowledge possessed by clerks, sole guardians of "the highest wijsdom of god in erthe." What ultimately motivates this long and vigorous refutation is surely Pecock's awareness of the proverb's implied communal acceptance and its transformational power: each repetition of this seemingly unremarkable saying reopens the possibility that "othire . . . wisdomes" rival the wisdom of clerks. Once the proverb broaches that idea, clerical wisdom no longer looks quite so unassailable. Pecock calls the "greatest clerks" proverb a "chalenge ayens clerkis," and, writing in the mid-fourteenth century, he was right to see challenges all around him to the clergy's claim to exclusive possession of all the wisdom that matters.[10] His forceful and protracted refutation acknowledges both the power proverbs can wield as a result of their claim to speak for the many and their uncanny ability to transform situations in ways from which there is little chance of going back.

In the textual world of the *Canterbury Tales*, where viewpoints are multiple and often in contest with one another, the "greatest clerks" proverb poses a hostile challenge to the preeminence of clerical wisdom. The angry and socially assertive miller Symkyn in the *Reeve's Tale* bears a striking resemblance to the "presumptuouse seier," the presumptuous proverb user whom Pecock seeks to refute (60.9). Symkyn cites the proverb to himself while resolving to outwit two Cambridge students and steal their grain:

| | |
|---|---|
| "They *wene* that no man may *hem* bigyle, | *believe; them* |
| ☞ But by my thrift, yet shal I blere *hir ye*, | *their eye, i.e., trick them* |
| For al the *sleighte* in *hir* philosophye. | *subtilty; their* |
| The moore *queynte crekes* that they make, | *ingenious tricks* |
| The moore wol I stele whan I take. | |
| ☞ In *stide* of flour yet wol I *yeve hem* bren. | *Instead, give them* |
| ☞ 'The gretteste clerkes been noght wisest men,' | |
| As *whilom* to the wolf thus spak the mare. | *once* |
| Of al hir art counte I noght a *tare*." | *weed* |
| (I.4048–56) | |

As the last two manicules replicated here from Speght's 1602 edition help to emphasize, Chaucer pairs the "greatest clerks" proverb with another proverbial expression, a resolution to give the hapless scholars the bran—here the worthless outer husks—instead of the good flour milled from their grain. By having a miller use the proverb in reference to actual grain, Chaucer puts an amusingly literal twist on a saying that is often metaphorical, as when the Wife of Bath expresses regret that, having passed the prime of youth, the good flour is gone and she is left to sell the bran (III.477–78, F299). In Symkyn's speech, the proverbial bran sustains its connection to the world created by the plot, a nice instance of Chaucer's capacity to reanimate the familiar imagery found in proverbs.[11] The effect is enhanced by another image of worthless plant matter in the last quoted line, the tare or weed that Symkyn evokes in his hostile valuation of the "art" or clerical training of the scholars (from Latin *ars*, 'a craft, skill, or body of knowledge'). In this fictional situation, Chaucer combines the "greatest clerk" saying with the proverbial images of worthless husks and weeds to accomplish just what Pecock accuses this proverb of doing: in a memorable verbal form, it challenges the preeminence of clerical wisdom.

As in Pecock's *Folewer*, in the encounter Chaucer imagines between Symkyn and the clerks in the *Reeve's Tale*, it sounds at first as though Symkyn evokes the more innocuous application of the proverb, as if his point were simply that the tale's two scholars are babes in practical dealings—"lat the children pleye" (I.4098). But the simplicity of university students in worldly matters might be expected to gratify rather than infuriate a miller bent on cheating them. Like Pecock's vehemence, the anger Chaucer depicts in the fictional Symkyn reveals that here too more is at stake. Symkyn resolves to outwit the two clerks despite "al the *sleighte* ['subtlety'] in hir philosophye" (4050). His use of the "greatest clerks" proverb is of a piece with his mocking invitation to the students to use their sophistical logic to distort reality by proving his house much larger than it is so that it can accommodate them more comfortably:

> "Myn hous is *streit*, but ye han lerned art;     *narrow*
> Ye konne by argumentes make a place
> A myle brood of twenty foot of space.
> Lat se now if this place may suffise,
> Or make it *rowm* with speche, as is youre *gise*."     *roomy; custom*
> (4122–26).

The openly competitive words spoken earlier by Symkyn confirm that the clerks' "art"—their clerical training—is the target of his hostility: "Yet kan a millere *make a clerkes berd* ['outwit a clerk'], / For al his art" (4096–97).[12]

To complete this contextualization of Symkyn's "greatest clerks" proverb, one further example from outside Chaucer's work demonstrates the politically charged use of this saying as a check on clerical folly. A long verse epistle in rime royal stanzas was written in 1487 or 1488 in the name of John Butler, Mayor of Waterford, and its citizens, addressed to the Archbishop of Dublin, Walter Fitzsimons. This pro-Tudor poem rebukes the archbishop for failing to intervene when a Dublin priest crowns a boy, described as an organ-maker's son, as King of Ireland, an open act of rebellion against Henry VII. It urges the archbishop, and by extension the Irish clergy in general, to heed the wisdom of the common people and put an end to this dangerous act of insurrection:

> Retourne ones, and forsake this folie,
> If anie there be revolved in your mynd;
> Correct yourself, amend it shortlie,
> And to your soveraigne lord be not unkind:
> The people tongues no man can bind.
> In such cases they saie, now and then
> The best clearkes be not the wysest men.[13]

Making explicit the claim to widespread assent conferred by a proverb's genre, these verses assign this saying to the irrepressible voice of the people, whose "tongues no man can bind." In the *Reeve's Tale*, Pecock's *Folower*, and this verse letter, rather than a truism or platitude, the proverb in question is better described as a flashpoint.

Of these three applications of the "greatest clerks" proverb, only Chaucer's speaker identifies it as the *moralitas* of an Aesopian fable by adding the words "As *whilom* ['once, long ago'] to the wolf thus spak the mare."[14] This attribution to an ancient literary source reminds us again of the impracticality of a binary division between popular proverbs and learned *auctoritees*, especially on the basis of origins. Extant in varying versions and languages, the fable features a horse or mule who, in response to a threat of humiliation or harm, persuades a predator—a lion, fox, or wolf—to seek information written on its hoof, with which it gives the predator a sharp kick. The morals that accompany the surviving versions of the fable differ, but all assert the unwisdom of the tale's literate predator: "not all who can read are wise."[15]

For premodern readers familiar with some version of the fable, Symkyn's angry *moralitas* calls up the image of a domesticated beast (a longstanding image for a peasant) who delivers a kick in the head to an educated but unwise predator (foxes and wolves served as images for a corrupt clergy). Not only does Chaucer's evocation of the fable amplify with violent imagery his fictional peasant's resentment toward the two clerks, it also joins that resentment to a larger cause, the critique of a corrupted clergy that preys on the third estate. This charge is especially evident in the clerical portraits in the *General Prologue*, where even the portrait of the idealized Parson serves as an opportunity to contrast this figure with clerics who neglect pastoral care in favor of ease or personal gain (I.507–14). Despite its utterance by the unsympathetic *cherl* Symkyn, the "greatest clerks" proverb carries a surplus of meanings that allow it to transcend its immediate context and to encapsulate a provocative claim to which the larger work repeatedly returns.

Through the perspective Chaucer creates for Symkyn, the reader sees how clerks trained in logic spark the anger of *cherles* by presuming to use their "argumentes" and "speche" to remake the physical world to their own specifications (I.4123, 4126). This perspective is of course only one of many on offer in the *Canterbury Tales*. Chaucer's works leave no doubt about his veneration for the learning acquired and conserved by clerks, and in the broadest sense of the word, Chaucer *was* a clerk. But by adopting a fiction in which socially diverse narrators tell their own stories, the *Canterbury Tales* presents competing wisdoms from competing perspectives, as against Pecock's fixed and hierarchical view from above.

Chaucer's campaign for the recognition of multiple wisdoms begins in the *General Prologue*. For the word itself, the *MED* (s.v. "wisdom") records essentially the same wide range of meanings we give it today, including sound judgment, sharp wit, spiritual enlightenment, practical knowledge, and the sage advice transmitted by proverbs. Just as the *General Prologue* exposes the inadequacy of the old feudal "three estates" model of clergy, knights, and peasants by presenting an array of occupations that reflect the social and economic complexity of late medieval England, so it demonstrates the insufficiency of a single model of wisdom. Even comic or ironic applications of Chaucer's vocabulary of knowledge and wisdom help to expand the hierarchical definition articulated by Pecock. Readers new to Middle English often notice the abundance of verbs of knowing in the *General Prologue*, the many forms of *knowen, kunne,* and *witen*. Nearly all its pilgrims are characterized in part by what they know and what they know how to do. Knowledge gleaned from scripture and from ancient *auctoritees* figures in the portraits of the Clerk, Monk (negatively, as what he spurns), Man of Law, Physician (who knows many books but not *the* Book), and Parson.

Many portraits, however, feature experiential knowledge, not all of it morally admirable. The expression "Wel koude he" is formulaic in the *General Prologue*: "Wel koude he *dresse his takel yemanly* ['care for his gear in a yeomanly manner']" (I.106); "Wel koude he *in eschaunge sheeldes selle* ['benefit from monetary exchange']" (I.278); "Wel koude he kepe a *gerner* ['granary'] and a bynne" (I.593). The Miller's and Cook's portraits offer ironic twists on the "wel koude he" formula: in the case of the Miller, "Wel koude he stelen *corn* ['grain'] and *tollen* ['charge for it'] thries" (I.562). In the Cook's portrait, the description "Wel koude he knowe a draughte of Londoun ale" (I.382) appears at first to refer to his occupational knowledge as a judge of good local drink, but later developments suggest that he has known personally all too many drafts of ale, all too well (IX.25–68). The Friar's experiential knowledge is also transgressive, at odds with his vocation: "Wel koude he" sing and play worldly entertainments that include "yeddynges," or narrative songs, and he knows taverns, innkeepers, and barmaids in every town (I.236–37, 240–41); similarly, the Summoner knows the secrets of the youths of his diocese (I.664–65) and how to trick someone ("Ful prively a fynch eek koude he pulle," I.652).

Chaucer describes the experiential knowledge of the five guildsmen as a form of wisdom: each of them "for the wisdom that he *kan* ['knows']" is equipped to hold a responsible position in the administration of the city (I.371). The Manciple is "wise in byyng of vitaille," so wise in his purchasing of provisions that his "*lewed* ['uneducated'] mannes wit" fraudulently surpasses "the wisdom of an heep of lerned men" (569, 574–75). The Wife of Bath, whose proverb-wielding is the subject of the next chapter, is Chaucer's leading challenger of the sententious clerical discourse I will refer to as "high Solomonic wisdom"—her prologue famously begins with the word *experience* set in opposition to learned *auctoritee*.[16] Her portrait in the *General Prologue* ends with a surge of knowingness born of experience: she "*koude muchel* ['knew a great deal'] of wandrynge by the weye," "Of remedies of love she knew per chaunce," for "she koude of that art the olde daunce" (467, 474–76). The "art" of the "old dance" describes the knowledge she has gained over the course of five marriages and other company she kept in youth, knowledge of the age-old rhythms of courtship and conflict between the sexes.

Thus the *General Prologue* undermines the opposition between the "lewed mannes wit" demonstrated by the Manciple and "the wisdom of an heep of lerned men" attributed to the lawyers he serves. It does so by demonstrating the many shades, degrees, and varieties of wit and wisdom, reputable and disreputable, found in the portraits of its "lewed" pilgrims as well as in clerical portraits. The superficial parroting of the language of scholarship by the purportedly "lerned" also complicates this opposition: the Prioress, who might be expected to possess some Latinity, engages with the liturgy only deeply enough to intone it in a seemly fashion (I.122–23); the Friar similarly pronounces his "In principio" very pleasantly (254); and, capping this series of superficial voicings, the Summoner, when drunk, roars out the Latin legal phrases he hears in court with all the comprehension of a talking bird (635–46). What the Pardoner knows how to do is to enrich himself by preaching sermons against avarice, "as he ful wel koude" (713), while the idealized Parson, a "lerned man, a clerk" (480), grows rich in holy thought and work but remains poor in material earnings, serving an institution depicted as rewarding its corrupted representatives and impoverishing the devout. To his scholarly learning, the Parson adds practical knowledge of how to subsist on the scarce means left from his meager income after his practice of Christian charity: "He koude in litel thyng have suffisaunce" (490).

The interaction, overlap, and rivalry in the *General Prologue* among different wisdoms serves as prelude to the varieties and sources introduced in the rest of the work, including the diverse wisdoms encoded in the work's "sentences and proverbes." Unlike Aristotelian logic, canon law, or what Pecock terms the "methafisik of god and of aungels" (55.13), proverbs could be wielded by "lerned" and "lewed" alike. In the *Canterbury Tales*, they speak for powerful institutions and for those who challenge them. Like Chaucer's framing narrative, the pilgrimage itself, the proverb too provides a plausible way of fictionalizing debate and fraternization across lines of class, gender, and religious vocation in a culture committed to permanent hierarchies of persons and of knowledge.

## PROVERBS AS PEASANT WISDOM

Little can be known about the historical realities of peasant speech, but in representing it within his fictions, Chaucer draws upon a longstanding belief that common people were adepts in proverb use and especially receptive to persuasion by means of them.[17] Although I follow custom in using modern English *peasant* and Middle English *cherl* interchangeably, it is worth noting that *peasant* is barely attested in English before the sixteenth century. English writers including Chaucer tended to group common or working men under the heading of *cherles*, including prosperous tradesmen in towns and cities as well as the rural laborers suggested by the word *peasant* (from Old French *païsant*). Medieval sources subscribe to at least two conflicting stereotypes about the language of *cherles*: their accomplished use of proverbs contrasts with an opposing vision of their speech as scarcely more articulate than the sounds of beasts.

The Rising of 1381 with its haunting specter of "the cherles rebellyng" (I.2459) occasioned fearful and derisive portrayals of the language and behavior of those held responsible for the revolt. Descriptions in Latin depict the insurgents as *rustici*, although historians have shown that a great many of them were not agricultural laborers from the country. Contemporary accounts of the Rising are particularly condemnatory of peasant speech.[18] To the ears of John Gower's dreamer in Book I of the *Vox Clamantis*, it seems that these supposed peasants "bray in the beastly manner of asses, some bellow the lowings of oxen. Some give out horrible swinish grunts ... and fierce barking weighed heavily upon the air of the city as the harsh, angry voice of the dogs flies about. The hungry fox wails and the cunning wolf howls into the air and calls together his runningmates.... Behold the loud din, the wild clangor, the savage brawling—no sound was ever so terrible before."[19] The chronicler Thomas Walsingham describes the shouting of *rustici*: "No words rang out amidst their horrifying clamour, but their throats bellowed forth all kinds of noises, or, to tell the truth, sounds more like the diabolical cries of peacocks."[20] Chaucer too employs—or parodies—such images in the *Nun's Priest's Tale* when its narrator compares the raucous barnyard sounds made by the pursuers of the fox who has captured Chauntecleer to the "hideous" noise made by the rebels of 1381 (VII.3375–401).

These negative representations of peasant speech are the most heightened of examples because the writers are reacting to what they perceive as rebelling peasants, but an admirably balanced study like Paul Freedman's *Images of the Medieval Peasant* shows how commonly even the ordinary, nonrebelling *rusticus* was portrayed by his contemporaries as a creature of beast-like stupidity or rapacity, his words heard only as meaningless noise.[21] As noted, these outright denials of mental life or expressive speech in *cherles* coexist with their contrastive reputation for proficiency in generating and using proverbs, and the storytelling *cherles* constructed by Chaucer's texts are of this latter variety, practiced wielders of proverbs. We saw in the previous chapter that B. J. Whiting's early attempt to distinguish the sayings of ordinary people from those of the highly learned was ultimately not feasible in practice and later abandoned, but the *belief* that peasants were sources, carriers, and audiences for proverbial wisdom has a very long history in Western culture. Anticipating Chaucer's proverb-citing *cherles* by well over a millennium and a half, Aristotle's *Rhetoric* notes that "rustics especially are fond of coining maxims and ready to make display of them."[22]

The authors of classical antiquity recognized a category of "rustic" proverbs, expressions thought to be coined or favored by rural agricultural workers, as when Livy describes the expression "Don't be an ass in a ditch," as "a saying that then became a rustic proverb [*rusticum prouerbium*]."[23] The *Etymologies* of Isidore of Seville (ca. 615–635), a major conduit for classical learning to the Middle Ages, offers this explanation for the proverb "Lupus in fabula" (The wolf [is] in the tale): "Peasants [*rustici*] say that a person would lose his voice if he saw a wolf in front of him. Thus the proverb, 'the wolf in the story,' is said to someone who suddenly falls silent." When Chaucer's contemporary, John Trevisa, renders this explanation in Middle English, he translates *rustici* as "churles."[24] *Cherles* would have learned proverbs from the speakers around them, just as they learned the idioms of their mother tongue, as well as coining their own—there was of course no dedicated fund of peasant wisdom for them to draw upon—but the *idea* that peasants possessed and could skillfully apply wise expressions intrigued and was useful to highly educated writers, including Chaucer.

The association between proverbs and peasants enjoyed considerable currency in medieval Europe, as is evidenced by the titles of collections such as *Proverbia rusticorum* and *Li Proverbe au Vilain*. In the latter, a French work of the twelfth century, each stanza is followed by a proverb and the refrain, "Ce dit li vilains" ('so the peasant says'). A fourteenth-century German legal document cited by Archer Taylor instructs pleaders before juries: "Whenever you can attach a proverb, do so, for peasants like to judge according to proverbs."[25] A scurrilous but eloquent wielder of proverbs is the fictional peasant Marcolf, who emerges victorious from a proverb contest with King Solomon in the versions of *The Dialogue of Solomon and Marcolf*, a multiform work apparently in circulation by the twelfth century or earlier, but now extant only in Latin and vernacular texts of the fifteenth and sixteenth centuries.²⁶ Chaucer never mentions Marcolf, but a casual reference to him in a poem by his younger contemporary, John Lydgate, suggests that the peasant's competition with the biblical patriarch was well known in Chaucer's England. Lydgate's poem complains of fools who climb into "chaires of worldly dygnyte . . . Marcolff to sitt in Salamonis *see* ['seat']."²⁷ Many traces of Marcolf's reputation survive in medieval English texts and pictorial representations, including references in the thirteenth-century *Proverbs of Hendyng*, where Hendyng, a fictional speaker of proverbs, is identified as "Marcolves sone." An English poem written by John Audelay around 1410–26 adopts the persona of "Marcolf the fool" in order to voice some sharp criticisms of church and state.²⁸ Whether the English writers and artists who allude to Marcolf before the appearance of the extant texts were familiar with earlier versions of the *Dialogue*, or whether he was simply known to them as a peasant victorious over Solomon in a proverb contest, either way Marcolf's reputation for success in competing against the ultimate avatar of proverbial wisdom is a prime example of the widespread association between peasants and skilled proverb use.

*The Dialogue of Solomon and Marcolf* also merits attention here because it depicts, in more starkly polarized form, a simpler version of the rivalries I am tracing in the *Canterbury Tales*, a struggle over what constitutes wisdom and whose wisdom matters. Helen Cooper has called the *Dialogue* "a powerfully suggestive analogue to Chaucer's methods in the *Tales*," and indeed the competitive exchange of tales across class lines in Chaucer parallels the contests in the *Dialogue* between peasant and patriarch, who exchange proverbs, riddles, and other verbal forms.²⁹ In the *Dialogue*, Solomon's proverbs touch upon many of the major themes of the biblical wisdom books from which the majority of his contributions are drawn: wisdom and foolishness; marriage and the nature of women; goodness and evil; truth and falsehood; the raising of children; the importance of keeping good company; and the benefits of modesty, moderation, industriousness, and patient acceptance of hierarchies. Drawing on his native wit alone, Marcolf must answer to all this established wisdom.

Marcolf's proverbs are an eclectic mix that includes parodic versions coined in direct mockery of Solomon's wisdom, proverbs in wide circulation, and a miscellany of other kinds of remarks.³⁰ The longest versions of the work run to about 140 exchanges of *proverbes*, broadly defined, as in Chaucer's usage of the term. On their own, Solomon's contributions to the proverb contest in the *Dialogue* can seem diffuse and obvious: "Go thou not wyth the evyll man or the brawelyng, lest thou suffre evyll for hym or peryle" (60a); "If thou make frendeshipe with a false and evylwylled man, it shal hyndre thee more than proffyte" (61a). On their own, many of Marcolf's contributions seem gratuitously repellant: "As a man wypyth his ars he doth nothing ellys" (26b); "He that etyth radyssh *rotys* ['roots'] coughyth above and undyr" (34b); "So whan the hownde shytyth, he berkyth noth" (57b).[31]

When these two contrastive discourses are juxtaposed, however, each reveals what is lacking from the other:

> 15a Solomon: "He that sowyth wyckydnesse shal repe evyll."
> 15b Marcolf: "He that sowyth chaf shal porely mowe."
> 19a S: "In an evylle wylled herte the spyryt of wysedome shalle not entre."
> 19b M: "As ye smyte with an axe in an hard tre, beware that the chippes falle not in youre *ye* ['eye']."
> 24a S: "Honoure is to be *yeven* ['*given*'] to the maistre, and the rodde to be feryd."
> 24b M: "He that is *wonte* ['*accustomed*'] to anointe the juges handes oftyn tymes he makyth his asse lene."
> 56a S: "Lete us ete and drinke; we shall alle deye."
> 56b M: "The hungery dyeth as wele as the full fedd."

In its abstract moral idealism, Solomonic wisdom often overlooks the body with its needs, appetites, and vulnerabilities, many of which weigh heaviest on those with fewest material resources, as Marcolf's most pointed rejoinders testify. In the exchanges above, Solomon speaks from the perspective of the judge and the well-fed; Marcolf speaks for the accused who starves his pack animal in order to pay the judge a bribe and for the hungry with no means to feast away the sorrows of mortality. As selectively represented in his dialogue with Marcolf, Solomon's proverbial wisdom comes to seem overly narrow, prescriptive, and lacking in compassion. The rival wisdom offered by Marcolf's proverbs merits a hearing, not because it refutes or displaces Solomonic wisdom but because, in the words of Natalie Zemon Davis, it "had a claim to tell some of the truth"; like Solomon and Marcolf, peasants and clerks "shared the same speech form—the proverb—and none had an absolute monopoly on wisdom."[32] The same can be said of the contrastive pairing that initiates the *Canterbury Tales*: the *Knight's Tale* offers elevated and moving philosophical ideas while the Miller—like Marcolf an advocate for the material body—trades on its physical pleasures and indignities, names its parts and functions bluntly, and asserts the validity of an alternative view of the human condition.

To be clear, I am not proposing "Solomonic" and "Marcolfian" proverbs as fixed categories—I am not bringing back Whiting's attempted dichotomy between learned sentences and popular proverbs in new guise. Rather, aside from the biblical proverbs repeated by Solomon, these designations depend upon context, on who utters the proverb and what work it does; on its *use*, not its origin.[33] Although the multiform *Dialogue* appears to have had numerous authors and accretions over the centuries—Davis makes the plausible suggestion that its exchanges may once have been played as a game, a kind of flyting or insult match[34]—Marcolf was likely a clerical creation, at least in part. Indications include the work's composition in Latin, its evocation of academic disputation, and the technical skill and familiarity with scripture revealed in Marcolfian responses that closely and scurrilously parody Solomon's biblical proverbs. These responses, about a fifth of those offered in the longest Latin versions of the contest, are carnivalesque mock-proverbs, not sayings that circulated among historical peasants, as in this example, in which Solomon's contribution echoes Ecclesiasticus 12:2:

> 138a Salomon: Benefac justo et invenies retribucionem magnam; et si non ab ipso, certe a Domino.
> [Do good to the just, and you shall find great recompense; and if not of him, assuredly of the Lord.]
> 138b Marcolphus: Benefac ventri et invenies eructuacionem magnam, et si non ab ore, certe a culo.
> [Do good to the belly, and you shall find great belching, and if not of the mouth, assuredly of the arsehole.][35]

By no means, then, can the imaginary peasant speaker's assortment of responses be identified literally with peasant speech, but among its varied sources, it draws upon a rich store of internationally circulating proverbs, many of which articulate positions resistant both to abstraction and to authority.[36] Bakhtin compares Marcolf to another fictional peasant, Sancho Panza, who counters the literary idealism of his knightly interlocutor, Don Quixote, with proverbs that serve to bring "the conversation down to a strongly emphasized bodily level of food, drink, digestion, and sexual life."[37]

The *Dialogue*'s proverb contest remains as open-ended as the contest for the supper in the *Canterbury Tales*. Solomon declares that he cannot go on: he represents an older, fixed, and authoritative discourse that is running out of viable precepts. Marcolf declares victory, but he has not vanquished Solomon's wisdom, only shown himself unexpectedly equal to improvising indefinitely in answer to it. Both speakers live on past the end of the *Dialogue*, as do the rival wisdoms they stand for. After Marcolf tricks Solomon into an unwelcome close-up view of "hys arshole and alle hys othre fowle gere" (63, 24.8), Solomon condemns him to hanging but rashly grants him the right to choose his own tree, and Marcolf can never find just the right one. As with Chaucer's paired tales, the paired *proverbes* of Solomon and Marcolf allow the contributions of both to take on meanings more complex in their juxtaposition than either could generate on its own. In Bakhtin's words, "A meaning only reveals its depths once it has encountered and come into contact with another, foreign meaning: they engage in a kind of dialogue, which surmounts the closedness and one-sidedness of these particular meanings, these cultures."[38] In "Speech Genres," Bakhtin makes this claim for all smaller genres embedded within larger ones, and it seems to me especially useful for understanding the various kinds of work that proverbs do in the *Canterbury Tales*. As the *Dialogue* does consistently, Chaucer at time uses Solomonic proverbs to suggest the "closedness and one-sidedness" of clerical wisdom, and his *cherles* use a miscellany of proverbs of their own to "surmount" or subvert it.

## "WHAT MAKE YE SO MUCHE OF SALOMON?"

In the fictions of the *Canterbury Tales*, a "heep" of learned clerks use proverbs in attempts to deceive, denigrate, or control *cherles* and women. Peasant and female figures use their own proverbs to argue back against the proposition that human wisdom is a closed, prescriptive, and disembodied system available only to the clerical and seigneurial figures represented by Solomon. The Hebrew Bible describes Solomon as "wiser than all men," and as a measure of that vast wisdom, he spoke three thousand proverbs (3 Kings 4:31–32).[39] Although the persistence of Solomon's presence throughout the *Tales* is not always noted, in *Melibee* and the *Parson's Tale* alone, he is cited by name some *sixty* times, and as I argue in chapter 4, a Solomonic proverb is central to *Melibee*'s unfolding and resolution. Eleven of Chaucer's twenty-four tales attribute proverbial words of wisdom to Solomon by name, and he is implicitly present in many more as the source of unattributed quotations from the biblical wisdom books, which were widely credited to his authorship in the Middle Ages.[40]

In some settings, especially the profuse citations in *Melibee* and the *Parson's Tale*, Chaucer's "Salomon seith" follows from his sources and serves simply to attribute a proverb to a preeminent authority. In other generic contexts, however, Solomon takes on more life and bears some resemblance to the imperious but ultimately somewhat hapless figure who contends with Marcolf in the *Dialogue*. In Chaucer, the kind of sententious wisdom Solomon personifies is authoritative in many of its applications but attracts opposition when it becomes repressive and threatens to eclipse other forms of knowledge. In the *Canon's Yeoman's Prologue*, to which we will return, clerical wisdom is explicitly identified with Solomon, in the guise of an overweening Canon, and it is deplored by a beleaguered *cherl*. When those pressed into the practice of alchemy by the Canon are all together, "Every man semeth a Salomon" (VIII.961), but their wisdom is ultimately folly. The Yeoman has at hand a stock of relevant proverbs, including this one, endorsed by "clerkes" themselves, to identify the problem with his master's wisdom:

| | |
|---|---|
| He is *to wys*, in feith, as I bileeve, | *too wise* |
| ☞ That that is overdoon, it wol nat *preeve* | *turn out* |
| *Aright*, as clerkes seyn; it is a vice. | *Well* |
| Wherefore in that I holde hym *lewed and nyce*. | *ignorant and foolish* |

(644–46, E203)

A man with "over-greet a wit" often misuses it, he continues, "So dooth my lord" (649–50). From the perspective of this Chaucerian *cherl*, the clerk who is too wise ends up more "lewed" and foolish than his servant.

What unites the *Dialogue of Solomon and Marcolf* and the *Tales* is the dynamic of *quiting*—not vanquishing but rivaling, matching, and paying back—that underlies both. As the *Miller's Tale* does not invalidate or replace the *Knight's Tale*, so Marcolf's counter-truths do not banish or disprove Solomon's proverbs; rather, they relativize them by disputing their claim to universality and revealing that they come from a particular perspective. Some of the Solomonic precepts that Marcolf counters—"Work all by counsel," "All things have their time"—recur throughout the morally serious literature of the Middle Ages, including the works of Chaucer.[41] Familiar today in the King James translation "To everything there is a season," the saying "All things have [their] time" ("Omnia tempus habent," Ecclesiastes 3:1) can be resonant and comforting in the right setting, but it can also be irksome and easily satirized, according to the context, the skill, and the audience awareness with which it is used. In *Troilus*, for example, Pandarus shares some traits with the overly sententious Solomon of the *Dialogue*. In a moment of emotional urgency—the distraught Troilus has just compared himself to a man told to wait patiently while he is hanging by the neck—Pandarus counsels him that "every thing hath tyme" (2.985–89). This ill-timed Solomonic advice leads the reader to sympathize with Troilus's earlier protestation: "thy proverbes may me naught availle" (1.756).[42] Irony in *Troilus* at the expense of Pandarus' sententiousness is mild, however, compared to the sharpened exchanges in the *Canterbury Tales*. Chaucer presents Troilus and Pandarus as near-equals in social terms, and their conflict lacks the hostility that eventually builds between Solomon and Marcolf or the anger that sparks between clerks and *cherles* in the *Tales*.

The Solomonic proverb "all things have their time" works across class lines in the *Tales* when an urban member of the third estate, the Host of the Tabard Inn, appropriates it to rib the pilgrim Clerk about his mirthless silence: "I *trowe* ['believe'] ye studie aboute som *sophyme* ['specious argument']; / But Salomon seith, 'every thyng hath tyme'" (IV.5–6). A *cherl* less jovial than the Host, the pilgrim Merchant attributes the same expression to "clerkes" and uses it sardonically to comment on how quickly May's affections are transferred from her lecherous old husband January to the attractive young Damian: "For alle thyng hath tyme, as seyn thise clerkes" (IV.1972). Chaucer's most entertaining subversion of this quintessential piece of high Solomonic wisdom comes in the *Friar's Tale*, where the speaker is not a *cherl* but the "feend"—the devil himself—though initially mistaken by the tale's summoner for a "yeoman" or common man (III.1457). Demonstrating the proverbial truth that the devil can quote scripture, the "feend" uses Solomon's proverb to postpone answering the summoner's impatient questions about how exactly he goes about entrapping unsuspecting souls: "Seyde this feend, 'but alle thyng hath tyme'" (III.1475). All in good time this summoner, portrayed as a corrupt official of a corrupted Church, will learn firsthand more than he ever wanted to know about hell and damnation. The placement of one of the best known of Solomonic proverbs in the mouth of the devil shows us the Marcolfian side of Chaucer's proverb use, countering and cutting down to size (*quiting*) but not refuting or replacing the serious evocations of Solomonic wisdom found elsewhere in the same work. The remainder of this chapter shows how *cherles* in the *Canterbury Tales* deploy proverbs to strike back at condescending clerks and assert rival wisdoms of their own.

PROVERBS AND THE REPRESENTED SPEECH OF *CHERLES*

In the tales told by the Miller, Reeve, Friar, Summoner, and Canon's Yeoman, we meet *cherles* who are cynical, angry, or highly distraught, in no mood for condescending streams of high Solomonic wisdom. Like Marcolf and the hypothetical merchant rebuked by Pecock, Chaucer's fictional *cherles* use *proverbes* to challenge the position that clerks possess the culture's "grettist and worthiest wijsdom" and to open up fresh perspectives and worldviews. Some of these expressions are very likely Chaucer's own coinages, but they are understood as proverbs because they are labeled or clearly used as such (the "perception of proverbiality" adopted in the previous chapter). Many others are identifiable as expressions in wide circulation.[43] Those that Chaucer imports from outside the *Tales* possess their own independent lives, histories, and ideologies, and they contribute to his ambitious effort to encompass a social vision far broader than was attempted by the majority of writers of his day.

    The speech of *cherles* does not make a subtle entrance into the *Canterbury Tales*. In his urgent haste to *quite* the *Knight's Tale*, the Miller bursts into the storytelling contest, shouting and swearing by Christ's arms, blood, and bones. He defies the Host and loudly refuses to await his proper place in the hierarchy of tellers (I.3120–33). The reader has already been primed to appreciate this rebellious peasant and the risqué tale to come. At the end of the *General Prologue*, Chaucer's fictional narrator stresses his responsibility to represent truthfully every word of every speech of each teller:

| | |
|---|---|
| Everich a word, if it be *in his charge*, | *his responsibility* |
| *Al speke he* never so rudeliche and *large* | *Although he speaks; freely* |

> Or ellis he *moot* telle his tale untrewe,     *must*
> Or *feyne thing*, or fynde wordes newe.     *falsify things*
> (733–36)

A few lines later, readers of this passage in Speght's 1602 edition could follow a pointing finger to a much-discussed proverb on artistic representation that Chaucer attributes to Plato but drew from his own proverb-conscious reading of Boethius's *Consolation of Philosophy*: "The wordes moote be *cosyn* ['cousin'] to the *dede* ['deed']" (741–42).[44] On one level, the saying purports to justify the bluntness involved in reproducing the language of those who speak "rudeliche and large." The poet's obligation is to repeat the tales as told, representing faithfully the speech of *cherles*. This tongue-in-cheek disclaimer—no author of fiction is forced to represent the direct speech of *cherles* or anyone else—at the same time suggests genuine concern about the constraints of decorum or established precedent that might lead a writer to "telle his tale untrewe" (735).

This seminal *proverbe* linking word to deed brackets the whole work as we have it by its repetition near the end in the *Manciple's Tale*, where its speaker also uses it to vindicate "knavyssh" or vulgar speech (IX.205) and amplifies it with another version linked more directly to the art of storytelling: "If men shal telle proprely a thyng, / The word moot cosyn be to the werking" (IX.207–10). It affirms the mature work of a poet credited, for example, with being the first English writer to imitate regional accents in the represented speech of fictional characters.[45] That the "lewed" Manciple (I.574), a self-described "boystous man" ('plainspoken, unlearned, crude', IX.211), apparently possesses sufficient learning to cite the "wise Plato" (IX.207) reminds us that "cosyn to the dede" represents a medieval standard of verisimilitude, not the literal contract to which writers of realistic fiction are often held today. It reminds us also that Chaucer's authorial voice can freely override the voices of his ostensible speakers, and it calls attention to new challenges facing an author whose innovation in the *Tales* includes extended representations of peasant speech.[46]

Because John the carpenter in the *Miller's Tale* is the first of many *cherles* to speak within the pilgrims' tales and because Chaucer's text constructs him as a surprisingly distinctive speaker, I examine the role of proverbs and related microgenres in his represented speech in some detail. Chaucer makes a point of the status of the tale's fictional storyteller: "The Millere is a cherl; ye knowe wel this" (I.3182). Given this emphasis, a perennial question is why

Chaucer creates a rebellious and sharp-dealing Miller who refuses to defer to any "bettre man" but then assigns to him a fabliau featuring a naïve *cherl* easily duped by a clerk. The "sentences and proverbes" exchanged between the two—Solomonic and imperative on the clerk Nicholas's side, docile and devout on John the carpenter's—point to a possible explanation. The tale's polarization of clerk and *cherl* is emphatic: for example, Chaucer's audience would not assume high educational attainment in a carpenter, even a wealthy one, but the narrating Miller nevertheless calls attention to John's lack of formal schooling. While the clerk Nicholas is introduced as the possesser of a copy of Ptolemy's *Almageste*, a relatively arcane astronomical tome, the *cherl*, by contrast, enters the tale as someone who "knew nat Catoun, for his wit was rude" (3208, 3227). John's unfamiliarity with Cato's *Distichs*, an elementary book of versified Latin proverbs, calls out his lack of progress into the Latinate world of clerical knowledge. A Speght-marked *proverbe* spoken by Nicholas draws attention to the tale's one-sided wisdom contest between clerk and *cherl*: "A clerk hadde *litherly biset his whyle* ['used his time poorly'] / *But if* ['unless'] he koude a carpenter bigyle" (3299–300).

A key part of the tale's preparation for its uproarious conclusion is Nicholas's proverb-assisted persuasion of the carpenter to vacate his marriage bed and spend the night in a wooden tub, in expectation of the return of a flood God promised would never come again. John's credulity also extends to accepting that, in preference to everyone else alive, God will allow his clerical lodger to save only himself, the carpenter, and the carpenter's wife. According to Speght's markings, in sheer numbers the "sentences and proverbes" spoken by John and Nicholas in this short tale are evenly matched at three each. The carpenter's three proverbs point up the contrast between his knowledge and that possessed by Nicholas. Two of them warn against what John sees as impious attempts by Nicholas to foresee the future, prying into the foreknowledge that is God's alone: "Men sholde nat knowe of Goddes pryvetee" (I.3454, G198), and "blessed be alwey a lewed man / That noght but oonly his bileve kan," the latter a blessing upon a "lewed" man who knows nothing but his "belief" or Apostles' Creed (3455–56).

The third and most intriguing of John's proverbs reenforces the devout simplicity of the previous two and demonstrates the elasticity of Speght's designation, "sentences and proverbes": "Where *wentestow* ['did you go'], Seinte Petres soster?" (I.3486). "Where did you go, Saint Peter's sister?" is not an obvious *sentence* or *proverbe* even in the capacious premodern sense, and this odd query is worth a closer look. Proverbs rarely take the form of questions; on the contrary, they tend toward definitive assertions that something is "always" or "never" the case. Like more conventional "sentences and proverbes," however, this one too creates a break with its immediate context abrupt enough to call for a reception different from the lines around it.

As he so often does with his microgenres, Chaucer specifies the expression's genre: this one is part of a "nyght-spel" (I.3480) or verbal charm that protects against threatening spirits of the night. Like many proverbs, charms were largely anonymous verbal forms that circulated in the spoken language as well as in writing, and even more than proverbs, they call for a voicing different from more ordinary speech: they were ritually performed, not simply spoken. In this case John performs his charm over the four corners of the room and the threshold of the exterior door, thus creating a type of *lorica*, or verbal protective armor, around the vulnerable household:

> Therwith the nyght-spel seyde he *anon-rightes*   *immediately*
> On foure halves of the hous aboute,
> And on the thressfold of the dore withoute:
> "Jhesu Crist and Seinte Benedight,
> Blesse this hous from every wikked *wight*,   *creature*
> For nyghtes *verye*, the white *pater-noster*!   *spirits (?); 'Our Father'*
> ☞ Where *wentestow*, Seinte Petres soster?"   *did you go*
> (3480–86)

References to Saint Peter and his relatives, images of walking and journeys, questions in direct address, and mentions of the Lord's Prayer (*pater-noster*) were all features of charms still circulating in Speght's day, as in the case of this one, preserved because a Protestant clergyman deplored its ignorant superstition in 1610:

> White Paternoster, Saint Peter's brother,
> What hast i' th' t'one hand? White booke leaves,
> What hast i' th' t'other hand? *Heaven yate keyes*.   *The keys to heaven's gate.*
>
> Open heaven yate and sticke hell yate:
> And let every *crysome* child creepe to its   *baptized*
>   owne mother.[47]

A version recorded in the thirteenth century demonstrates that by Chaucer's time, Saint Peter's sister and a "Paternoster" of a specified color already figured together in a charm. Robert Grosseteste, Bishop of Lincoln, objects to healers who use nonsensical charms, citing this example:

| | |
|---|---|
| Grene pater noster | |
| *Petris leue soster.*[48] | *Peter's dear sister* |

Despite this evidence of clerical disapproval, John's "nyght-spel" works with his more conventional proverbs to establish him as the tale's most sincerely devout Christian speaker.

While some medieval and early modern clerics disapproved of healing and protective charms, others took a more benevolent view of them when performed by "simple" but pious Christians; for example, a clerical manual, the *Doctrinal of Sapyence* (printed by Caxton in 1489), advises that those who use charms "synnen ryght grevously" unless they are "symple people and so ignoraunt of symplesse / that by ignoraunce they be excused."[49] John's "nyght-spel" is consistent with his two previous proverbs in establishing his identity as a simple and unquestioning Christian working man. On the eve of Nicholas and Alison's assignation, John settles down for the night in his kneading trough, and with characteristic piety, "This carpenter seyde his devocioun / . . . and biddeth his preyere" (I.3640–41). Not just his proverbs but nearly every piece of his dialogue supports John's characterization as an innocently pious laborer, as when he urges Nicholas to cease sighing over his dire prognostications and instead, "Thynk on God, as we doon, men that *swynke* ['work']" (3491).

Another embedded microgenre, the religious oath, works with John's *proverbes* to distinguish him as by far the tale's most pious speaker. Unsurprisingly, neither of the misbehaving clerks, Nicholas or Absolon, is given to using devout oaths, except ironically or profanely. Absolon asks a married woman for a kiss "For Jhesus love" (I.3717); so pleased is Nicholas with Absolon's indignant reaction to kissing Alison's behind that he swears roundly "By *Goddes corpus* ['God's (i.e., Jesus's) body'], this goth faire and weel" (3743). Alison quite wonderfully swears by the "hooly blisful martir," Thomas Becket, that she will go to bed with Nicholas (3290–92). By contrast, John's oaths are earnest petitions: "I am *adrad* ['afraid'], by Seint Thomas, / It stondeth nat aright with Nicholas. / God *shilde* ['forbid'] that he deyde sodeynly!" (3425–27). His "Help us, Seinte Frydeswyde!" requests the aid of a locally venerated saint with particular relevance to the tale's Oxford setting (3449).⁵⁰

Why should the Miller, depicted as a *cherl* who defers to no one, take such pains to establish the *cherl* within his own tale as the simple Christian working man whose religious thought is limited to obedient recitation of the Apostle's Creed and the prayers known as the Ave and Paternoster? Why does Chaucer use the embedded microgenres in John's peasant speech so consistently to support the stereotype of the pious "lewed man," wholly content to know only what the priest has taught him and thus easy prey for Nicholas's machinations? In a short but substantive piece rarely cited in more recent discussions of the tale, Alan J. Fletcher argues that in the character of John the carpenter, Chaucer's imagined Miller satirizes an "ideological stereotype" promoted by late medieval clerical works: "the idealized credal simplicity of the estate of labourers."⁵¹ (*Credal* refers to the basic Christian beliefs stated in the Apostle's Creed, taught by the clergy and memorized by the laity.) The proverbs and other microgenres in John's peasant speech provide additional support to the argument that Chaucer's John the carpenter conforms to the stereotype that the Miller mocks in his tale.

Fletcher quotes pertinent examples from sermons and other contemporary clerical works of the recommendation to the "lewde man" that "it is enough for you to believe as Holy Church teaches you and leave the clerks alone with their arguments."⁵² A Middle English sermon, modernized here, emphasizes the undesirability of religious questioning from a carpenter or other working man:

> For now every uneducated [*lewde* here can also mean 'lay'] man has become a clerk and talks in his [clerical] terms. Who, I ask you, is bolder in talking of the mystery of the sacred knowledge [translating *priuyte*, Chaucer's *pryvetee*, see below] that is contained in the holy sacrament of the altar, bolder in disputing the high matter of destiny and foreknowledge of almighty God? Who inserts himself more readily into the sacraments and devout observances of Holy Church than does an uneducated [*lewde*] weaver, tailor, or a carpenter? And yet truly, to tell the truth in plain terms, it seems no better than for a cow to bear a saddle.⁵³

In language that also recalls Reginald Pecock's objections to the "presumptuous" tradesmen who deny that clerks are the wisest men, the sermon writer laments that ordinary people now encroach upon clerical knowledge, daring even to opine about God's *pryvetee*, those sacred secrets that John the carpenter piously warns Nicholas against peering into (I.3454). Using a *proverbe* worthy of but not present in Chaucer, the sermon writer draws a very firm line between the high knowledge of clerks and what is appropriate to discussion by "lewde men": speaking about "high matter" suits a carpenter or other tradesman only as well as wearing a saddle suits a cow. A version of the same proverb serves a related cause in the *Dialogue of Solomon and Marcolf*, where Solomon attempts to silence his opponent, "It becomth no *foles* ['fools'] to speke or to brynge forth any wyse reason" and Marcolf lays bare the patriarch's contemptuous meaning with characteristic animal imagery, "It becomyth not a dogge to bere a sadylle."[54]

As deployed by Chaucer's insubordinate Miller within the cynical world of fabliau, the clergy's wishful image of the obedient and unquestioning Christian laborer does not fare at all well. The tale warns early on that "clerkes *ben ful* ['are very'] subtile" (I.3275), and it hints rather broadly that perhaps the "lewed" but sincere Christian working man should look more deeply, if not into God's secrets, at least into the secrets of the clerks who exploit his ignorance. With the brilliant economy characteristic of the whole tale, before he hops into the carpenter's bed with the carpenter's wife, Nicholas's last instruction to John in his tub sums up in two words the religious discourse the clergy wishes to hear from working men—"*Pater-noster, clom* ['hush']!" (3638)—that is, prescribed prayer and silence.

As Fletcher has argued on the basis of contemporary clerical sources and as my attention to the construction of John's peasant speech further supports, the tale told by Chaucer's rebellious Miller satirizes a *cherl* who represents in exaggerated form the ideally pious working man promoted by clerics: obedient, unquestioning, and naïve to the point of simple-minded. Nicholas's three proverbs contribute to the Miller's picture of a "subtile" clerk who takes advantage of the conveniently unquestioning piety of a Christian laborer. The first of these, as we've seen, sets up the one-sided wisdom contest between them and voices Nicholas's resolution to outwit the carpenter: "A clerk hadde *litherly biset his whyle* ['used his time poorly'] / But *if* ['unless'] he koude a carpenter bigyle" (I.3299–3300). In his comically elaborate effort to mislead John into vacating his marriage bed, Nicholas first asks him to swear that he will not repeat the sacred knowledge Nicholas has shared: "to no wight thou shalt this conseil *wreye* ['betray'] / For it is Cristes conseil" (3503–4). Nicholas's repetition of the word *conseil* leads up to his second *proverbe*, one of the best known and most self-validating of Solomonic wisdom expressions, "Werk al by conseil"—'Act according to [good, wise] counsel in all things'.⁵⁵ When John hears that Noah's flood will return and asks if there is no way to save his wife, Nicholas's response is a deft parody of clerical condescension:

| | |
|---|---|
| "Why, yis, for Gode," quod *hende* Nicholas, | *mannerly* |
| "If thou wolt werken after *loore* and *reed*. | *instruction; advice* |
| Thou mayst nat werken after thyn owene *heed*; | *judgment* |
| For thus seith Salomon, that was ful trewe: | |
| ☞ 'Werk al by *conseil*, and thou shalt nat rewe.' | *Always follow [wise] counsel* |
| And if thou *werken wolt by* good conseil, | *will follow* |
| I *undertake*, withouten mast and seyl, | *pledge* |
| Yet shal I saven *hire* and thee and me." | *her* |
| (3526–33) | |

The focal point of this speech is the Solomonic proverb, framed here with a full line of introduction: "For thus seith Salomon, that was ful trewe." If John will "werk al by conseil," obediently following Nicholas's instruction, and if he carefully avoids using his own judgment ("Thou mayst nat werken after thyn owene heed"), he and his wife will be saved from drowning.

Nicholas's three-proverb persuasion of John ends with another widely used expression, "send the wise and say nothing" (W399), a version of today's "A word to the wise is sufficient":

☞ "Men seyn thus, 'sende the wise, and sey no thyng.'
Thou art so wys, it needeth thee nat teche.
Go, save oure lyf, and that I the biseche."
(I.3598–3600)

Directly after warning him not to exercise his own judgment and urging him instead to follow wise advice, Nicholas flatters the carpenter's wisdom, defined as doing exactly as his clerical interlocutor instructs. John's proverb use is no match for Nicholas's annexation of Solomonic authority, and at the end of the tale, John is universally ridiculed for having taken some nonsense into his head about a flood. His neighbors laugh, and his speech is for naught: "what so that this carpenter answerde, / It was for noght; no man his *reson* ['explanation'] herde" (3843–44). Consistent with the rebellious spirit displayed in his prologue, the Miller ends his tale with the suggestion that only injury and ridicule await *cherles* who naïvely "werk al" by the Solomonic counsels of self-serving clerks. John's boundless credulity is laughable, but it is double-edged laughter, as the Miller ridicules not so much the carpenter himself as the demeaning clerical stereotype of ideal Christian simplicity he embodies, an ambitious effect for fabliau, a genre in which characterization is often stereotyped, but in ways that are much more rudimentary.

The clerks at the end of the *Miller's Tale* stand together to their mutual advantage: "every clerk *anonright* ['immediately'] heeld with oother" (I.3847). As with the clerks, Chaucer also represents the pilgrims of highest social rank, the *gentils*, as capable of speaking in one voice. They join unanimously in praising the *Knight's Tale* as a "noble storie" (I.3109–13), and they also speak in unison in requesting a morally instructive tale from the Pardoner (VI.323–26). But the *cherles* of the *Canterbury Tales* exhibit no such cohesion: they quarrel with one another as well as with their "betters" in a disorderly pushback against the authority of the more unified orders above them. The work's first hint of this division is the imagined response to the *Miller's Tale*, expressed by a saying that proves so relevant to the project of the *Canterbury Tales* that Chaucer cites four versions of it. Although most listeners were amused by the tale, "Diverse folk diversely they seyde" (I.3857). Proverbs rarely employ the past tense, and Speght does not mark this line, arguably just part of the narrative. But when it reappears with a different rhyme word in the *Squire's Tale*, the poet adds a second line that receives a manicule from Speght, a line that ties Chaucer's repeated expression more closely to a well-known ancient proverb: "Diverse folk diversely they *demed* ['judged']; / As many heddes, as manye wittes *ther been* ['there are']" (V.202–3, H230).[56]

According to Erasmus, "Nothing is more widely known" than the Latin version of this proverb, "Quot homines, tot sententiae" ('As many men, so many opinions', or, as the second element was also translated in his day, 'so many minds'). Although this proverb can comment wryly on the human propensity to be more opinionated than informed, Erasmus embraces the diversity of viewpoints it acknowledges, observing that there would be far fewer of the religious controversies that roiled his times if theologians took it to heart.[57] The quadruple repetition of Chaucer's "diverse folk" saying in the *Tales*—applied to diverse circumstances with diverse levels of irony—suggests that he too embraces the variety of opinions it claims as part of the human condition. The reader who accepts Speght's invitation to pause over the translated Latin proverb in the *Squire's Tale* might note how it encapsulates some of the work's most original aspects: the social diversity of its tellers, the generic variety of their tales, their disagreements about a tale's *entente*, and the further variety of voices and points of view embedded in its microgenres, including its proverbs. "As many heddes, as manye wittes ther been" (V.203) can also mean "As many wisdoms as heads," thus adding its ancient authority to Chaucer's proposition that wisdoms are multiple and more widely distributed than the clergy might wish to acknowledge.

As the reader moves from the *Miller's* to the *Reeve's Tale*, rivalry over whose knowledge, whose wisdom, and whose proverbs matter intensifies and grows angrier. While the Miller resolves to "quite the Knyghtes tale" (I.3127)—to answer story with story—the Reeve's promised *quiting* targets not the tale but its teller:

> This dronke Millere hath ytoold us heer
> How that bigyled was a carpenteer,
> *Peraventure* in scorn, for I am *oon*.  *Perhaps; one*
> And, by youre leve, I shal hym quite anoon.
> (3913–16)

Nearly all aspects of the Reeve's performance suffer from his vengeful motive, his proverbs included. In Speght's edition, his morosely sententious prologue on the miseries of aging is studded with manicules. It ends with two misused expressions that help to reveal how anger has darkened his proverb use along with his perspective. He justifies his resolve to avenge himself on the Miller with the first of these sayings, "leveful is with force force of-showve" ('It is permissible to repel force with force', 3912, F491). A parallel proverb similarly misapplied by Melibeus is helpfully explicated by Prudence in *Melibee*: what both expressions condone is self-defense in the moment, not premeditated revenge.[58] The Reeve's prologue ends with a second dubiously applied proverb, a twist on the well-known biblical expression with which Jesus upbraids the faultfinder who does not try to remove the substantial *balke* ('beam') from his own eye before criticizing the minor *stalk* ('bit of straw') or tiny mote in his neighbor's eye (3919–20).[59] In using his proverb to attack the Miller for allegedly defaming him while offering no acknowledgment of his own faults, the Reeve shows that he has missed its point. The proverb-conscious reader leaves this prologue alerted to the corrosive effects that revenge as a motive can have on proverb use as well as on storytelling.

In the *Reeve's Tale*, Chaucer's representation of rival wisdoms mines a darker vein. While in the *Miller's Tale*, a clerk exploits the naïveté of the clergy's ideal *cherl*, the situation is reversed in the *Reeve's Tale* when the scheming *cherl* Symkyn takes advantage of what he calls the "nycetee," or naïve foolishness (I.4046), of the two Cambridge University students, sending them chasing after their horses while he steals the grain they have come to monitor. The proverb Reginald Pecock attacks with such unremitting vigor serves as a focal point for this rivalry: "The gretteste clerkes been nought wisest men" (4054). The clerks themselves worry that his sharp intellect will allow the *cherl* to triumph, as in the student John's lament:

| | |
|---|---|
| "Oure *corn* is stoln; men wil us fooles calle, | *grain* |
| *Bathe* the wardeyn and oure felawes alle, | *Both* |
| And *namely* the millere, *weylaway*!" | *especially; alas* |

(4111–13)

John later expresses his fully justified worry that he will be made to play the fool in a comic tale, a "jape" to be told at his expense. His wish to avert ridicule leads him to a proverb:

| | |
|---|---|
| "And when this jape is tald another day, | |
| I *sal* been halde a *daf*, a *cokenay*! | *shall; fool; weakling* |
| I wil arise and *auntre* it, by my fayth! | *risk* |
| ☞ 'Unhardy is *unseely*,' thus men sayth." | *unhappy* |

(4207–10)

His proverb, which might be translated "Unbold is unhappy," is an analogue of the modern expressions "Fortune favors the bold (or brave)" and "Nothing ventured, nothing gained" (U3, F519). Like so much in this tale, the clerk John's proverb is darkly ironic at its speaker's own expense: the valiant deed it empowers him to "auntre" ('risk, dare') is moving a baby's cradle so that the miller Symkyn's wife gets into his bed instead of her husband's after she goes "out to pisse" (4215); he then "leith on soore" and "priketh harde and depe as he were mad" (4229, 4231). The chivalric language that mingles here with blunt fabliau diction emphasizes the proverb's biting irony: both "auntre" and "priketh," in the sense of spurring a horse, are formulaic words describing knightly behavior in Middle English romance. Sir Thopas is a parodic "knyght auntrous" said to "priketh north and est" (VII.757, 909). *Auntre* is a cognate of *adventure*, and in the examples cited by the *MED* (s.v. "auntren," v. 3 and 4), knights "auntren" their lives, saving ladies and exposing themselves to "grete perell." In the mouth of the oafish clerk constructed by the Reeve's narrative, a proverb encouraging brave action is misapplied as incitement to an assault that is anything but heroic.

In addition to fueling competition in miniature wisdom contests, proverbs were also useful in mediating situations of acute social tension across class lines. In negotiating with Symkyn, the student John makes use of four proverbs, all of them maniculed by Speght and amusingly rendered in the Northern dialect Chaucer imitates in representing the clerks' speech. The first two are John's attempts at diplomacy in explaining to Symkyn why they are standing in for the college's purchasing agent, when their true aim is to circumvent the miller's thieving. His proverbs justify the arrival of two university students carrying bags of grain, explaining their behavior as a matter of necessity: "Nede has na peer" ('Need has no rival'—that is, 'necessity prevails') and, immediately following, "*Hym boes* ['he must'] serve hymself that has *na swayn* ['no servant'], / Or elles he is a fool, as clerkes sayn" (I.4026–28).[60] Since the Whitings found no other examples of this expression (S919), this may be an instance in which Chaucer adds the designation "as clerkes sayn" to create the perception of proverbiality. Tension mounts at the prospect of the clerks spending the night in the miller's peasant house, and we have already seen his taunts to the clerks about using their sophistical logic to remake his small dwelling place to suit their needs. John responds to these taunts with two more proverbs, the first of which affirms, more truthfully than tactfully, that however small Symkyn's house, it will have to do in the absence of an alternative: "I have herd seyd, 'Man sal taa of twa thynges: / Slyk as he fyndes, or taa slyk as he brynges'" ('A man must take [one] of two things: such as he finds, or such as he brings', 4129–30, T15).

A version of the proverb "take such as you find" plays a similar role in mediating across class lines in the late fifteenth-century Scottish text, *The Taill of Rauf Coilyear*. A peasant speaker (a *carll*, the Northern form of *cherl*) is represented as a skilled wielder of proverbs who uses them to negotiate the social tensions brought on by his offer of shelter to a stranded guest of a higher social rank. He recognizes the knightly status of his lodger, but with comic results he fails to identify him as the Emperor Charlemagne. Rauf the coal seller is as prickly as the miller Symkyn about sharing his space across a social divide, and it takes five proverbs to work out the terms by which a *carll* can accommodate a socially superior guest, one of them a version of the expression found in the *Reeve's Tale*: "With-thy thow wald be payit of sic as thow fand / Forsuith, thow suld be welcum to pas hame with me"; that is, "Assuming you would be satisfied with 'such as you find,' in truth, you should be welcome to come home with me."[61] That one must accept simple accommodations when no better can be had is obviously more tactful coming from Rauf, the peasant host, than from the clerical lodgers in the *Reeve's Tale*. In both cases, however, whether the proverb comes from the social superior or the prickly inferior, Chaucer and the anonymous author of *Rauf Coilyear* depict their characters using proverbs to mediate relations between men of unequal status forced by unusual circumstances into close proximity. In the case of Chaucer's Symkyn, however, the reader will likely conclude that it is John's second proverb that secures the night's lodging: "With empty hand men may *na haukes tulle* ['lure no hawks']; / Loo, heere oure silver, redy for to spende" (I.4134–35, H89).

We have seen the vengeful misinterpretation that the Reeve puts on the proverb "leveful is with force force of-showve" in his prologue, and his tale ends with two proverbs in the same vein, the first heralded by a full line identifying its genre and affirming its truth:

> Lo, swich it is a millere to be fals!
> And therefore this proverbe is seyd ful sooth,
> ☞ "Hym thar nat wene wel that yvele dooth."     *see below*
> A *gylour* shal hymself bigyled be.     *deceiver*
> (I.4318–21)

Speght marks as one proverb what might also be seen as two, as in the Whitings' index (E185, G491); the first admonishes that 'He who does evil need not expect good'; the second fits the first more closely to the situation at hand: 'A deceiver shall himself be deceived'. In the mordant spirit of the Reeve's whole performance, these final proverbs purport to supply conventional morals for an amoral tale when his obvious aim is getting in two last blows against the pilgrim Miller. The Reeve's concluding words, "Thus have I quyt the Millere in my tale," identify for the third time the true target of his narrative and of his proverbs (3864–65, 3916, 4324). Thief and hothead that he is, as well as a soundly beaten scapegoat for the pilgrim

Miller, the Reeve's Symkyn nevertheless emerges as another socially assertive and rebellious *cherl*, whose proverb, "The gretteste clerkes been noght wisest men," reasserts in compressed form the challenge to clerical superiority first put forward by the pilgrim Miller when he refuses to yield his place in the storytelling contest to the Monk.

The claim of clerks to a monopoly on the culture's highest truths looks even more tenuous when the reader encounters the acrimonious exchange between Friar and Summoner. Both their tales generate sympathy for *cherles* beleaguered by religious authority. The *Friar's Tale* presents a rapacious summoner with no scruples about seizing in the name of the Church a poor person's every possession, unless it be "to hevy or to hoot" (III.1436), 'too heavy or too hot', a livelier equivalent—perhaps ripe for revival?—of today's "to take everything that is not tied (or nailed) down." The tale's two peasant speakers, the carter whose load of hay is stuck in the mire and the impoverished old widow Mabely, say very little. Rather than proverbs, their microgenres are curses, the carter's a temporary expression of annoyance at the horse that provides his livelihood, the widow's a heartfelt wish for the damnation of the predatory summoner. Both invite the reader to consider the relation of word to *entente*. Brief as they are, Mabely's speeches quickly establish her as a pious speaker reminiscent of John in the Miller's tale. Her oaths too are devout petitions: "Now, lady Seinte Marie / So wisly help me out of care and synne" (1604–5). Old, ill, and so poor that her most valuable possession is a new pan, she utters a curse against the summoner, comic but all the stronger by contrast with her initial piety: "Unto the devel blak and rough of hewe / *Yeve* ['give'] I thy body and my panne also!" (1622–23). In response to the summoner's clueless quest for information about the afterlife that awaits him, the devil assures him that upon arriving in hell, the experiential knowledge he gains will confer the equivalent of an advanced degree in theology: "thou shalt knowen of oure *privetee* ['secrets'] / Moore than a maister of dyvynytee" (1637–38). By means of his damnation, this victimizer of the poor will rise to the lofty equivalent of a learned clerk.

As with other tales said to *quite* one another, the meanings of the *Friar's Tale* only take their full shape after the pilgrim Summoner hits back with his own tale of a friar who, with the usual entitlement of clerical figures in fabliaux, denigrates the intellect of the *cherl* Thomas, as well as encroaching upon his home, wife, income, and the bench on which his cat rests. In this one-sided wisdom contest, the friar's plentiful proverbs merit our attention;

the tale's *cherl* is a man of few words, and his most notable communicative act is his notorious fart, the parodic wisdom expression with which he responds to the pompous *proverbes* of the friar in the tale. The friar assures Thomas that he is very careful not to overtax the intellect of ordinary people like himself by teaching directly from the Bible; scripture, after all, "is hard to yow." Instead, he teaches "al the *glose*"—the clerical commentary (III.1791–92). Predictably, since the friar is collecting for a new church building as well as for the sustenance of his friary, the self-interested "glossing" he substitutes for scripture itself promotes charitable giving to his mendicant order. His hypocrisy is revealed by wry touches such as the contrast between his protestations of strict abstinence and his detailed instructions for preparing him an epicurean meal, but most important for our purposes is his overt declaration of the superior efficacy of clerical prayers and the clergy's more extensive knowledge of "Cristes secree thynges":

| | |
|---|---|
| "Oure *orisons* been moore effectueel, | *prayers or petitions* |
| And moore we seen of Cristes secree thynges, | |
| Than *burel* folk, although they weren kynges." | *secular or unlearned* |
| (1870–75) | |

He goes on to inform Thomas that the humility and self-denial practiced by friars ensures that "oure preyeres / . . . Been to the hye God moore acceptable / Than youres . . ." (1911–14).

In a further display of condescending clerical wisdom, the friar delivers to the sick man a long pitch for a donation that features ten "sentences and proverbes" by Speght's count.[62] A close look at the first of these will suffice to illustrate how self-serving is their application, how likely to frustrate the listening *cherl*, and how complexly layered and sharp-edged is Chaucer's use of proverbs in sending up the friar as a parodic wisdom figure. After Thomas laments the sums already given to the friars to pray for his recovery with no result, the friar begins his lecture by rebuking him with a well-known New Testament proverb: "The werkman worthy is his hyre" (III.1973, W655). Spoken by Jesus, the saying affirms the value of his disciples' evangelism by comparing the alms freely given to them on their travels to a workman's well-earned "hire" or wages. The friar literalizes these metaphorical workman's wages, chiding the *cherl* for expecting friars to pray for him without monetary compensation for their "labour": "Thou woldest han oure labour al for noght" (1971–73). Not only is this a proverb more likely to antagonize than to persuade a bedridden manual laborer, it was also a particularly potent expression at the time. The scriptural context from which it is drawn, Luke 10:1–12, figured in heated contemporary debates about the legitimacy of the mendicant orders as successors to Christ's apostles. Thus the friar's misapplied proverb broadens the scope of Chaucer's critique by importing into the *Canterbury Tales* a brief expression that stands in for a larger controversy.[63] As the sick man grows more exasperated, the friar bends nine more proverbs toward his goals of self-aggrandizement and material gain. Like that of other pontificating clerics in the *Tales*, the friar's wisdom has Solomonic associations. Three of his proverbs derive from the Solomonic wisdom books, two of them attributed indirectly to the patriarch as "the wise [one]" and "he that so wel teche kan" (1988, 2085).[64]

The ailing *cherl* famously rewards the "labour" of this fatuous wisdom figure with a generous fart, payment in kind for the friar's long-winded harangue, as critics have long noted. In response to the friar's pretentions to high Solomonic wisdom, Thomas employs the same tactics as the peasant Marcolf, who uses scatological jests and other sensational effects to break into a proverb-fueled clerical discourse represented as monologic, self-contained, and impervious to other perspectives:

70a Solomon: *Whoo* ['*woe*'] to that man that hath a
   dowble herte and in bothe weyes wyll wander.
   (Ecclesiasticus 2:14)
70b Marcolf: He that wolle two weyes go muste eythre
   his ars or his *breche* ['*britches*'] tere ['*rip*' or '*tear*'].
71a S: Of habundaunce of th'*erte* ['*heart*'] the mouth
   spekyst. (Matthew 12:34, Luke 6:45)
71b M: Out of a full *wombe th'ars trompyth* ['belly the arse trumpets'].
81a S: Alle reyght pathys goon towardes oon weye.
81b M: So done alle the veynes renne towardes the ars.[65]

Marcolf's scatological proverbs serve as symbolic equivalents of farting and arse-baring, mocking gestures intended to disrupt the cultural authority of Solomon's wisdom, which to the *Dialogue*'s anonymous authors has come to seem overly narrow, prescriptive, and hierarchical.

Thomas's fart achieves the same sort of shock effect. The affronted friar protests that "this olde cherl . . . / Blasphemed hath oure hooly covent" (III.2182–83). He interprets it as an insult not just to himself and his order but "*per consequens*, to ech degree / Of hooly chirche" (2192–93). A long series of hostile remarks from the "lord of that village" and his lady follow, directed not just at Thomas's rude act but also at the conundrum he poses: how can his bequest be shared among the friars with perfect fairness? The responses of lord and lady lay heavy emphasis on Thomas's status as *cherl* and on the temerity of his irreverent treatment of a clerical figure: "I seye a cherl hath doon a cherles dede"; "How hadde this cherl ymaginacioun / To shewe swich a probleme to the frere?"; "O *nyce* ['foolish'], proude cherl, I *shrewe* ['curse'] his face!"; "Ey, nyce cherl, God lete him nevere *thee* ['thrive']!"; "What, lo, my cherl, lo, yet how *shrewedly* ['wickedly'] / Unto my confessour to-day he spak!" (2206–241). The lord and his lady speculate that one who sets such a condition must be a fool or possessed by a demon. In the end, the cleverness of the solution proposed by the squire Jankyn—that in anticipation of sharing equally in the gaseous bequest, the noses of the friars be positioned at equal intervals around a cartwheel, Thomas's confessor below its hub and the ailing *cherl* on top—moves all but the friar from ire to admiration, both for the squire's solution and for Thomas's subtle but not insoluble conundrum:

| | |
|---|---|
| The lord, the lady, and ech man, *save* the frere, | *except* |
| Seyde that Jankyn spak, in this matere, | |
| As wel as Euclide dide or *Ptholomee*. | *Ptolemy* |
| *Touchynge* the cherl, they seyde, subtiltee | *Speaking of* |
| And heigh wit made hym speken as he spak; | |
| He nys no fool, ne no *demonyak*. | *possessed person* |
| (2287–94) | |

Both the tale and the tacit wisdom contest within it conclude with the condescending cleric silenced, Jankyn rewarded for his erudite solution, and the *cherl* commended for the "heigh wit" and "subtiltee" with which he responds to the friar's sententiousness.

The distinctive proverb use of one last cherl, perhaps the most aggrieved of all, will serve to conclude this chapter's argument. In yet another twist on the template of a duel in proverbs between cleric and peasant, the Canon's Yeoman, a self-described "lewed" man, engages in a one-sided proverb contest with his clerical master in absentia. Speght identified twenty-one "sentences and proverbes" in the Yeoman's performance,[66] yet the Yeoman's represented speech shares none of the windy sententiousness with which Chaucer satirizes the proverb-spouting friar in the *Summoner's Tale*. As with the often-metaphoric flour and bran image literalized by the grain-stealing miller in the Reeve's Tale (I.4053), familiar metaphors in many of the Yeoman's proverbs are refreshed and strengthened by their connection to the material world created by the plot.[67] "They that *han been brent* ['have been burnt'], / Allas, kan they nat flee the fires heete?" (VIII.1407–8) is an interrogative version of the widely attested proverb, "A burnt child dreads the fire" (C201), but "they who have been burnt" is also a literal description of the plight of the Yeoman and his fellows. In his former unwisdom, he continued to take part in failed alchemical experiments even when his face became scorched from blowing on the fire. Similar is his use of the Speght-marked expression "blered is myn ye" (VIII.730, E217). Having one's eye bleared usually serves as a metaphor for being deceived, but here it also applies to the disfiguring effects of his occupation. A few of the Yeoman's "sentences and proverbes" are simply idiomatic phrases that caught the editor's eye, such as that Speghtian favorite, "a twenty devel waye" or "in the name (or manner) of twenty devils" (VIII.782), but the majority strike direct blows aimed at the spurious wisdom of his absent clerical master.[68]

When the two first gallop up to overtake the pilgrimage, they are dirty and ragged, and the Canon is sweating profusely, as though he is already in the hell suggested by the fire imagery that runs through the Yeoman's performance. Reacting to the ambiguity in the Canon's appearance, the Host tentatively equates the Canon's alleged possession of wisdom with his clerical status: "certein it wolde seme / Thy lord were wys . . . Is he a clerk, or noon? Telle what he is" (VIII.594–95, 616). According to the Yeoman, "he is gretter than a clerk"; his Canon possesses such "subtilitee" that he can pave the road to Canterbury with silver and gold. Pressed by the Host to explain why a clerk with such valuable knowledge appears so impoverished, the Yeoman can no longer contain the grief and frustration his master's purported wisdom has caused him:

| | |
|---|---|
| He is *to wys*, in feith, as I bileeve. | too wise |
| ☞ That that is overdoon, it wol nat *preeve* | turn out |
| *Aright*, as clerkes seyn, it is a vice. | Well |
| Wherefore in that I holde hym *lewed and nyce*. | ignorant and foolish |
| ☞ For whan a man hath *over-greet a wit*, | too much cleverness |
| Ful oft *hym happeth to mysusen* it. | it happens that he misuses it |
| So dooth my lord, and that me *greveth soore*. | grieves me sorely |
| (644–50) | |

The idea that an overweening pride tips the man who is "too wise" into the category of fool or charlatan is deeply ingrained in medieval proverb tradition, as the two expressions marked here by Speght suggest.

A wealth of well-known "sentences and proverbes," both biblical and secular, lay readily at hand to aid premodern writers in destabilizing the opposition between wisdom and folly.[69] The proverb with which this chapter began, "The greatest clerks are not the wisest men," belongs to this large family, and in the longest versions of the *Dialogue of Solomon and Marcolf*, at least ten of Marcolf's responses work in some way to mock or challenge Solomon's preeminent wisdom. When later in the work Solomon states that "God . . . fulfylled me wyth *sapience* ['wisdom']," Marcolf's reply is "He is holdyn wyse that reputyth hymself a fole."[70] As a path to genuine wisdom, Saint Paul recommends the direct opposite of the alchemist Canon's use of his "over-greet . . . wit": "If any man among you seem to be wise in this world, let him become a fool, that he may be wise. For the wisdom of this world is foolishness with God" (1 Corinthians 3:18–19). The "wisdom" of Chaucer's alchemist Canon is wholly "of this world," applied only to a futile struggle with intractable physical matter. In the eyes of his servant the Canon, he appears equally as ignorant and foolish ("lewed and nyce") as the pontificating friar in the *Summoner's Tale*, and perhaps even more venal.

Driven to near madness by the repeated failure of the effort to turn base metal into silver and gold, the Yeoman makes a critical speech at the end of his long autobiographical account. The speech may have been intended to serve as the climax of the Yeoman's confessional prologue rather than as the end of Part One of his tale, as modern editors follow the Ellesmere manuscript in labeling it.[71] In a protest against his master's pretensions to Solomonic wisdom, his proverbs come tumbling out one after another:

| | |
|---|---|
| And whan we been *togidres everichoon*, | *all together* |
| Every man semeth a Salomon. | |
| ☞ But al thyng which that shineth as the gold | |
| Nis nat gold, as that I have herd told; | |
| ☞ Ne every appul that is fair at eye | |
| Ne is nat good, *what so* men *clappe or crye*. | *whatever; say or shout* |
| Right so, lo, *fareth it* amonges us: | *it happens* |
| He that semeth the wiseste, by Jhesus, | |
| ☞ Is moost fool, whan it cometh to the *preef*; | *proof* |

And he that semeth trewest is a theef.
(VIII.960–69)

All three manicules mark proverbs that apply not just to the Canon but more generally in the *Tales* to a clergy that is wedded to the gold of this world, guilty of theft both literal and metaphoric, and rendered foolish by boasting of its own wisdom.

The simple imagery in the Yeoman's still-familiar proverb—"al thyng which that shineth as the gold / Nis nat gold"—runs through much of the *Canterbury Tales*. It appears literally in the *General Prologue* in the form of the Prioress's "brooch of gold ful sheene" (I.160) and the Monk's love-knot "of gold ywroght" (I.196–97). The Parson's portrait includes the image of the "lewed" parishioner left to rust like base metal by a clergy that may glitter with incongruous ornaments but has little share in the incorruptibility of gold: "if gold ruste, what shal iren do? / For if a preest be foul, on whom we truste, / No wonder is a lewed man to ruste" (I.500–502). The Yeoman's performance is placed in dialogue with that of the Second Nun (VIII.554–58), a pairing that contrasts a sweating clerical charlatan who fails to "multiply" or produce precious metals to a saint who succeeds in multiplying converts to her faith and remains miraculously "coold" in a boiling cauldron (VIII.521). In contrast with the soul-deadening pursuit of precious metal by the alchemists, in the *Second Nun's Tale*, gold appears in the form of illuminated letters in a text of sacred scripture seen in a vision (VIII.202, 210).

To the familiar clerical abuses called out in the portraits of the *General Prologue*—the flouting of the monastic rule, the lining of clerical pockets with resources meant for the poor, and the peddling of fake relics to naïve country folk—in this chapter I have sought to add a grievance recurrent throughout the work and played out in exchanges of proverbs between clerks and *cherles*. These tacit and sometimes one-sided proverb contests critique the self-aggrandizing and exclusionary view of wisdom adopted by so many of Chaucer's clerks and its effect on the physical and spiritual well-being of *cherles*. The Canon has compelled his Yeoman to take part in the "illusioun" foisted on ordinary people by corrupted clerks: "To muchel folk we doon illusioun, / And borwe gold . . . / And make *hem wenen* ['them believe'] . . . / That of a pound we koude make *tweye* ['two'] / Yet is it fals. . . ." (VIII.673–78). By the time the Canon's Yeoman tells his sorry tale, the journey to Canterbury is nearly at an end, and in a characteristically Chaucerian turn of events, this latecomer to the pilgrimage, a disfigured and impoverished *cherl*, seems to be its one potential convert, positioned to make a genuine change in his life, maybe. This possibility is compressed into the unassuming proverb mentioned earlier in chapter 1, an expression recorded in English before Chaucer was born and still often heard today, "Bet than never is late" (1410, L89). Its usual contexts now are much more prosaic, but as spoken by the Yeoman, it compresses into five words the theological promise of salvation for the repentant even at the last possible moment. In words also quoted earlier, Erasmus says of a different adage, "You see what an ocean of philosophy, or rather of theology, is opened up to us by this tiny proverb."[72]

CHAPTER 3

---

# THE RIVAL WISDOMS OF CLERKS AND WOMEN

> England is the paradise of women. . . . Yet it is worth noting that though in no country of the world [are] the men so fond of, so much governed by, so much wedded to their wives, yet hath no language so many proverbial invectives against women.
> —JOHN RAY, *A Collection of English Proverbs*, 1678

A metaphor from Erasmus quoted in chapter 1 captures the proverb's succinctness, tenacity in the memory, and impetus to further reflection: "An idea launched like a javelin in proverbial form strikes with sharper point on the hearer's mind and leaves implanted barbs for meditation."[1] But Erasmus's image represents the proverb as a weapon; striking with a sharpened point and leaving implanted barbs also figures injury and pain. As we saw in the previous chapter, the same qualities that give the proverb its transformational power also confer its capacity for inflicting damage, especially in premodern cultural settings where its prestige was high. Despite the devaluation of the proverb as a rhetorical force in the modern world, we have seen that even today many argue that the proverb "Boys will be boys" works to justify gender inequality. In the *Wife of Bath's Prologue* and *Tale*, Chaucer speculates about the impact of antifeminist proverbs on women and marital relations in a culture in which gender was viewed as binary and the proverb's influence was much greater than today.

Generations of scholars have recognized that in the *Wife of Bath's Prologue*, Chaucer fictionalizes an idiosyncratic response in a feminine voice to an existing body of antifeminist writings explicitly acknowledged within his text.[2] Largely absent from the voluminous scholarship on this prologue, however, is consideration of its antifeminist proverbs *as proverbs*, expressions circulating within a culture that recognized them as belonging to a particularly potent verbal form.[3] The persuasive powers we have noted in the proverb—its ready familiarity, claim to communal acceptance, and ability to label and transform situations—made it an ideally efficient instrument for asserting masculine superiority and containing the threat posed by recalcitrant women. But the premodern literary culture that venerated proverbs also fostered strategies for contesting and resisting their authority. After the harrowing exchanges of weaponized proverbs in her prologue, the tale models a healthier, less destructive form of proverb use than wielded either by antifeminist clerks or by one of Chaucer's most complex textual constructs, the embattled Wife herself.

This chapter argues that Chaucer's Wife of Bath serves as a proverb-disputing and proverb-dispensing feminine wisdom figure, a controversial anti-Solomon with some intriguing parallels to another of Solomon's adversaries, the fractious peasant Marcolf we met in the previous chapter. By disputing the antifeminist proverbs transmitted by clerks (members of the clergy, those in training for it, and by extension, other highly educated male writers), Alison of Bath challenges the clerical claim to a monopoly on the culture's highest wisdom—on all the knowledge that matters most.[4] In constructing this performance, Chaucer provides a fresh angle of attack on the same sweeping clerical claims that anger or distress the *cherles* we saw in chapter 2. The Wife's discourse responds in two ways to the special powers of antifeminist proverbs: it verbally opposes them, and yet it also internalizes and acts out the damaging contents of her culture's much-repeated stock of proverbs on the wickedness of women.

To contextualize this reading of the *Wife's Prologue* as a debate in proverbs against the false Solomonic wisdom of antifeminist clerks, I present some examples of the genre that adopt Solomon as a rival or adversary to women, first from outside Chaucer's work and then from the *Canterbury*

*Tales* outside the Wife's performance. Next, I examine the challenges this prologue poses to an antifeminist clerical discourse that, like the Wife's fifth husband, knows "mo proverbes / Than in this world ther growen gras or herbes" (III.773–74). A final section moves to the *Wife of Bath's Tale* to show how it completes the proverb rescripting project begun in her prologue. The performance Chaucer creates for the Wife speaks eloquently about the damage that antifeminist proverbs inflict, but it also offers a glimpse of how proverbs might function in a discursive world somewhat less misogynist, if still a far cry from the "paradise of women" proclaimed by proverb collector John Ray in the epigraph to this chapter.[5]

PROVERBIAL INVECTIVES AGAINST WOMEN

Even if we are skeptical of Ray's claim that seventeenth-century England was "the paradise of women," there is no doubt about his final proposition, that his native language abounded in "proverbial invectives against women." Courtesy of the Whitings' index, a quick sampling of English proverbs mainly before 1500 shows why proverbs about women gave cause for concern. The Whitings cite sixty-five expressions in which the first significant noun is *woman* or *women*. Three are wholly positive: women are helpful in need (W536), efficacious in prayer (W544), and steadfast (W548). Six are more ambivalent: women are fair when young (W490), possess nine lives like a cat (W510), have subtle or quick wits (W514 and W531), desire sovereignty (W539), and, unlike men, are "always ready" (W523). The remaining fifty-six proverbs in this sampling, about 86 percent, offer a faithful index of medieval misogyny: women are whores, chatterers, fools, vindictive, inconstant and changeable, spendthrift, lawless, inclined to take up with strange men, deceptive, evil, man's ruin, quarrelsome, meddlesome, willful, shameless, self-justifying, uncontrollable, power-hungry, and inwardly rotten (W484–549). A sermon from the thirteenth-century *Lambeth Homilies* warns that it is with good reason that women are called the devil's mousetraps (W530). While the dispute Chaucer gives the Wife is mainly with the misogyny and condescension of Latin clerical culture, we've seen that Latin and vernacular proverbs were regularly exchanged for one another as translation exercises in the schoolroom, and many proverbs from the Latin Vulgate Bible were widely quoted in vernacular translation. For premodern English readers, both Latin and vernacular proverbs would have been part of the cultural backdrop for the Wife's case against antifeminist proverbial "wisdom" and in favor of a more humane and judicious form of proverb use.

The *Wife's Prologue* has much of interest to say about what Chaucer calls the *proverbe*, and I continue the practice discussed in chapter 1 of using the word as Chaucer does, as a blanket term covering a variety of expressions. Chaucer's *proverbe* includes sayings known to have circulated in more-or-less fixed form—the "proverb proper" for some proverb scholars, especially those who study living traditions. It also includes probable new coinages that create "the perception of proverbiality" by claiming to be venerable pieces of wisdom, as well as the generally longer and more loosely worded "sentence" or "sententious remark" that, despite the familiarity of its idea, "has not crystallized into specific current form and which anyone feels free to rephrase to suit himself."[6] In long quotations, I also continue the practice of marking with manicules (fists, pointing hands) the expressions Thomas Speght identifies as "sentences and proverbes" in his 1602 Chaucer edition, where his use of just one typographic marker for both indicates that the reader response he anticipates for these expressions did not depend upon any distinction between *sentence* and *proverbe*.[7]

The *Wife's Prologue* makes effective use of rhetorical questions and apostrophes to various absent listeners. The two work in combination when Chaucer's speaker asks rhetorically whether the proverb-spouting masculine voices she apostrophizes cannot find proverbs ("parables") that posit "resemblances" to something other than innocent wives (III.368–70).[8] And well she might ask: her prologue cites a profusion of derogatory "wisdom" aimed at women and wives, much of it the fruit of Chaucer's own proverb-conscious reading of Latin and French literature.[9] The "resemblances" drawn by these antifeminist proverbs and quoted in the *Wife's Prologue* liken sharing a home with a woman to living with a roof that leaks and a fire that smokes (278); a woman resembles a vegetation-destroying worm (376), a lion or a foul dragon (776) and a gold ring in a sow's nose (785); a woman's love is likened to a wild fire so destructive it will "consume every thyng that brent wole be" (375).

These and many other sayings, not all of them antifeminist, help to make the *Wife of Bath's Prologue* and *Tale* the most explicitly proverb-oriented portion of the *Canterbury Tales* outside the *Tale of Melibee*, which also addresses the ethics of proverb use, as we will see in chapter 4. As a rough index of the proverb density of this prologue and tale as it might strike a premodern reader, Speght's pointing hands direct attention to a total of 61 "sentences and proverbes" in the 1,264 lines of the Wife's performance: 36 in her prologue and 25 more in the brief tale.[10] Eighteen of those in her tale occur in rapid succession in the long lecture on true nobility or *gentilesse* delivered to her reluctant bridegroom on their wedding night by the shape-shifting old woman.

In the introduction to his anthology, *Woman Defamed and Woman Defended*, Alcuin Blamires cites five main textual sources for clerical antifeminist writing as it reached late medieval vernacular writers, including Chaucer: (1) "a relatively small number of gloomy remarks about women in Proverbs, Ecclesiastes, and Ecclesiasticus, the account of the Fall and Eve's punishment... and the Epistles of St. Paul"; (2) "apophthegms" drawn from a small set of Latin authors from classical antiquity, including Ovid, Juvenal, Virgil, and Valerius Maximus (a first-century collector of anecdotes and sententiae); (3) "statements" from the works of the Church fathers; (4) secondary "extracts" from these earlier sources, especially Jerome's notorious antimatrimonial tract, *Against Jovinian* (a major source for the *Wife's Prologue*); and (5) "numerous anonymous Latin or vernacular proverbs."[11] Remarks, apophthegms, statements, extracts, and anonymous proverbs: in other words, in the broad premodern sense of the word adopted here, medieval antifeminist discourse was, to a very substantial degree, a matter of antifeminist *proverbes*. The Wife and her avatar, the old woman in her tale, also use the term *auctoritee* to refer to such extracts and their authors, an indication of their cultural prestige (III.1, 1208). While the English proverbs about women noted above come from widely disparate sources and show much more variety, in the prestigious literary texts produced by clerks a surprisingly small corpus of sayings on the evils of women was repeated throughout a wide range of late medieval genres, as Blamires' anthology clearly demonstrates.

Christine de Pizan remarks on this dispiriting consistency among antifeminist writers in the *City of Ladies* (1405), written just after Chaucer's death: "it seems that they all speak from one and the same mouth." As she contemplates their writings on women, Christine's first-person speaker continues, "Like a gushing fountain, a series of authorities, whom I recalled one after another, came to mind, along with their opinions on this topic." (For someone of her social class in the fifteenth century, "de Pizan" was still a place name rather than a surname; hence the custom of referring to the author as Christine.) The image of a "gushing fountain" (*une fontaine resourdant*) captures the way these remembered sayings flood the female speaker's mind uninvited, "one after another," leading her to despair.[12] Christine's wit can be sharp, and her image of a "gushing fountain" may also be a covert swipe at the note of masculine self-pleasuring in evidence in much antifeminist discourse. The same narrow and invidious tradition exerts the same inundating effect in the *Wife's Prologue*.

To a twenty-first century reader, the antifeminist proverbs circulating primarily among the members of an ostensibly celibate male clergy in the later Middle Ages suggest a strange combination of revulsion, erotic attraction, condescension, curiosity, fear, and self-protection. Many of these much-repeated antifeminist *proverbes* derive originally from the biblical wisdom books attributed to Solomon in the Middle Ages, and, as we will see, some of the most frequently cited expressions have been radically decontextualized or altered to produce a "wisdom" more sweepingly condemnatory of women than the original sayings in scripture. The circumstances that supported the proliferation of such sayings, with their atmosphere of man-to-man sharing behind the backs of women, are hard to imagine in our world, where what were once described as the "secrets" of women's bodies have now been demystified by readily available sources from medical websites to advertisements for intimate products. Similarly, it was easier for antifeminist writers to attribute sinister "secrets" to women's minds at a time when the thoughts of women writers were only sporadically recorded and shared.

Medieval antifeminist writers accused women of concealing until marriage the inherent evils of their gender, as noted with indignation in the Wife's narrating voice:

> Thow seyst that we wyves wol oure vices hide
> Til we be *fast*, and thanne we wol *hem* shewe—     *married; them*
> Wel may that be a proverbe of a shrewe!
> (III.282–84)

The most scurrilous of medieval antimatrimonial and antifeminist writings throve on insinuations that, prior to marriage, women hid not just moral vices but also bodily monstrosity, dirt, and contagion. If a man should doubt the existence of these concealed perils, Boccaccio writes in *Il Corbaccio*, "let him search the secret places where they in shame hide the horrible instruments they employ to take away their superfluous humours."[13] The means he recommends for verifying the existence of these horrors would not have been readily available to schoolboys training on proverbs or to celibate clerics, and thus the nature of these repulsive "secrets" must often have been left to the masculine imagination. As with the mysteries of their bodies, the unknowability of women's minds also posed a threat: *Il Corbaccio* holds that women "secretly consider any man a fool who loves them ... and they know how to hide it"; similarly, the final book of Andreas Capellanus, *On Love*, asserts, "There is not a living woman who does not make pretense of what is untrue, and invent lies with reckless ingenuity."[14] These materials often claimed to be satirical, as their absurd exaggerations suggest, or they have been labeled as satire by modern scholars, but the satiric point of their vituperation remains unclear, and Chaucer creates a fictional character who, like Christine de Pizan, fails to appreciate its wit.

Profuse as the proverbs are in the *Wife's Prologue*, they are not the only lexical terrain over which the Wife wages a pitched battle, and before focusing on her proverbs, it is worth pausing briefly to acknowledge another of the microgenres to which she objects and to recognize her prologue's larger generic affiliations. Another notable antifeminist staple is the brief cautionary tale or negative exemplum, drawn from biblical and classical literature and featuring transgressive female figures such as Eve and Clytemnestra who give title to the "book of wikked wyves" from which the Wife's fifth husband reads (III.685). Chaucer also reworked larger literary forms to produce this highly original piece of writing. Widely accepted models for the *Wife's Prologue* itself include the *confessio*, or literary confession, and the *sermon joyeux* or mock-sermon, and Susanna Fein has more recently demonstrated the influence of fabliau.[15] In addition, I argue for the importance of another underlying generic structure, the dialogue or debate in proverbs, in this case featuring a disruptive female wisdom figure who relies on her ready wit to defend against an established tradition of proverbs that proclaims the worthlessness of women.

If, as the evidence indicates, premodern readers were more aware than we are of the proverbs in their reading, more *interested* in them, it would have been easier for them to see the extent to which the *Wife's Prologue* functions as a proverb contest. Well before the hundred-year lifespan of Speght's proverb-marked edition in print, manuscripts of the *Canterbury Tales* reveal this prologue as one of the most heavily annotated sections of the whole work. Scribes and readers emphasized its proverbs by providing Latin equivalents, source citations, and expressions such as *nota bene* and *nota proverbium*.¹⁶ Even in the absence of these marginal indicators, the poet's own verbal framing often highlights the presence of proverbs. As elsewhere in Chaucer's writing, most of the proverbs in the *Wife's Prologue* are clearly marked off from the text in which they are embedded. In a humorously extended example of such explicit framing, the Wife expresses her approval of a proverb attributed to the second-century mathematician and astronomer, Ptolemy.¹⁷ She emphasizes its genre by twice labeling it a *proverbe* and by defining its speaker as a wisdom figure ("the wise astrologien"); she then purports to walk her late husband (apostrophized as "olde dotard") through a bawdy application of the wisdom in question:

> Of alle men yblessed moot he be,
> The wise astrologien, Daun Ptholome,
> That seith this proverbe in his Almageste:
> ☞ "Of alle men his wysdom is the hyeste
> That *rekketh nevere* who hath the world *in honde.*"   *does not care; in his control*
>
> By this proverbe thou shalt understonde,
> Have thou ynogh, *what thar thee recche or care*   *why should you care*
> How *myrily* that othere folkes fare?   *merrily*
> For, certeyn, olde dotard, by youre leve,
> Ye shul have *queynte* right ynogh at eve.   *sexual gratification*
> (III.323–32)

The speaker's distinctive voice flows through the fixed but voice-permeable boundaries of the Speght-marked expression, re-accentuating with her own taunting tones the solemnity of a proverb about what constitutes wisdom.¹⁸ Chaucer adapts it to the transgressive purposes of the Wife, who takes it to mean that wisdom is a matter of minding one's own affairs and not looking for trouble. If satisfied with the sexual gratification he receives from his wife, a wise man does not concern himself with what others might be enjoying. This boldly licentious application recruits the authority of the "wise astrologien" in support of unlimited freedom of action for wives when so many antifeminist proverbs seek to justify strict limits.

Drawing strength from the proverb's special nature as a memorable, culturally sanctioned, and potentially transformative utterance, the antifeminist proverb served as a particularly consequential verbal tool or weapon against women, and in her prologue, Chaucer gives his fictional

Wife a variety of intriguing responses to it. Her tale then continues the proverb-related project begun in her prologue: it offers an idealized vision of the role proverbs might play in reshaping gender relations in a magical world in which a woman can function as a wisdom figure who succeeds in rescripting masculine language and behavior from abuse of women to support for feminine self-determination.

TWISTED WISDOM

As we saw in the previous chapter, in the medieval imagination the biblical patriarch King Solomon personified an authoritative cultural wisdom expressed primarily in the form of the many proverbs circulating under his name. The biblical wisdom books—Proverbs, Ecclesiastes, The Song of Songs, Wisdom, and Ecclesiasticus—were regularly attributed to his authorship in the Middle Ages, and Chaucer includes "The Parables of Salomon," a designation given either to a section of the book of Proverbs or to the whole, among the contents of the antifeminist anthology from which Jankyn reads so incessantly to his wife (III.679).[19] Many of the "resemblances" to which the Wife objects, the comparisons that antifeminist proverbs draw between women and baleful images such as serpents and wildfires, derive from the wisdom books and therefore carried Solomon's authority. In fairness to the patriarch to whom these books were attributed, it should be said that they abound in "gloomy remarks" about men as well as women, and balanced and affirmative sayings about women can also be found there. A core set of Solomonic proverbs, however, came to Chaucer preselected for their antifeminism by key sources for the *Wife's Prologue*, including Jerome's notorious antimatrimonial tract *Against Jovinian* and the misogynist rant of the Jealous Husband in Jean de Meun's continuation of the *Roman de la rose*.[20] Not only were these antifeminist proverbs preselected; in some conspicuous cases, mild or neutral sayings were also truncated, altered, wrenched out of context, or misconstrued to produce memorable expressions that cast women as wicked by their very nature and thus in urgent need of masculine control.[21]

As the personification of an abstract, highly authoritative, and seemingly timeless form of wisdom, Solomon had by Chaucer's day long served as something of a magnet or lightning rod for rival figures bent on challenging the received opinions voiced in the wisdom books. The Marcolf of the previous chapter who answers the patriarch's proverbs with earthy and anti-authoritarian proverbs of his own is such a figure. The Wife of Bath takes up an antagonistic position also held by others of Solomon's disputants, including the biblical Queen of Sheba, who tests the patriarch with hard questions (3 Kings 10:1), and the "foolish woman," "full of allurements, and knowing nothing at all," who counters Solomon's moral wisdom with an enticing proverb of her own: "Stolen waters are sweeter, and hidden bread is more pleasant" (Proverbs 9:13, 17). In *The Dialogue of Solomon and Marcolf*, Marcolf recruits a company of anti-Solomonic disputants, the female subjects of Solomon's kingdom, who rise up against their king and denounce his wisdom.[22] Solomon's unnamed wife in the thirteenth-century French *Queste del Saint Graal* (*Quest for the Holy Grail*) is a less oppositional figure than Marcolf or the Wife of Bath, but she nevertheless makes it clear to her husband that her ingenuity (*engin*) is at least as essential to solving a practical problem as his abstract moral wisdom.[23] I mention these Solomonic rivals as precedents, not sources or models, for Chaucer's female anti-Solomon. These varied figures help to reveal another dimension of Chaucer's fictional Wife, and thus in just this one regard—resistance to high Solomonic wisdom by a woman or a peasant—they merit a place beside such direct and long-acknowledged literary models for the Wife as Ovid's Dipsas and Jean de Meun's *La Vieille*.[24]

Like Marcolf and Solomon's wife in the *Queste del Saint Graal*, the Wife of Bath relies on a native cleverness she calls her *wit* and on a ruse she calls a *soutiltee* (III.400, 426, 576). Similar language characterizes Marcolf in the English *Dialogue*: he is introduced as "right subtill and wyse of wyt" and Solomon describes him as succeeding "by crafte and subtylte."[25] Often the province of the unschooled, impoverished, or otherwise marginalized, this is the "lewed mannes wit" that Chaucer opposes to "the wisdom of an heep of lerned men" in the *General Prologue* (I.574–75), a cleverness that shades easily into trickery and deception, especially when practiced by those who lack the power to act more directly. In his classic study of French chivalric works, Robert W. Hanning writes that medieval characters mentally enlivened by native wit (*engin* in his French works) "have their own special charm—sometimes exhilarating, sometimes cynical, always profoundly human—as they embellish the world to make it better (or at least other) than it is and surmount life's obstacles by manipulation and circumnavigation rather than by brute force or irresistible goodness."[26]

When Marcolf uses his wit to challenge Solomon's authoritative wisdom in the *Dialogue*, he is accused of excessive talking, and efforts are made to silence him.[27] The Wife, too, is interrupted, in her case by male clerical figures, the Pardoner and the Friar, and the latter jokes about her (genuinely) lengthy prologue (III.163–87, 829–56). Both Marcolf and the Wife persist nevertheless in speaking their minds, at times with an air of near desperation, and in Marcolf's case an increasingly authoritarian Solomon and his counselors menace him with escalating threats of imprisonment and physical punishment. The Wife is also battered in her resistance to Solomonic wisdom, but she nevertheless perseveres in defending her rival form of knowledge, imagining (especially by means of her tale) new solutions for the woes of marriage, and advocating for a more capacious view of the current world than the circumscribed wisdom of Solomon and other ancient masculine *auctoritees* can encompass.[28]

In proverb contests fueled by antifeminist "wisdom," a central question is whether "women"—half the population—were, uniformly and by nature, either good or evil. Few arguments can seem more futile now, but practice in arguing both sides of yes-or-no questions such as "Should a man marry?" had been part of a training in rhetoric since antiquity, and premodern authors prolonged this artificial, hyper-polarized debate for centuries with undiminished enthusiasm.[29] The biblical wisdom books themselves foster a binary view of all creation: "Good is set against evil, and life against death: so also is the sinner against a just man. And so look upon all the works of the most High. Two and two, and one against the other" (Ecclesiasticus 33:15). By their very form, proverbs make a natural medium of exchange for hyperbolically dichotomized conflicts such as the debate over woman's nature: their black-and-white rhetoric ("always," "never," "all," "none") suits them ideally to "situations characterized by conflict, skepticism, or other kinds of oppositionally structured mental dispositions."[30] Selectively quoted and deceptively truncated Solomonic proverbs were staples of debates about women's nature, and the practices that produced them are crucial to understanding the proverb use fictionalized in the *Wife's Prologue*.

Such a debate occurs in *Dives and Pauper* ('The Rich and the Poor Man'), a long prose dialogue in English probably written shortly after Chaucer's death.[31] There, a discussion of the deadly sin of lechery leads swiftly and predictably to the threat women pose to men's souls. The worldly layman figure, Dives, holds women responsible for assenting to the lusts of the flesh, but Pauper maintains on the contrary that men are readier to propose sexual acts, and the proposer of a wicked deed is morally more culpable than the assenter. With the battle lines thus drawn, Solomon comes immediately to the fore as the relevant authority. Dives asserts, "Solomon said much about the evil of women"; Pauper responds, "And Solomon said much about the good of women." By means of selective citation and omission, each speaker enlists "Solomon" as an advocate for his own side.[32]

In an exchange that highlights the bookish nature of these debates and their penchant for selective quoting, Dives repeats a much-cited proverb from the notoriously antifeminist twenty-fifth chapter of Ecclesiasticus: "All malice is short to the malice of a woman." As though the Bible were open before them, Pauper, for the defense, calls attention to the considerable praise in "the next chapter," that is, in Ecclesiasticus 26, where the good woman's virtues are lauded: "Hyr disciplyne & hyr nurture is the gifte of God, & the holy woman & chaste is grace upon grace."[33] As an example of the selective quoting characteristic of these uses of Solomonic sayings, in order to uphold the pro-woman side, Pauper must omit a series of statements about the wicked woman found in verses 8–15 of Ecclesiasticus 26, where the Solomonic speaker likens a woman to a scorpion and names among her vices jealousy, drunkenness, impudence, and a propensity for opening her quiver to every arrow.

A much livelier debate in proverbs featuring Solomon on the nature of women takes place in the *Dialogue of Solomon and Marcolf*. The initial proverb exchange between the two is the best-known part of the work, but they engage in a series of wisdom contests. In a later contest, positive and negative sentiments regarding women's nature are once again taken from the wisdom books and sorted into two opposing discourses, as in *Dives and Pauper*, but this time Solomon is not just a written authority cited by the disputants. Rather, both the praise and the blame of women come directly from the mouth of the hapless Solomon figure personified in the subversive *Dialogue*. In a selective patchwork of positive quotations, drawn especially from the portrait of the virtuous woman in Proverbs 31:10–31, Solomon begins by celebrating women's nature with unqualified praise. Marcolf resolves to draw his rival into self-contradiction: "albeit that ye now prayse thaym ovyr moche, *or* ['before'] ye slepe ye shal dysprayse thaym as faste" (17.28).[34] Marcolf's inventive wit enables him to spin damaging fictions about Solomon's intentions and circulate them among his female subjects, turning them against their ruler. He undermines the king's best-known judicial act by announcing that Solomon has decided, after all, to divide in half the infant claimed by two women. He informs them that the king will implement a new policy of providing seven wives to each husband, to which an outraged spokeswoman responds that such an arrangement is "aboven any mannys myght or power," and seven husbands to each wife would be a more sensible arrangement (20.11). In a chorus, his angry female subjects taunt Solomon with his reputation as an antifeminist: "Ye are an evyle king and youre sentences ben false and unrightfull. Now may we wel here and se that it is trouthe that we have herd of you, and that ye have of us sayde evyll, and therto ye skorne and mocke us before oure vysages that we se it" (20.13–14). The primary meaning of "sentences" here is his judicial sentences, but, given his reputation for proverbial wisdom and the multitude of proverbs he speaks in the *Dialogue*, a play on his "false and unrightfull" sayings about women is likely as well, especially given the women's accusation that Solomon has "of us sayde evyll."

With his female subjects thus roused to furious rebellion against him, Solomon reverses his former praise and delivers a tirade against women. Illustrating how the same relatively small group of antifeminist proverbs recurs in these debates, Solomon's rant includes the bitter "resemblances" with which Jankyn berates the Wife of Bath: "There is no hede more worse than the serpent, and there is no malyce to the malyce of a woman, for it were bettyr to dwelle wyth serpentys and lyons, than wyth a wyckyd woman" (21.1, cf. Ecclesiasticus 25:22–26). Having goaded Solomon into self-contradiction, Marcolf announces his victory in their final verbal contest: "Now have ye spokyn aftyr myn intent. For ones thys daye ye praysed women out of alle mesure, and now have ye dispraysed thaym as moche. That is it that I sought, always ye make my saying trewe" (22.5–6).

Not only do the combatants in these debates quote selectively from their Solomonic sources, those on the antifeminist side also carry their claims to a perversely exaggerated level and in some cases flaunt their own illogic. "All women are known to be also liars," we learn from the notorious final section of Andreas Capellanus's late twelfth-century Latin treatise *De Amore*, "There is not a living woman who does not make pretense of what is untrue and invent lies with reckless ingenuity.... Moreover all women are drunkards.... No woman can keep a secret.... Every woman in the world is also lustful." His authority for these claims? "This is why Solomon in his great wisdom ... made a general pronouncement on her vices and depravity. His words are: 'There is no good woman.'"[35] Similar hyperbole comes from the late thirteenth-century Latin *Lamentations of Matheolus*, circulated widely in Jehan LeFèvre's French translation from the 1370s. "Matheolus," the first-person speaker of the *Lamentations*, openly acknowledges the illogic of such claims while continuing to refer to them as "logical." He concedes that what is true of some women cannot be validly predicated of all: "if some women are evil and perverse and abnormal, it does not necessarily follow that all of them are so cruel and wicked. . . . Logic hates this kind of argumentation." But the pain in the speaker's heart caused by his regretted marriage to a widow leaves him no choice but to push his position "to its logical, if extreme, conclusion, which is that no good woman exists."[36]

Despite having acknowledged his fallacious reasoning, the speaker of the *Lamentations* adds Solomon's authority to his "logical" conclusion about the worthlessness of all women: "Solomon, in his works, makes an amazing comment, which supports my case, for he exclaims, 'Who could find a virtuous woman?' The implication here is, of course, that this would be impossible. Since he says this, who am I to disagree? . . . Thus there is no woman worth anything at all; I don't need to look for further proof. That's enough logical demonstration."[37] In the context from which it is wrenched, far from supporting the case for the worthlessness of women, the "amazing comment" in Proverbs 31:10 about the *mulier fortis*—the virtuous (or valiant, strong, trustworthy) woman—initiates a well-known description of this idealized feminine figure. Rather than an "amazing comment" on the worthlessness of women, the biblical utterance is a rhetorical question attributed in 31:1 to King Lamuel (understood by later commentators as an alternate name for Solomon), speaking as instructed by his mother. "Lamuel" does not ask who "could find" such a woman (with the implied answer, "no one"); rather, the question is what fortunate individual "shall find" such a woman, and the Vulgate verse continues, "far and from the uttermost coasts is the price of her."[38] The speaker expresses wonder not just at the rarity of this paragon but also at her *value*. An additional twenty verses list her virtues, including acts of charitable giving and other good works, loving care for her household, and judicious use of language: "She hath opened her mouth to wisdom, and the law of clemency is on her tongue" (Proverbs 31:26). Only through willful disregard for meaning in context does "Matheolus" arrive at his "logical" conclusion: "Thus there is no woman worth anything at all."

One of Chaucer's prime sources for the antifeminist proverbs of the *Wife's Prologue*, Jerome's late fourth century antimatrimonial tract, *Against Jovinian*, set an early precedent for twisting biblical wisdom expressions to make them more damning of women. It claims, for example, that Solomon classes "a wife" with the greatest of evils, when the evil specified in

Proverbs 30:23 results from marriage to a "hateful" or "odious" wife. Jerome anticipates the obvious objection to this distortion by trying to claim that even the *prospect* of marrying a hateful woman is not worth the risk posed by marriage: "But if you reply that it is a *hateful* wife, I will give you the same answer as before—the mere possibility of such danger is in itself no light matter."[39] He also supplies "an evil woman" as the direct cause of the sadness that in Proverbs 25:20 is said to consume a man's heart as a moth eats away a garment and a worm destroys wood. In context, a variety of disappointments, including "a man that beareth false witness against his neighbour" and trust in "an unfaithful man in time of trouble," inflict this heart-destroying sadness; living with a "brawling woman" doesn't enter the list of afflictions until 25.24.[40] Jerome employs his misleadingly presented proverb as part of a larger claim to disclose "what this Solomon with his many wives and concubines thought of marriage."[41] In a list of proverbs to which she objects, the Wife of Bath cites Jerome's doctored version, in which the many sadnesses that can consume the human heart have been narrowed to the ruin of the married man by his wife: "Thou seyest, right as wormes *shende* ['destroy'] a tree, / Right so a wyf destroyeth hire housbonde" (III.376–77).

Chaucer's interest in the use and misuse of Solomonic proverbs by antifeminist writers is not confined to the *Wife's Prologue*. In two relevant passages from elsewhere in the *Canterbury Tales*, Proserpina in the *Merchant's Tale* and Prudence in the *Tale of Melibee* take issue with the willful misinterpretation by their husbands of a Solomonic proverb, one that Blamires aptly describes as "obsessively quoted" by antifeminist writers.[42] In his search for mortals who are good, wise, and just, the speaker of Ecclesiastes laments, "One man among a thousand I have found, a woman among them all I have not found." Completing the thought, the passage continues, "Only this have I found, that God made man right, and he hath entangled himself with an infinity of questions. Who is as the wise man?" (7.29–30). The references to "man" (Vulgate *homo*, 'man or human') confirm that the speaker's pessimism extends to all mortals, not just women. In a sampling of one thousand, one good man and no good woman reflects the longstanding belief in women's moral inferiority to men, but 999 wicked men to a single right-minded one is hardly a ringing affirmation of masculine superiority. The misuse of the same proverb by another source for the *Wife's Prologue*, Jean de Meun's Jealous Husband, shows how easily a pessimistic view of all humanity could be distorted into the claim, on Solomon's authority, that no good women exist: "I have not yet found any, however many I may have tested. Not even Solomon could find them . . . for he himself affirms that he never found a stable woman."[43]

A dispute over the meaning of this same infamous proverb occurs in the brilliant comic scene from the *Merchant's Tale* in which Pluto and Proserpina—transformed from pagan deities into a Fairy King and Queen who inhabit a corner of an Italian garden—engage in a marital spat. Appalled by the ease with which May dupes her jealous husband January, Pluto assures his wife that "ten hondred thousand" examples could easily be brought to bear on "The tresons whiche that wommen doon to man" (IV.2239-40). Like other antifeminists before him, he falls back on the authority of "Salomon, wys, and . . . / Fulfild of sapience," whose words "Ful worthy been . . . to memorie / To every *wight* ['person'] that wit and reson *kan* ['knows']." He cites the results of the patriarch's search for a morally right individual:

| | |
|---|---|
| "Thus preiseth he yet the *bountee* of man: | goodness |
| ☞ 'Amonges a thousand men yet foond I *oon*, | one |
| But of wommen alle foond I *noon*.'" | none |
| (2246-48) | |

Proserpina offers a sounder interpretation of the proverb than her husband, asking that its meaning (*sentence*) in context be considered. Though her response includes some conciliatory language ("sire, ne be not wrooth"), it addresses directly one of the most egregious examples of antifeminist misuse of proverbial wisdom. In the last two quoted lines below, Proserpina vents some frustration with her husband's abuse of Solomonic wisdom and Chaucer thereby calls attention to its misuse by antifeminist writers:

| | |
|---|---|
| "But, sire, ne be not wrooth, al be it so, | |
| Though that he seyde he foond no good womman, | |
| I prey yow take the *sentence* of the man; | meaning |
| He mente thus, that in sovereyn *bontee* | goodness |
| *Nis noon* but God, but neither he ne she. | Is none |
| Ey! For verray God that *nys but oon*, | is but one |
| What make ye so muche of Salomon?" | |
| (2286-92) | |

Why indeed, Chaucer seems to ask through this unlikely fairy speaker, do masculine *auctoritees* make so much of Solomon and the tendentious antifeminist "wisdom" they attribute to him?

Pluto does not cite any of the "ten hondred thousand" examples of women's dishonesty and fickleness to which he alludes with characteristic antifeminist hyperbole. In contrast, despite the comic setting, Chaucer gives Proserpina what I read as valid support for her claim that "Wommen ful trewe, ful goode, and vertuous" can be, and always have been, found:

> "Witnesse on hem that dwelle in Cristes hous;
> With martirdom they preved *hire* constance.   *their*
> The Romayn *geestes* eek make remembrance   *historical narratives*
> Of many a verray, trewe wyf also."
> (IV.2282–85)

These are resonant lines to appear in a playful scene amid a tale full of dark ironies, but as the Host affirms in a proverb with larger implications for the *Canterbury Tales*: "A man may seye ful sooth in game and pley" (I.4355, S488).

Proserpina's observations—that saints' legends bear witness to the constancy of women martyred for Christ, that Roman history includes accounts of exemplary women, and that old books are valued sources of "remembrance"—occur in serious contexts elsewhere in Chaucer's work. The exemplary "mayde and martyr, Seint Cecilie," is the protagonist of the *Second Nun's Tale* (VIII.28). The *Legend of Good Women* includes the virtuous matron Lucretia, whose story is told by the Roman historian Livy and whom Chaucer praises in language close to Proserpina's: "the verray wif, the verray trewe Lucresse" (1686). Well-known lines from the prologue to the *Legend* observe that, were it not for old books, the key of "remembraunce" would be lost (25–26). Proserpina's attention to "the sentence of the man"—the proverb's meaning in context—models an important point about proverb use. In addition, her recourse to the exemplary women of Roman literature and the Christian saints as testimony to the existence of virtuous women foreshadows the defense against antifeminism that Christine de Pizan mounts in the *City of Ladies*. Women from ancient history help to populate Book II of the *City*, and the female Christian saints populate Book III, as both groups shelter in Christine's metaphorical city, a defensive structure that serves as an allegory for her book.

Like the Wife of Bath, Chaucer's Proserpina is a complex verbal construct, and her promise to give May and all women after her the ability to lie boldly even when caught in the act fosters an antifeminist stereotype

(IV.2265–75). Her accusations against Solomon as a lecher and idolater are based in scripture, but the passionate force of her *ad hominem* outburst against him—"I am a womman, *nedes moot I speke* ['I must speak'], / Or elles swelle til myn herte breke" (IV.2305–6)—may be Chaucer's ironic comment on the heightened emotion, at times near-hysteria, that characterizes both sides of these rancorous, proverb-fueled gender debates. Despite exposing her husband's proverb as a misuse of Solomonic wisdom in support of a spurious claim about the utter worthlessness of women, Proserpina nevertheless vents her anger on the patriarchal figure who has come to personify the antifeminist proverbs circulating in his name. Just as the Wife claims that she managed to *quiten* "word for word" ('match, rival, pay back') the antifeminist proverb use she attributes to her early husbands (III.422), Proserpina's stated aim is to return verbal harm for verbal harm in response to Solomonic antifeminist discourse: "I shal nat spare, for no curteisye, / To speke hym harm that *wolde us vileynye* ['wishes shame on us']" (IV.2309–10). Most important for our purposes is this female speaker's effort to deflate Solomon's authority and discredit one of the most sweeping and ubiquitous of antifeminist proverbs. Most of her protests are addressed to her husband: "*What rekketh me of* ['what do I care about'] youre auctoritees?" "What make ye so much of Salomon?" (IV.2276, 2293). But her reference to written slanders suggests that these remarks are also addressed to Solomon himself and to the many antifeminist authors who draw on his authority: "I sette right noght, of al the vileyne / That ye of wommen write, a boterflye!" that is, "I do not set all the wickedness you write about women even at the worth of a butterfly" (IV.2303–4).

In an entirely different tone but with identical outcome, in the *Tale of Melibee* another married couple debates the interpretation of the same "obsessively quoted" Solomonic proverb. A more deferential wife than Proserpina, Prudence listens "*ful debonairly* ['very graciously'] and with greet pacience" to her husband's citation of the "one man in a thousand" proverb, from which Melibeus draws the usual fallacious conclusion, "alle wommen been wikke" (VII.1064, 1057). Only after she has listened to "al that hir housbonde liked for to seye" does Prudence request "licence for to speke" (1064). Translated closely from the *Livre de Mellibee et Prudence*, Chaucer's model for *Melibee*,[44] Prudence's exegesis closely resembles that given to Proserpina. Prudence too holds that the proverb's point is not that good women do not exist but that no one possesses "sovereyn bountee save God allone" (1079). Where Proserpina cites Roman matrons and Christian saints as positive examples of womanhood, Prudence points out that Jesus was born from a woman and a woman was the first to be entrusted with announcing his resurrection (1074–75).

The intertextual connection between Proserpina's refutation of Solomon's proverb and the passage in *Melibee* adds authority to a speech easy to read only for its comic dimension as part of a supernatural marital spat. Outside the *Wife's Prologue*, then, the *Canterbury Tales* depicts two female figures who provide sounder and more responsibly contextualized interpretations of a key Solomonic proverb than their husbands. By including these two interpretive acts performed by fictional women, Chaucer reveals his interest in imagined feminine responses, not simply to a clerical culture seemingly saturated with antifeminist proverbs but more specifically to the misuses of language, sources, and logic involved in some of the most common proverbial condemnations of women.

### THE CRITIQUE OF ANTIFEMINIST PROVERB USE IN THE *WIFE'S PROLOGUE* AND *TALE*

The Wife's personal war on antifeminist proverbs is far more vividly imagined than the literary challenges to Solomonic wisdom we have seen thus far. It gains additional strength from its setting within a larger work that offers other forms of resistance to the monopoly on wisdom claimed by an overbearing clergy. Alison of Bath is one of Chaucer's most complex textual constructs, and I hope that the proverb-conscious reading of her *Prologue* and *Tale* that follows will reveal another of the character's many dimensions: her role as a proverb-citing and proverb-disputing female anti-Solomon. Her *Prologue* mounts a searching critique of antifeminist proverb use, deepened by an exploration of its effects on its targets, and her *Tale* models a possible path toward reform.

Unlike the Wife, neither Proserpina, a "queene of Fayerye," nor Prudence, whose allegorical dimensions I discuss in chapter 4, is represented as an ordinary woman. Thus, no naturalistic explanation need be offered for their ready access to Latin scripture and capacity to address the misinterpretation of a Solomonic proverb. Only in the more fully realized portrait of the Wife does Chaucer imagine in precise detail, down to the table of contents of Jankyn's book, the circumstances by which an unusually heavy dose of antifeminist proverbs might reach an ordinary married woman from the middle ranks of society. The *Prologue* demonstrates the corrosive effects of this exposure on such a figure, offering further support for my argument that Chaucer and his readers saw proverbs as verbal forms with significant real-life implications, in this case as potential shapers of the culture's attitudes toward women.

The giddy atmosphere of absurd exaggeration and perverse titillation that characterizes so much consciously antifeminist writing reflects the dubious assumption, or the jocular pretext, that most women would remain oblivious to its contents. The idea that antifeminist materials were surreptitiously exchanged by men behind the backs of women finds explicit statement in a mid-fourteenth century work, Richard de Bury's Latin prose *Philobiblon* (*The Love of Books*), in which a personified book describes the antagonism between a woman and a clerk's personal library. The woman, "that biped beast whose cohabitation with the clergy was forbidden of old," scolds the clerk's books for taking up too much household space, diverting attention from herself, and usurping funds that could be better used for her personal adornment—commonplaces from arguments against clerical marriage. Citing standard antifeminist authorities, this personified tome opines that a woman has even more justification than she realizes for antipathy toward the books of a clerk, as she would learn if she could "see our inmost hearts"—that is, "if she had read the book of Theophrastus or Valerius, or only heard the twenty-fifth chapter of Ecclesiasticus with understanding ears."[45] The book speculates about how a woman would react if she were somehow exposed to the antifeminist works contained within the clerk's library, most of them in Latin like Richard's own book, and concludes that if she ever encountered their contents, the hostility and scolding already natural to women would surely increase.

A possible Chaucerian comment on antifeminism's "behind her back" posturing is the moment in the *Nun's Priest's Tale* when the strutting cock Chanticleer, debating with the hen Pertelote, ostentatiously translates for her the proverb, "*Mulier est hominis confusio*" ['woman is man's ruin']: "Madame, the *sentence* ['meaning'] of this Latyn is, / 'Womman is mannes joye and al his blis'" (VII.3164–66). I will return in my conclusion to the many possible interpretations of this mistranslation, but one relevant here is that it shows a masculine figure taking advantage of a feminine figure's lack of training in Latin as an opportunity to slander her with impunity, behind her back and yet to her face. While Pertelote apparently never learns the derogatory import of her avian husband's proverb, the *Wife's Prologue* takes up the thought experiment proposed by Richard's personified book. How might an ordinary woman, of little formal education and few scruples in dealing with her elderly spouses, but with a ready wit and considerable spirit, react when faced with the hyperbole, slanders, and flagrant illogic of antifeminist proverbs?

Chaucer sets up this thought experiment by creating the clerk Jankyn who forces her to listen to readings from the same *auctoritees* that Richard's speaking book specifies. A former university student, Jankyn presumably translates these Latin clerical works for her, though Chaucer does not specify this, and some scholars take the Wife as the English translator. Or perhaps in a work of fiction we are meant simply to overlook the language issue. Whatever the case, what matters is that she hears these readings with what Richard de Bury calls "comprehending ears," at least until one of hers is deafened by Jankyn's retaliatory blow when she tears a leaf, or maybe three, out of this book even as he reads from it (III.667–68, 790–91). She has much to say about the *proverbes* contained therein, and the sorrow and pain they inflict.

The Wife's copious citations of these "sentences and proverbs" are sometimes counted among the character's intellectual inconsistencies, as contradictions of her *Prologue*'s opening contention that experience alone is "right ynogh" to qualify her to speak of the woe that awaits women in marriage. What she says, however, is that speaking from experience would be sufficient to carry her point even if ("though") not a single written authority "were in this world." On the contrary, however, all too many masculine *auctoritees* impinge on her fictional world. She responds first to the proverbs she accuses her first three husbands of harassing her with, then to those that are read aloud to her "every nyght and day" by a fifth husband who "knew of mo proverbes / Than in this world ther growen gras or herbes" (III.682, 773–74). Rather than being polarized against her daily *experience*, *auctoritees* have played an integral role in shaping that experience. The antifeminist proverbs in the *Wife's Prologue* come in two dense clusters: those she attributes to her first three husbands (224–385), falsely, as it turns out, and those that feature in Jankyn's oppressive readings (627–787). A third dense cluster occurs in her tale, where a powerful supernatural figure, read by many as a wishful version of the Wife herself, turns the tables in her extended marriage-bed lecture, in which a female figure addresses a stream of proverbs to a distressed male (1109–216). This feminine wisdom figure—the possessor of the knowledge that has saved her new husband's life—models a different and more genuinely instructive form of proverb use. Each of these clusters serves its own purposes, and I take up each in turn.

PROVERB CLUSTER 1: "I QUITTE HEM WORD FOR WORD"

In this first cluster of proverbs, attributed to the Wife's first three husbands, Solomonic wisdom speaks from a subsequently denied, but nevertheless insistently quoted, chorus of disembodied male voices, voices that stand in for antifeminist proverb tradition and its users. Like the peasant Marcolf and Chaucer's *cherles* in the previous chapter, the Wife lays claim to an alternative to Solomonic wisdom, born of her daily experience of the "wo that is in marriage." On this topic, she declares herself "expert in al myn age" (III.174), an early use of this now-ubiquitous word, here in the sense of 'experienced, wise through experience' (*MED*, s.v. "expert," adj. 1). Her rivalry with Solomon breaks the surface early in the *Prologue* when she first aspires not to his fabled stock of proverbs or his moral wisdom but to his enjoyment of marital partners:

> Lo, heere the wise kyng, daun Salomon;
> I *trowe* he hadde wyves mo than oon.     *believe*
> As wolde God it *leveful* were unto me     *Would to God;*
>                                             *permissible*
>
> To be refresshed half so ofte as he!
> Which *yifte* of God hadde he for alle his wyvys!     *gift*
> (35–39)

While the antifeminist pretext is that Solomon's experience with multiple wives led to his condemnation of women, this bawdy opening salvo celebrates wives as a gift of God and also serves as a reminder that by no means did this "wise kyng" practice the celibate avoidance that one might expect to result from the aversion to women so forcefully (and often speciously) attributed to him in the antimatrimonial discourse of clerks.

As a feminine rival to "the wise kyng, daun Salomon," the Wife constructs an alternative discourse of transgressive women's "wisdom." "A wys womman" will win her desired lover by whatever means are available; "a wys wyf" will lie to her husband and ask her maid to swear to it (III.209, 231–34). Addressing an imagined audience of "wise" married women—"Now herkneth . . . / Ye wise wyves" (225–26)—she launches her first and strangest foray into proverb use, the long series of antifeminist proverbs that she accuses her first three husbands of berating her with when they were drunk (379–83). The Solomonic associations of many of the proverbs in this cluster are readily apparent. One expression to which the Wife objects combines several verses from Proverbs: "Thow seyst that *droppyng* ['leaking'] houses, and *eek* ['also'] smoke, / And chidyng wyves maken men to flee / Out of *hir owene* ['their own'] houses" (278–80). In Proverbs 19:13, a contentious woman is compared to a dripping roof, and in 27:15, to a leaking roof on a cold day. But if, as is usually assumed, the reference to smoke as an irritant derives from Proverbs 10:26, the biblical reference is to domestic discomfort caused not by a wife but by a masculine sluggard (Latin *piger*). Small wonder that the ample quotation of antifeminist proverbs in this section, to which will be added a second cluster from Jankyn's book, has led some scholars to regard the *Wife's Prologue* itself as a piece of antifeminist writing.[46]

There is no denying the profusion of antifeminist *proverbes* in the *Wife's Prologue*. When quoted in overtly antifeminist contexts, these proverbs speak with the authoritative masculine voice of a revered author or, when anonymous, with the air of communal sanction that accompanies the premodern proverb. But in the *Wife's Prologue*, the distinctive feminine voice Chaucer creates for his best-known fictional character surrounds and infiltrates these expressions of antifeminist "wisdom," exposing and contesting their misogyny. Bakhtin's theory of embedded utterances is useful here: when a small but complete genre is "absorbed" into a larger one, its "clearly delimited" boundaries remain in place, but they become porous and allow the voice that surrounds them to flow through, an effect that in this case goes a long way toward containing and disarming the Prologue's noxious proverbs.[47] A reader hears them not simply intoned in the deep masculine voice of Solomonic authority but as contested and "re-accentuated" by the indignantly protesting voice Chaucer creates for the Wife. To quote at greater length a passage that begins with the Solomonic proverbs discussed above:

| | |
|---|---|
| ✥ Thow seyst that *droppyng* houses, and *eek* smoke, | *dripping; also* |
| And chidyng wyves maken men to flee | |
| Out of *hir* owene houses; *a benedicitee!* | *their; [God] bless you* |
| What *eyleth swich* an old man for to chide? | *ails; such* |

Thow seyst we wyves wol oure vices hide
Til we be *fast*, and thanne we wol *hem shewe*—     *i.e., married; show them*

Wel may that be a proverbe of a *shrewe*!     *scoundrel*
(278–84)

The speaker's expressions of disapproval and frustration—"a benedicitee!," "What eyleth swich an old man for to chide?," "Wel may that be a proverbe of a shrewe!"—combined with her personalization of their slanders—"Thow seyst *we* wyves wol *oure* vices hide" (my emphasis)—allow readers to hear these galling words of "wisdom" not only as a derogatory masculinist discourse supposedly carried on behind the backs of women but also as slander actively deplored and contested by an imagined feminine voice.

As in the quotation above, a curious and noteworthy aspect of the voicing of this first proverb cluster is its heavily repeated accusation "thou sayest," followed by an unexpected *volte face* at the end. The Wife attributes the proverbs in this section to her first three husbands by means of some *thirty* repetitions of forms of "thou sayest," "thanne seistow," "thus seistow," interspersed with vehement denunciations of that masculine "thou" who so persistently "seyest": "olde dotard shrewe," "olde barel-ful of lyes," "Sire olde fool," "Moote thy welked nekke be tobroke! ['May your withered neck be broken']" (III.291, 302, 357, 277). After thirty-plus repetitions and variations on "thou seyest," the Wife announces quite startlingly that her husbands did not say any of it. Although she swore, and induced her accomplices to swear, that "thus they seyden in *hir* ['their'] dronkenesse," nevertheless, "al was fals": it seems they did not assail her with antifeminist proverbs when drunk; they were, she declares, "ful giltelees" (379–85). That women serve their own ends by making false allegations against their husbands is a familiar charge in antimatrimonial and antifeminist discourse; the Wife's subsequent boast that she covered her own behavior by falsely accusing her husbands of having lovers is a typical example (391–99). But accusing her husbands of a malign form of *proverb use* in which they apparently never engaged is a much more interesting false allegation, and, as far as I know, one unique to Chaucer.

If it was not her earlier husbands who spoke these bitter proverbs against women, as the Wife so casually admits at the end of her long recital, perhaps the reader is meant to ask who *did* say them—who is this overbearing "thou"? Her litany is so extensive, her reversal of it so offhand, and this alleged method of husband management so improbable, that interpretation beyond the literal level of the plot seems warranted. A possible answer is that "Solomon" spoke these proverbs, or better, they were spoken by an antifeminist literary tradition that adopted Solomon as one of its foremost *auctoritees*. The repetition of the "thou seyest" formula, along with the misogyny of the quoted proverbs and the blurring of the identities of the different husbands falsely accused of uttering them, gives this first onslaught of proverbs an almost surreal quality, as though it is hard even for the fictional speaker to separate fabrications from painful past experience. The repeated accusations of malign proverb use so insistently addressed to "thou" might also encompass her largely male listening audience—how many of these imaginary pilgrims might have used proverbs such as these? Perhaps these accusations also gave pause to Chaucer's original readers; how many of them, having repeated antifeminist proverbs, might answer to the charge "thou seyest"?

Perhaps we are to assume that "al" this part of her narrative "was fals"—not only did her "olde husbondes" not speak these proverbs, as she admits, but neither did she accuse them of it at the time. It is even possible to read this entire account as part of a yarn the Wife spins for the benefit of the "wyves" she apostrophizes at its opening, promising to instruct them in how to interact with their husbands—"Thus shulde ye speke" (III.226)—and for her listening pilgrim audience. In other words, this derogatory proverb use could be a fiction she invents after, and perhaps as a result of, Jankyn's incessant recitation of antifeminist proverbs. If, as seems important later in the prologue, she acquires these learned antifeminist proverbs from readings by her fifth husband, then her account of falsely accusing her first three husbands of using them might be best understood as a tall tale, one designed to reveal the lasting effect they have had on this complexly imagined fictional character.

If we take the proverbs in this first cluster as standing in for the whole tradition of antifeminist writing, the emphasis on the Wife's having "quited" or paid back these imaginary proverb users "word for word" helps to explain the adoption in her prologue of their methods of selective and out-of-context quotation. In her own argumentation, she rivals, matches, and pays back in kind the misuses of *auctoritees* committed by antifeminist writers. In the important passage that concludes this first proverb cluster, she declares victory over her "olde husbondes" and their alleged abuse:

> For, by my trouthe, I *quitte hem* word for word,   *repaid them*
> As helpe me verray God omnipotent,
> Though I right now sholde make my testament,
> I *ne owe hem nat* a word that *it nys quit*.   *do not owe them;*
>                                                  *hasn't been repaid*
>
> I broghte it so aboute by my wit
> That they moste *yeve* it up, as for the beste,   *give*
> Or elles hadde we nevere *been in reste*;   *lived in peace*
> For thogh he looked as a *wood* leon,   *crazed*
> Yet sholde he faille *of his conclusion*.   *to attain his goal*
> (III.422–30)

This passage stands out for its emphatic opening lines of formal oath-taking, in which the speaker pledges her "trouthe" before God—even if she were on the edge of death and making her final "testament"—that not a single word of their alleged abuse went unrequited: "I quitte hem word for word," and again, even more emphatically, "I ne owe hem nat a word that it nys quit."

Ironically, this avowed repayment in kind has at times led to criticism of the character's flawed intellect, as witnessed by her misuse of sources. Probably the most definitive of these detractors, D. W. Robertson, wrote in the mid-twentieth century of the Wife's misleading effort to enlist Saint Paul in her defense of sexuality in marriage: "The support for her position that Alisoun is able to derive from St. Paul is obtained only by quoting him out of context or by disregarding the obvious implications of what he says."[48] Yet as we have seen, taking proverbs out of context and "disregarding the obvious implications" of what a writer says describes precisely what antifeminist writers so flagrantly do, as Chaucer was well aware. Both Prudence and Proserpina urge that misusers of the "one man in a thousand" proverb look at its speaker's intent, judged by its meaning in context (IV.2286–90, VII.1076–80). The selective quotation and disregard for context that Robertson and other scholars of his era emphasized as intellectual and moral failings of the Wife are indeed part of the fabric of her prologue, but, as Carolyn Dinshaw pointed out over thirty years ago in a pioneering feminist reading, the specious argumentation Chaucer gives the Wife mocks the methods by which antifeminist writers such as Jerome and Jean de Meun arrived at their slanders.[49] Thus the character's emphatic declarations about *quiting* her husbands' antifeminist discourse draw the reader's attention, not just to her war on the substance of antifeminist proverbs but also to the openly irresponsible methods by which those proverbs were altered and applied.

In her declaration of victory over husbands one through three, the Wife claims that she brought about the desired outcome by her "wit" (III.426), that quick, sharp, and amoral faculty that women and peasants in medieval literature often draw upon to counter the high wisdom clerics claimed for themselves. Stepping back from the literal account of this alleged interaction between the Wife and her first three husbands, we can read it as another instance of verbal sparring between authoritative Solomonic wisdom and a stalwart challenger determined to match, rival, and pay it back. We can see in the Wife a kind of female Marcolf, less profane and more refined in her speech, but whose means of verbal competition against a more powerful opponent are morally ambiguous at best.[50] And the opponent Chaucer pits her against is indeed powerful, a chorus of male voices that stands in for antifeminist proverb tradition. Even if the husbands in the Wife's narrative did not voice these defamatory expressions, someone did, many times over—it is in the nature of proverbs to be repeated, and it is in the nature of antifeminist writing to repeat its proverbs obsessively.

PROVERB CLUSTER 2: "NO WOMMAN OF NO CLERK IS PREYSED"

By depicting the Wife's deception, scolding, and ill-treatment of her early husbands amid a flood of proverbs proclaiming that this is what women were born to do, Chaucer reveals how the stereotypes these proverbs convey have distorted the character's nature. We have seen that *quiting* in the *Canterbury Tales* can be an effective and humorous way of cutting a rival's words down to size and revealing their blind spots, as when the Miller announces that he will tell "a noble tale" with which to "quite the Knyghtes tale" (I.3126–27). *Quiting* can also be destructive to a teller's language use, however, as when the Reeve vengefully sets out to *quiten*, not the Miller's *tale* but the Miller himself, by means of a fabliau notably darkened by the aggressive motives attributed to its fictional teller (3916). In the *Wife's Prologue*, the act of *quiting* a discourse riddled with antifeminist proverbs leaves its disfiguring mark on the thought and language of the requiter.

This second wave of antifeminist proverbs, brought on this time by Jankyn's readings from his "book of wikked wyves," is more painfully dispiriting than the first, both to its first-person speaker and to sympathetic readers. In contrast to her lack of respect or affection for the derided elderly husbands—those debilitated stand-ins for Solomon—the now-aging Wife expresses love for her fifth husband, younger and better educated than she, and Chaucer depicts her as taking to heart the harsh proverbs Jankyn cites in judgment of herself and other women. For premodern readers and writers, the combination of "sentences and proverbes" and physical beatings from her husband that the Wife endures in this fifth marriage might recall the use of rod and switch in inculcating the proverbs so central to elementary education.[51] For well over a hundred lines (roughly III.650–787), the reader experiences along with the narrating Wife the protracted misery of a second round of antifeminist proverbs. Chaucer specifies the contents of the notorious book from which Jankyn reads with such pleasure, complete with *Against Jovinian* and the "Parables of Salomon":

| | |
|---|---|
| He hadde a book that gladly, nyght and day, | |
| For his *desport* he wolde rede alway; | entertainment |
| He *cleped* it Valerie and Theofraste, | called |
| At which book he *lough* alwey *ful faste*. | laughed; very hard |
| And *eek* ther was somtyme a clerk at Rome, | also |
| A cardinal, that *highte* Seint Jerome, | was called |
| That made a book agayn Jovinian; | |
| In which book *eek* ther was Tertulan, | also |
| Crisippus, Trotula, and Helowys, | |
| That was abbesse nat fer fro Parys, | |
| And *eek* the Parables of Salomon, | also |
| Ovides Art, and bookes many on, | |
| And alle thise were bounden in *o* volume. | one |
| (669–81) | |

To the narrating Wife, it seems that Jankyn read "nyght and day," "alway," "every nyght and day" (669–70, 682). On and on he goes: "*Tho* ['then'] redde he me" (twice), "No thyng forgat he," "He tolde me *eek* ['also']," "Thanne tolde he me" (721–57). Without respite, "He spak moore harm than *herte may bithynke* ['the heart can imagine']" (772), until it was clear that "he wolde nevere *fyne* ['cease'] / To reden on this cursed book al nyght" (788–89). Once again, thanks to the speaker's running commentary, we hear the antifeminist proverbs in this section "re-accentuated" by the distinctive feminine narrating voice, this time inflected by suffering as well as indignation.

Jankyn's oppressive readings illustrate once again the bookish character of medieval antifeminism, and here the emphasis on the material book culminates in the Wife's assault on her husband's favored volume. Chaucer and his contemporaries were doubtless able to quote familiar biblical proverbs from memory, as we still do today when we say "Eat, drink, and be merry," or "There is nothing new under the sun" (Ecclesiastes 8:15, 1:10). But the prologue also represents Jankyn paging through his Bible to locate a proverb with which to rebuke his wife:

| | |
|---|---|
| And thanne wolde he upon his Bible seke | |
| That *ilke* proverbe of Ecclesiaste | *same* |
| Where he comandeth and forbedeth *faste* | *firmly* |
| Man shal nat *suffre* his wyf *go roule* aboute. | *allow; to roam* |
| (III.650–53, citing Ecclesiasticus 25:34, unmarked by Speght) | |

Chaucer here names the book of Ecclesiasticus as the proverb's source, but like other medieval writers, he would have attributed to Solomon this authoritarian voice that "comandeth" obedience and "forbedeth" a husband to allow his wife freedom of movement.[52]

As I have suggested, the experience of hearing these sayings reaccentuated by a powerfully imagined feminine voice may in itself have had a strong impact on Chaucer's contemporary readers by bringing the vituperation written by "clerkes . . . withinne *hire* ['their'] oratories" out of the cloister and into an ordinary domestic setting (694). As with the first proverb cluster, here too the voice Chaucer creates for the Wife stubbornly resists an invidious form of proverb use:

| | |
|---|---|
| But al for noght, I sette noght an *hawe* | *hawthorn berry* |
| Of his proverbes *n'of* his olde *sawe* | *nor of; sayings* |
| Ne I wolde nat *of hym* corrected be. | *Nor would I by him* |
| I hate hym that my vices telleth me, | |
| And so doo *mo*, God *woot*, of us than I. | *more; knows* |
| (III.659–63) | |

Her pugilistic response to Jankyn's "proverbes" and "his olde sawe"—ripping leaves from his book and landing a blow with her fist that sends him reeling backwards into the fireplace (788–93)—suggests to the reader that his proverbs did matter more than a hawthorn berry, despite her protestations of imperviousness. But Chaucer's larger point is well taken: no one's moral character improves in response to denigration in the guise of high Solomonic wisdom, some of it misquoted or falsely interpreted, and all of it constituting an ugly underside of premodern proverb use.

In addition to the prohibition on allowing a wife freedom of movement quoted earlier, Chaucer cites four other expressions as illustrations of Jankyn's antifeminist proverbs, three of them noted by Speght, who, perhaps to his credit, seems a little less meticulous than elsewhere about calling each antifeminist proverb to the reader's attention.[53] Here is Jankyn, as he "spak moore harm than herte may bithynke":

&gt; "Bet is," quod he, "thyn habitacioun
Be with a leon or a foul dragoun,
Than with a womman usyng for to chyde.
&gt; Bet is," quod he, "hye in the roof abyde,
Than with an angry wyf doun in the hous;
They been so wikked and contrarious,
They haten that *hir* housbondes loven *ay*."  *their; always*
&gt; He seyde, "A womman cast hir shame away,
Whan she cast of hir smok," and forthermo,
"A fair womman, but she be chaast also,
Is lyk a gold ryng in a sowes nose."
(III.775–85)

Except for the claim that women cast away their modesty when they undress, which is adapted from a classical expression found in Jerome's *Against Jovinian*, these antifeminist chestnuts, including the unmarked final saying about the gold ring in a sow's nose, originate in the Solomonic wisdom books.[54] Instead of reveling in how she *quited* their alleged utterers, as in her earlier account of her response to the proverb use of the three elderly husbands, this time the Wife speaks of the demoralizing effect on herself of Jankyn's recitation:

Who wolde *wene*, or who wolde suppose,  *believe*
The wo that in myn herte was, and *pyne*?  *pain*
(786–87)

While Richard de Bury has his personified clerical book imagine that a woman's natural tendency to "chide" would escalate if she were exposed to Latin antifeminist writings, Chaucer gives his character a more complex set of reactions. First comes the combative account of how she paid back the proverbs she falsely attributed to the "giltelees" elderly husbands—making of them, I have argued, stand-ins for the disembodied male voices of antifeminist proverb tradition. But then follow her expressions of sorrow and pain brought on by the contents of the volume Jankyn shares with such consistent hilarity: "At which book he *lough* ['laughed'] alwey ful faste" (672).

With their unremitting emphasis on feminine contentiousness, lasciviousness, deception, weakness of mind, and metaphorical monstrosity, Jankyn's daily and nightly readings to his wife stand in for the potential infringement of antifeminist proverbs on women's wellbeing in premodern culture. Some would have encountered them directly, as with the relative few like Christine de Pizan who read for themselves Latin and vernacular antifeminist clerical texts. For women with little to no literacy training, "an heep of lerned men" (I.575) were available to serve as conduits: not just clerics but also educated male relatives and husbands, with motives that doubtless ranged from well-intended efforts at building character to the deliberate infliction of pain.

If we take the clerical tradition of antifeminist proverbs—that relatively small body of expressions used by writers who seemed to Christine to "speak with one mouth"—as the ultimate identity of the "thou" who speaks these slanders of women, both the first onslaught and then those introduced through Jankyn's readings, we see how insidiously they operate, sometimes with the identity of their original bearers only half-remembered, misattributed, or wholly suppressed. They have the capacity, in Christine's words, to bring their hearers to the point of believing that "God formed a vile creature when He made woman."⁵⁵ Not only do antifeminist proverbs assert the derogatory "resemblances" to which the Wife objects (III.368–70), her prologue suggests that, over time, by persistently "likening" women to destructive forces and insensate objects, "sentences and proverbes" also have the power to help *create* those resemblances.

An example of this power is the Wife's claim to the ability to lie openly, a boast she supports with an antifeminist proverb:

> Now herkneth hou I baar me proprely,
> Ye wise wyves, that kan understonde.
> Thus shulde ye speke and *bere hem*    *swear to a*
> *wrong on honde,*    *false accusation*
> ☞ For half so boldely kan ther no man

Swere and lyen, as a womman kan.
(III.224–28)

She attributes her success in manipulating her early husbands to that amoral "wit" alleged to be native to women from birth, again citing an antifeminist proverb as authority for this claim:

| | |
|---|---|
| For al swich wit is *yeven* us in oure byrthe; | *given* |
| ☞ Deceite, wepyng, spynnyng God hath *yive* | *given* |
| To wommen *kyndely*, whil that they may lyve. | *by nature* |
| And thus of *o* thyng I *avaunte me*: | *one; boast* |
| Atte ende I *hadde the bettre* in ech degree, | *got the upper hand* |
| By *sleighte* or force, or by som maner thyng, | *trickery* |
| As by continueel murmur or grucchyng. | |
| (400–406) | |

The marked proverb circulated in learned circles in concise Latin form: "fallere, flere, nere / Statuit deus in muliere" ['God instilled in woman the capacity to deceive, weep, and spin']. The words "And thus" that follow it in the fourth quoted line suggest a causal connection between the proverb's claims that these traits are native to women and the Wife's attribution of them to herself, making of the proverb a self-fulfilling prophesy.[56]

Here too we can turn to Christine de Pizan, who deplores a version of the same proverb, for evidence that a writer of Chaucer's day could recognize how this expression and others like it helped to sustain negative perceptions of women. Acknowledging the authority carried by proverbs in her culture, Christine's first-person speaker in the *City of Ladies* laments the use by men of a softer version of these weaponized words, in which "to deceive" is replaced by "to speak" (with the implication "too much"): "men have burdened me with a heavy charge taken from a Latin proverb, which runs, 'God made women to speak, weep, and spin,' which they use to attack women" (I.10.3).[57] Interestingly, despite the substantial distance between Chaucer's battle-scarred, amoral Wife and Christine's principled, reason-guided first-person speaker, both deploy the same defensive strategy against this proverb: reappropriation, or adopting as praise what was meant as denigration, a recourse often favored by those in positions of lesser power.

Christine's Lady Reason, personifying the speaker's own reason, does not boast of being guilty of the proverb's charges against women in the rebellious manner of Chaucer's dame Alys, but she does accept them, albeit in the softened version that substitutes speech for deception: "this proverb is so true that it cannot be held against whoever believes or says it" (1.10.3). Yes, Reason explains, it is true that women weep, but Christ too shed tears of compassion, and he honored the tears of Mary Magdalene; his mother's tears moved Saint Augustine to convert. Yes, women spin, but their clothmaking contributes to the comfort of all humanity. Yes, women speak, and as a woman writer, Christine resists most strongly and at greatest length the proverb's demeaning of women's language. Unlike "our contemporary pontiffs," Reason argues, Christ valued women's speech, citing examples from scripture (I.10.5). Reason's tart contrast between the antifeminism of Latin clerical culture ("our contemporary pontiffs") and the higher authority of Christ recalls an equally pointed opposition in the *Wife's Prologue* (III.26–29), where the antimatrimonial glosses produced by "men" are contrasted with the encouragement in Genesis to "wexe and multiplye," a "gentil text" that comes from God. Like Reginald Pecock in the previous chapter, Christine too regards extended refutation of a proverb as an effective means of argument when a pervasive cultural attitude is at stake. She devotes the equivalent of about four pages in a modern printed edition to disarming this proverb of just seven words in its Latin version, another reminder of how our dismissive view of proverbs distances us from the seriousness with which they were taken by premodern readers and writers.

In the famous passage from the *City of Ladies* quoted briefly above, Christine's speaker directly acknowledges the negative shaping power of misogynist sayings wielded by clerks. Her response to reading the proverb-heavy *Lamentations of Matheolus* is worth quoting at greater length:

> And so I relied more on the judgment of others than on what I myself felt and knew. I was so transfixed in this line of thinking for such a long time that it seemed as if I were in a stupor. Like a gushing fountain, a series of authorities, whom I recalled one after another, came to mind, along with their opinions on this topic. And I finally decided that God formed a vile creature when He made woman.... As I was thinking this, a great unhappiness and sadness welled up in my heart, for I detested myself and the entire feminine sex, as though we were monstrosities in nature.[58]

Although the imaginary Wife's nursing of her personal grievances contrasts with the disciplined refutations of proverbs spoken by Christine's allegorical ladies, both late medieval texts depict at length the pain, sadness, and deformation of self that result from exposure, direct or indirect, to the twisted proverbial "wisdom" that makes up so much antifeminist writing. Both testify to the premodern belief that, for better and worse, proverbs produce effects in the world. In her prologue, the Wife remains locked into a reactive position as an anti-Solomon, "paying back" the patriarch and those who adopt and misquote his sayings, *quiting* them word for word, and in the process acting out the stereotypes these proverbs promulgate. As a source of respite and hope, Christine offers her book as an allegorical walled city where women can take refuge from antifeminist writings. In the Wife's performance, the potential for remediation comes in her tale where, at least in the magical world of Arthurian romance, a female wisdom figure can model a healthier, more genuinely instructive, *wiser* form of proverb use.

### PROVERB CLUSTER 3: "LAT THE WOMMAN TELLE HIRE TALE"

If Chaucer had kept to what most scholars accept as his initial plan to give the Wife the tale now assigned to the Shipman, a fabliau in which a wife successfully outwits, deceives, and extorts money from her husband, her performance would have offered the reader little help in imagining more constructive forms of proverb use than the embattled uses described in her prologue.[59] Instead, he made the more intriguing choice of the Arthurian romance we know as the *Wife of Bath's Tale*, where he completes a rehabilitation project barely begun in her prologue. Beginning as it does with a rape, the tale's vision of a better world for women is not the one we would imagine today. Its symbolic *contrapasso*, by which the sin against one feminine figure is redeemed by granting freedom of choice to another denies justice to the assaulted maiden on the literal level of the tale's plot. Yet among the tale's chief accomplishments is its depiction of a feminine wisdom figure who succeeds in rescripting masculine language and behavior, drawing upon the educative power of *proverbes* to transform her new husband's callous disparagement into an affirmation of her right to choose. While the prologue demonstrates the capacity of antifeminist "wisdom" to deform the culture's images of women and women's images of themselves, the tale suggests the potential for ethically used "sentences and proverbes" to help remediate hostile gender relations.

A telling moment in the *Wife's Prologue* foreshadows the remediation attempted in the tale. Amid the first wave of antifeminist proverbs initially attributed to her early husbands, the Wife makes a brief attempt at rescripting these attacks. Breaking the pattern of following the formula "thou seyest" with an antifeminist *proverbe*, she models for her husbands an alternative discourse:

| | |
|---|---|
| Thou sholdest seye, "Wyf, go wher *thee liste*; | *you please* |
| *Taak youre disport*, I wol nat *leve* no talys. | *Enjoy yourself; believe* |
| I knowe yow for a *trewe* wyf, dame Alys" | *faithful* |
| (III.318–20) | |

This effort to transform what a disparaging masculine voice says into what it *should* say comes to fruition at the end of her prologue, when a chastened Jankyn utters a version of the prescribed rewording:

| | |
|---|---|
| "Myn owene trewe wyf, | |
| Do *as thee lust* the terme of al thy lyf; | *as you please* |
| Keep thyn honour, and keep *eek myn estaat*." | *also my social position* |
| (819–21) | |

This preliminary glimpse of language reform in the *Wife's Prologue* is played out at greater length in her tale, where a supernatural figure, regarded by many as the Wife's wishful image of herself, is equally committed to reeducating and rescripting a male antagonist, in this case the rapist knight. From her position of supernatural power, the tale's wise woman can be more scrupulous than the Wife in her methods, but the outcome, a husband who forgoes verbal abuse and grants his wife freedom of choice, is the same.

In the shift from prologue to tale, through an interruption by the Friar, Chaucer again signals that it is not so much secular husbands who are the primary focus of the critique mounted here as the theoretically celibate clerks primarily responsible for antifeminist discourse, with its attacks on women and its purposeful disparagement of marriage. Earlier in the Wife's recital, the Pardoner (one of several ambiguously clerical figures in the *Tales*) interrupts to assert that listening to the Wife has persuaded him not to marry (III.164–68), an irony given that the point, or the ostensible point, of much antifeminist discourse was to discourage matrimony among males associated with the Church. One of the prologue's best-known passages is an attack on clerks that openly accuses them of a hypocritical misogyny: aside from holy saints, they never speak well of any woman; then, in their "dotage," when their sexual performance is no longer worth an old shoe, they sit at their desks and write attacks on women (688–710). When the Friar breaks in to jest about her lengthy preamble, she interprets this second interruption as an attempt at suppression and commences her tale with an icy request for his permission to continue speaking: "If I have licence of this worthy Frere" (855).

The story matter of her tale that follows, with its roots in Celtic fairy lore, draws upon a tradition of female sovereignty that offers powerful resistance to the clerical antifeminism depicted in the Wife's performance, as Richard Firth Green points out in *Elf Queens and Holy Friars*.[60] To the points he makes about the resistance inherent in the tale's traditional plot, I would add another counterforce against the antifeminism of clerks: the tale's representation of an idealized form of proverb use as a means of moral transformation. When the women of Arthur's kingdom choose rehabilitation for its rapist knight as an alternative to the death sentence pronounced by the king, they commit to a program of reeducation. They send him off to research the question of what women most desire, a question he can only answer by listening to women. The climax of this prescribed course of listening is his attention to the very long and proverb-dense lecture the wise old woman delivers in their marriage bed, to which we will return. At 107 lines (III.1109–216), it takes up fully a quarter of the tale; it exceeds by a few lines even Theseus's extended oration at the end of the much longer *Knight's Tale*.

As a result of his heinous assault, no longer may the knight "do al as hym liketh" however it may affect others; now, to keep his "nekke-boon from iren," he must commence his program of reeducation (III.914, 906). It often happens in Arthurian romance that the adventure of which a knight is morally most in need arises apparently out of nowhere: it is *his* adventure, it chooses him, called up by some flaw or failing in him. So it happens with the group of dancing ladies the knight comes upon, seemingly by chance, after a year of futile searching. In peril of his life and with time running out, he approaches eagerly ("ful yerne"), "In hope that som wysdom sholde he lerne" (993–94). His eagerness to acquire "som wysdom" calls into being the tale's shapeshifting and proverb-dispensing feminine wisdom figure. She remains behind the others in her aged and ugly guise, apparently assumed for pedagogical reasons, to judge by the vocabulary of instruction with which Chaucer surrounds her.

In her supernatural wisdom, the old woman knows already when she meets him that this rapist knight is on the wrong path with no way forward: "Sire knyght, heer forth ne lith no wey" (III.1001). She recognizes his need for instruction: "I shal thee teche" (1019). When the knight returns to court, he faces a judge and jury that could only exist in this imaginary woman-centered world:

> Ful many a noble wyf, and many a mayde,
> And many a wydwe, for that they been wise,
> The queene hirself sittynge as a justise,
> Assembled been, his answere for to heere.
> (1026–29)

To this panel of wives, maidens, wise widows, and his queen, the knight correctly repeats what he has learned:

> ☞ "Wommen desiren to have sovereynetee
>   As wel over hir housbond as hir love,
>   And for to been in maistrie hym above."
>   (1038–40, W539)

As Speght's pointing hand indicates, the knight's newly acquired wisdom takes the form of a *sentence* or *proverbe*, a precept that in its generality rises above individual experience. By memorizing and accurately repeating it, the knight demonstrates his own "maistrie" over one of the most elementary lessons of the premodern schoolroom, and the old woman once again asserts her role as instructor: "I taughte this answere unto the knyght" (1050).

To recite correctly what counts as a wise saying in the Wife's imaginary women's world is a start, but has this deeply compromised and unpromising pupil understood it? Will he be able to apply it when the right situation arises, the key to effective proverb use, according to thinkers from Erasmus to Walter Benjamin and Kenneth Burke? When King Arthur responds to the queen's intercession on behalf of the knight by suspending his death sentence and leaving it to her to choose whether the knight will live or die (III.898), he utters the first of the tale's many significant repetitions of forms of the verb *chesen*, 'to choose'. These repetitions emphasize freedom of choice as a necessary precondition of a woman's *sovereynetee*. The first sign that the knight has made a little progress is when, instead of simply breaking his word and refusing her, he pleads with his prospective bride not to ask for marriage as a reward for her instruction: "For Goddes love, as chees a newe requeste!" (1060). Having promised to grant what she asks if it be in his power, he acknowledges her right to choose the reward.

His distress when the new couple is brought to bed creates a striking reversal of the conventional marriage-bed scene. The groom tosses and turns like a blushing bride while his self-assured new spouse "lay smy-lynge everemo," wondering aloud whether all Arthurian knights share her bridegroom's standoffishness on their wedding night (III.1086–90). He has kept his word, but with the protest that his new bride is old, ugly, and of low degree. As a result, she offers a point-by-point scholarly refutation, and, despite his intended sarcasm, the Friar is right to speak of the Wife as engaging in "scole-matere" (1272). It constitutes the third and last dense cluster of "sentences and proverbs" in the Wife's performance, eighteen in a row by Speght's count.[61] The last eleven of these, marked with their tiny fists, appear on the page from Speght's 1602 edition that serves as a frontispiece to this book.

To us a series of proverbs seems an implausible method for bringing about moral transformation, and many modern readers are understandably skeptical of the speech's power to complete the reeducation of the knight. But for premodern audiences, for whom proverbs were the start and basis for schooling, "the stuff and the proof of learning," the educative power of well-chosen *auctoritees* was real.[62] Despite the humor in the juxtaposition of a series of eighteen earnest "sentences and proverbs" to the erotic setting of the marriage bed, her tale does not hold the contents of the speech up to ridicule. It represents one of the densest gatherings of *proverbes* in the *Canterbury Tales* outside of *Melibee*, and its *auctoritees*—Dante, Seneca, Boethius—were among the most venerated by Chaucer and his culture.

The knight's disparagement of his bride as ugly, old, and of low degree offends against Christian charity as well as against chivalry and respect for the wisdom of age. The wise woman responds with the standard Christian teaching that true *gentilesse*, nobility of character, is measured by virtuous behavior rather than rank or wealth. As one of her *proverbes* holds, "he is gentil that dooth gentil dedis" (III.1170, D131). Some of the egalitarian proverbs that help to make up her speech are found in varying versions throughout medieval literature, but that does not make them tired truisms; rather, their idealism was in acute tension with the realities of an openly hierarchical society. Having served hereditary *gentils*, Chaucer witnessed firsthand the fissure between the Christian values espoused by the old woman's proverbs and the actions of the powerful in a steeply stratified society. Expression of these values and the many challenges posed to them by the political realities of his day recur throughout his works, including the *ballade* titled "Gentilesse" by modern editors and "Moral balade of Chaucier" in manuscript. According to this poem, unless an individual refrains from vice, "He is noght gentil, thogh he riche seme, / *Al were he* ['Although he wears'] mytre, croune, or diademe" (13–14).

The *proverbes* with which his new bride answers the knight's defamation make the counter-assertions that riches are no indication of nobility of character, that the poor can be rich in virtue, that age is to be respected, and that marital fidelity and strength of character can compensate for lack of youth and beauty. Many of them receive the expansive framing we have seen elsewhere in Chaucer's verse. The most extended example involves a three-line preparation for a "sentence" from a revered poet:

> "Wel kan the wise poete of Florence,
> That highte Dant, speken in this sentence.
> Lo, in swich maner rym is Dantes tale:
> ☞ '*Ful selde* up riseth by his branches smale         *very seldom*
> Prowesse of man, for God, of his goodnesse,
> *Wole* that of hym we clayme oure gentilesse.'"        *Wills*
> (III.1125–30)

The named *auctoritee*, Dante, is affirmed as "wise" in the first quoted line, and the expression's genre, *sentence*, is specified in the second. The image of a man's worth arising, not from the "small branches" of his human ancestry, but from the goodness of God, echoes *Purgatorio* 7.121–23. Gracious but firm, the speech responds to a knight callous enough to rebuke what appears to be a poor old woman for her poverty:

> ☞ "Poverte a *spectacle* is, as *thynketh me*,         *optical lens; it seems to me*
> Thurgh which he may his *verray* freendes see.        *true*
> And therefore, sire, *syn* that I *nought yow greve*,  *since; do not injure you at all*
> Of my poverte namoore ye me *repreve*."               *reprove*
> (1203–6)

With the authority conferred by her *proverbes*, this imaginary wise woman speaks in a learned and reflective voice, respectful ("sire") and yet forceful ("Of my poverte namoore ye me repreve"), requiring civil treatment from the knight whose life she has saved.

Although she does not comment on the role of proverbs *per se* in the old woman's education of the knight, Susan Crane writes that he has been "changed by her words." The knight "accepts her culturally authoritative arguments concerning the regulated behavior of true gentility," a view of the old woman's successful instruction that other critics have shared.[63] Just before her speech, he addresses his new wife as "my dampnacioun" (III.1067). After it, when she asks him to choose whether he wants a wife who is young and beautiful but likely to be unfaithful, or an old, ugly wife whose fidelity is assured, he "avyseth hym and *sore siketh* ['sighs heavily']," but "atte laste" he puts himself in her "wise governance" (1228–33). Having learned not just to repeat the *proverbe* that saves his life but also to apply it, he offers his apparently ugly, old, and lowborn wife the right to self-determination or *sovereynetee*. "My lady and my love, and wyf so deere, . . . / Cheseth youreself which may be moost plesance / And moost honour to yow and me also" (1230–33). Without the protracted misery and spousal violence required for marital reconciliation in the *Wife's Prologue*, they reach an accord, and the knight's words directly recall those spoken earlier by the reformed Jankyn: "Myn owene trewe wyf, / Do *as thee lust* ['as you please'] the terme of al thy lyf; / Keep thyn honour, and keep *eek myn estaat* ['also my social position']" (819–21). As noted earlier, Jankyn's words in turn echo the Wife's first attempt to rescript the oppressive antifeminism she attributes to her first three husbands. Through the power of *proverbes* designed to enlighten rather than berate, the wise woman models the ethical use of language briefly imagined by the Wife in her *Prologue*, when she tries to overwrite what antifeminist male voices say about women, altering "thou seyist" to "Thou sholdest seye" (318–20).

True to the tale's vision of feminine "wysdom" as a means of transforming masculine behavior, in this third and final cluster of proverbs, Chaucer's wise woman does not respond to her new spouse's injurious words with defamatory "antimasculinist" proverbs, even though his initial act of violence against women is far more serious than Alison of Bath's transgressions against her husbands. In contrast to the antifeminist slurs in the *Wife's Prologue*, the *proverbes* spoken by the feminine wisdom figure in the tale are not twisted or misconstrued in a specious effort to demonstrate that all men are wicked. Even though the Wife and the supernatural being in her tale share some traits, including a fondness for long speeches, this imagined better self is not a combative anti-Solomon created in the teller's own image but rather, in accordance with the premodern understanding of the role of *proverbes* in moral education, she is a genuine teacher. She too *quites* her husband "word for word," but only in the sense that she takes up and refutes each of his charges individually.

In contrast to their use as assault weapons in the Wife's turbulent domestic life, in this imaginary world proverbs are tools to reason with and instruct. Pushing back against a clerical culture of virulent antifeminist proverbs held more urgency for Chaucer and his original readers than it does for us, and thus many modern readers experience justifiable discomfort, disappointment, or anger when the knight is rewarded with a loving and lovely wife. Vindication for the old woman is not reparation for the survivor of his brutal assault. But it is also true that the tale does not take his crime lightly: he faces a death sentence until the old woman shares her life-granting wisdom and he shows himself to have understood the role of choice in the attainment of female sovereignty. In the context of the Wife's whole performance, prologue and tale work together to expose and counter a proverb-centered clerical discourse with the capacity to inflict damage on all women.

Only in fantasy, as in the imaginary golden "olde dayes of the Kyng Arthour" (III.857), could a supernatural female wisdom figure model the ethical use of "sentences and proverbes" to reeducate a knightly representative of a misogynist culture and reform his criminal behavior. Yet one of the most appealing properties of medieval romance is its ability to imagine different and better worlds. Such imaginings can serve as an impetus toward change, and in this case a vision of reformed proverb use offers one step toward more equitable gender roles. Like Erasmus after him, Chaucer recognizes the suasive power wielded by compact, culturally affirmed, and memorable verbal forms, and in the Wife's performance he depicts their capacity to inflict injury but also their potential to instruct and repair. One of the uses of "sentences and proverbes" in the *Canterbury Tales* is to afford both *cherles*, as we saw in chapter 2, and the ordinary woman featured in this chapter the means to answer back, to contest the idea that clerks possess all the truth and wisdom that matter as well as the authority to impose their vision of wisdom on the rest of society.

CHAPTER 4

PROVERB AND STORY IN THE
TALE OF MELIBEE

Salomon seith, ☞ "Werk alle thy thynges by
conseil, and thou shalt never repente"
—*Melibee*, VII.1003

Chaucer focuses attention on the relationship between proverb and story in a startling passage near the middle of the *Canterbury Tales* as we have it, an arresting moment that signals the importance of what is to come. In the prologue to *Sir Thopas*, the Host's eyes fall for the first time upon the first-person narrator, singling him out for a turn in the storytelling game. The two attempts at storytelling by this fictional representative of the author within his work—the short, interrupted "rym" of *Sir Thopas* and the long prose *Tale of Melibee*—have long been recognized as "extreme and total" opposites.[1] One aspect of this contrast, however, the "extreme and total" contrast in their proverb use, has gone unremarked by modern readers. A proverb-conscious reader of Thomas Speght's 1602 Chaucer edition, however, might have noticed the complete absence of pointing hands in *Sir Thopas*, the only Canterbury tale in which the editor could find no wisdom expressions at all. Nor did Whiting find proverbs or "sententious remarks" in *Thopas*, nor to my knowledge has anyone else: the only whisper of (mock) sententiousness I find is the amusing (but not proverbial) observation that the many maidens who lie awake at night pining for Sir Thopas would be better off getting their sleep (VII.742–44).[2]

The margins of *Melibee*, however, teem with Speght's manicules. He marked two hundred "sentences and proverbes" in *Melibee*, the most of any Canterbury tale, and he might have marked many more if not for the diminishing returns: a system of emphasis loses its force when too much of a text is called out for special attention.[3] In *Melibee*, proverbs engulf the narrative to the extent that it is hardly a tale at all. More accustomed to reading proverbially, premodern readers might have looked for meaning in the dramatic contrast between the two tales. This chapter argues that, judged as a story, *Melibee* is even more problematic than the deliberately parodic *Sir Thopas*, but once we recognize *Melibee*'s proverbs as the main event and its story as a subsidiary feature, its purpose and function in the *Canterbury Tales* come sharply into focus and become much more comprehensible. This reading of *Melibee* also helps to explain why Chaucer would include such a work in a fiction of live storytelling and why he translates his source with such uncharacteristic, sentence-by-sentence fidelity.

If any Canterbury tale rewards the kind of proverb-conscious reading undertaken in this book, that tale would be *Melibee*. As Betsy Bowden and Christopher Cannon have argued, its overwhelming abundance of proverbs is hardly surprising. Like its ultimate source, Albertanus (or Albertano) of Brescia's thirteenth-century Latin *Liber consolationis et consilii* (*Book of Consolation and Counsel*), *Melibee* includes among its generic affiliations a literary genre influential from antiquity through the premodern period and still occasionally produced today: the proverb collection.[4] Unsympathetically but not inaccurately, J. Burke Severs offers this characterization of the author's method: "Usually Albertano states an idea succinctly, then piles up repetitious supporting quotations from various authorities, medieval and classic."[5] Collecting sententiae from various sources and "piling them up" into pertinent categories is a familiar method in proverb collections. Erasmus's *Adages* is also "repetitious": he included as many authorities as he could find to present variations on a particular thought. To read *Melibee* with this generic affiliation in mind, as I do in this chapter, is not to deny its relationship to other literary forms such as the mirror for princes or moral allegory; medieval works are rarely if ever "pure" examples of a single genre, if such a thing is even possible.[6] I intend this reading of the tale as a proverb collection to be additive rather than reductive—another illuminating way to look at this curious "tale."

Along with four others, *Thopas* and *Melibee* belong to the group of tales traditionally known as Fragment VII, six tales connected to one another by narrative links long accepted as Chaucer's work. Chaucer scholars have labeled it the "language," "literature," or "surprise" fragment, and many have placed emphasis on the insight these six tales provide into Chaucer's maturing ideas about his poetic art.[7] The generic variety within this group is truly spectacular: the Shipman's racy and cynical fabliau is succeeded by the Prioress's Miracle of the Virgin, a special instance of the saint's legend; from the "pilgrim narrator," first the brief and sparkling parody of English metrical romance and then the long, earnest proverb collection framed by a slender story. Next, from the Monk, comes a lugubrious collection of tragedies depicting falls of the great, paired with the Nun's Priest's inspired, multi-genre variant on the beast epic, which embraces a worldview as comic as the Monk's is tragic. Most Chaucerians agree that the *Nun's Priest's Tale* of the rooster Chauntecleer comes closer than any other part of the work to conveying Chaucer's mature ideas about literary making. Of the three pairs of tales in this sequence, the last two, the *Monk's Tale* and *Nun's Priest's Tale*, are most revealing of all about the role of proverbs in Chaucer's implicit *ars poetica*. I reserve them for the next chapter; here, after a very brief look at its pairing with *Sir Thopas*, I focus on *Melibee* and its many implications for understanding proverb use in the *Canterbury Tales*.

THE PROVERB IN THE *THOPAS-MELIBEE* LINK

The arresting means by which Chaucer reintroduces his first-person narrator in the *Prologue to Sir Thopas* draws attention to the upcoming two tales and their narrative link, a sequence that raises important questions about authorship and artistry. For a good long stretch between the introduction to the *Man of Law's Tale* and the *Prologue to Sir Thopas*, a reader following the order of the tales in the Ellesmere Manuscript adopted in modern editions receives little direct prompting to think about Chaucer's fictional "I," the supposed recorder of these tales, or about the relation of this complex textual construct to its author. This aspect of the work was last foregrounded in the Man of Law's lengthy complaint about an overly prolific, unskilled poet called Chaucer who has already told all the stories worth telling—if not in one book, then in another (II.45–96). Eleven tales and tellers later, without warning, comes that powerful moment in the *Prologue to Sir Thopas* in which the narrator reports that "at erst" (for the first time) the Host "looked upon me" (VII.694). Even for readers who know the work well, this unexpected focus on the narrating "I" retains its capacity to surprise and unsettle. It captures the disconcerting experience of suddenly becoming the center of attention in a large group after having grown comfortable in the role of passive listener.

Eyes downcast, portly around the waist like the Host, huggable as a doll—Chaucer's comically embodied poetic speaker straddles two worlds. Set apart from the other fictional storytellers by the pretext that he is recounting the whole journey, this speaker is set apart also by Chaucer's propensity for slipping unannounced from a naturalistic narrating voice limited to a single human perspective into an authorial perspective that knows no such limits.[8] In a group of strangers, who besides the character's creator could offer the insight, for example, that in his legal practice the Man of Law "semed bisier than he was" (I.322)? Even within the fictional world created by the text, something preternatural or otherworldly about this Chaucerian "I" attracts the notice of the Host, leading him to ask, "What man *artow* ['art thou']?" and to remark that "He semeth elvyssh . . . / For unto no wight dooth he daliaunce," or, as we would say, he doesn't socialize with anyone (VII.695–704).

Captured by the Host's imagined gaze, this liminal figure—one foot in the author's world and one in the illusory world of the author's making—embarks on his own effort to win the supper set as a prize for the tales of "best sentence and moost solaas"—tales that afford the most significant meanings *and* the greatest pleasure (I.798). In the link between *Thopas* and *Melibee*, the Host reminds the fictional narrator of these criteria by asking for "som murthe or som doctryne," apparently willing to settle for one or the other from this unpromising storyteller whose first tale has failed to please (VII.935). *Thopas* offers more mirth than the Host realizes, but little in the way of the insight indicated by *sentence*, while *Melibee* raises the question of how much *sentence* (or how many sententiae) a narrative can carry without falling to its knees. Thus, the link between the two seems a particularly promising place to begin this exploration of Chaucer's ideas about the relation of proverb to story.

In the *Thopas-Melibee* link, the transition from the only proverbless tale to the most proverbful of all, Chaucer's fictional speaker beseeches the reader not to blame him if it seems that he uses more *proverbes* than the reader might expect in the upcoming "tretys":

> lordynges alle, I yow biseche,
> If that yow thynke I varie as in my speche,
> As thus, though that I telle somwhat moore
> Of proverbes than ye han herd bifoore
> *Comprehended* in this litel tretys heere,          *Included*
> To enforce with th'effect of my mateere....
> Blameth me not.
> (VII.953–61)

I want to look closely at this odd disclaimer, which seems to me a telling, if characteristically ambiguous, comment on the function of proverbs in poetry. Most assume that "this litel tretys heere" is a slighting reference to the lengthy upcoming tale of *Melibee*, also called "a litel thyng in prose" in line 937.[9] Its teller appears to apologize in advance for textual variation from a known previous version: "though I nat the same wordes seye / As ye han herd ... I preye / Blameth me nat" (959–61). The speaker justifies this variation with a significant scriptural parallel: just as the four gospels differ in their versions of the crucifixion narrative while remaining faithful to the same ultimate truth, so the ultimate *sentence* of *Melibee* remains the same despite the addition of "somwhat moore / Of proverbes." Reconciling variant versions of a text without undermining their authority was a salient issue of the day: gospel harmonies—works that sought to weave conflicting versions of the same sacred narratives into authoritative wholes—were circulating widely across Europe in the thirteenth and fourteenth centuries.[10] Although the whole link is woven with ironies and interpreting it calls for cautious footing, the analogy Chaucer draws between variation among sacred gospel accounts and textual variation between his work and other extant versions suggests a poet thinking through serious questions of poetic authority.

Taken literally, however, the speaker's plea that his audience will forgive him for adding more proverbs to the upcoming *Tale of Melibee* makes little sense. How many readers—let alone the disparate assortment of fictive pilgrim listeners—could make the necessary close textual comparison or would have sufficient mastery over this very long work to spot a few new additions to its two hundred and more proverbs? *Melibee* in fact contains many *fewer* proverbs than the *Liber consolationis* compiled by Albertanus, the Erasmus of his day.[11] It remains disputed whether Chaucer knew the work of Albertanus directly, or only through his immediate source for

*Melibee*, the substantially condensed French translation composed after 1336 by Renaud of Louens. A few proverbs and some significant language near the end of *Melibee* are found in Albertanus, but absent from Renaud, and these bits of evidence leave open the possibility that, though he translated from Renaud, Chaucer was also familiar with Albertanus's well-known work.[12] If so, Chaucer's statement in this link that the upcoming work has been told at different times in different ways by different authors—"told somtyme in sondry wyse / Of sondry folk"—may refer to its prior existence in a longer Latin version and a shorter French version (VII.941–42). Judgments about the extent of Renaud's excisions cannot be certain in the absence of the particular manuscript he worked from, especially since manuscripts of Albertanus were sometimes abridged by their own copyists, but Renaud appears to have cut whole sections, trimmed Albertanus's long lists of proverbs, and reduced his work to about two-thirds of its former length. Items in lists are particularly open to variation in a manuscript culture, and Severs judges that Renaud "selected at will among the abundance of quotations, sometimes satisfying himself with one or two, sometimes indulging himself more fully, sometimes even rejecting the whole lot."[13]

It appears, however, that in translating the *Livre de Mellibee*, Chaucer added only about three proverbs to Renaud's reduced stock, as well as subtracting at least one, hardly a net change to merit so elaborate a disclaimer. Even those meager additions may be questioned since we cannot be certain that the manuscript of Renaud's work that Chaucer read did not already include the two proverbial warnings against undue haste present in Chaucer but absent from the extant manuscripts of Renaud.[14] If, as has been persuasively argued, Chaucer translated his *Melibee* with the willful boy king Richard II in mind, a more notable addition to Renaud is the admonition, "A litel thorn may prikke a kyng *ful soore* ['very sorely'], and an hound wol holde the wilde boor" (VII.1326). The proverb Chaucer appears to have subtracted may also reflect Richard as audience: "Woe to thee, O land, when thy king is a child" (Ecclesiastes 10:16).[15] These changes are not insignificant but they nevertheless represent a very small number of meaningful alterations in a very long work, copied by hand in a manuscript culture, where variation is the norm. *Melibee* is in fact an atypically faithful translation for Chaucer, deepening the mystery of why this of all tales should induce anxiety, or mock-anxiety, about variation from prior versions, when Chaucer's more usual approach is exuberant reworking, combining, and subverting of his source materials.

As a step toward a solution, Jill Mann makes the sensible suggestion that the apparently false claim that Chaucer has added proverbs to *Melibee* in numbers sufficient to merit an apology serves as "simply a way of drawing attention to the heavily proverbial nature of his source, and beyond this, to the importance of proverbs, and the communal experience they embody, within his own poetry."[16] Agreed on all counts: Chaucer's apology acknowledges the importance of proverbs to the premodern writer's craft and highlights the presence of many hundreds of them in the *Canterbury Tales*. As applied to *Melibee*, however, a work already so dense with proverbs that they stretch its slender framing story nearly to the breaking point, the notion that the poet would risk the supposed disapproval of his audience by adding "somwhat moore / Of proverbes" must also involve an element of irony.

Why would Chaucer claim that he has added proverbs to *Melibee*? Adding even more proverbs seems unlikely to improve it as an entry in a fictional storytelling contest. To a compendium of proverbs such as Albertanus originally created, adding more would only enhance its value, but once Chaucer places his version in a fiction of face-to-face storytelling—once *Melibee* represents itself as a *tale*—the expectations of its readers change. As acts of storytelling, neither *Thopas* nor *Melibee* fully achieve the ambitious goals for his fiction that Chaucer pursues in the *Canterbury Tales*, but the pairing reveals some of the most important raw materials from which he crafted his mature work: the lively vernacular storytelling tradition of English verse romance in one case and the voluminously learned international fund of "sentences and proverbes" in the other. Despite centuries of study of Chaucer's literary sources, including ample attention to the individual romances parodied in *Sir Thopas*, international proverb tradition has remained his great under-acknowledged source. *Melibee* is Chaucer's treasure house of proverbs, and he repurposes them in highly creative ways in other Canterbury tales, as we will see.

The significance of the curious disclaimer about added proverbs in the *Thopas-Melibee* link is heightened by its echo, "Blameth me nat," of the tongue-in-cheek authorial apology at the end of the *Miller's Prologue*. There, the reader unwilling to hear a "cherles tale" is famously invited to "Turne over the leef and chese another tale" and enjoined to "Blameth nat me if that ye *chese amys* ['choose wrongly']" (I.3177–81). This earlier disclaimer also expresses concern about a poet's responsibility to his "mateere." A key term in medieval literary theory, *mateere* (Latin *materia*) indicates the as-yet unformed substance that awaits shaping into words.[17] In the *Miller's*

*Prologue*, Chaucer's speaker playfully exculpates himself for using stylistically low language in representing the speech of *cherles*, adopting the transparent pretext that he is forced to do so or else he must "*falsen* ['falsify, misrepresent'] som of my mateere" (3175). Including "cherles" among his tellers and assigning them risqué tales is of course a voluntary choice in a work of fiction. But if the only perspective on offer were that of a high chivalric romance told by a knight, or that of a tract on penitence offered by a parson, what would be falsified or misrepresented is nothing less than the diversity of Chaucer's social world. As much as the storytelling of a knight or a priest, in this ambitious last literary project, the stories told by *cherles* and by an ordinary woman also constitute "som" of the poet's "mateere."[18]

Like the earlier disclaimer in the *Miller's Prologue*, the apology before *Melibee* also uses humor and irony to cloak a serious concern about the poet's responsibility in repurposing existing genres to suit new contexts. I read its characterization of proverbs as serving "to enforce with th'effect" of the poet's "mateere" as a brief but telling comment on the effective placement of proverbs, something Erasmus regards as a high-stakes compositional challenge for a premodern writer: "It is not everyone who can aptly and fittingly insert a proverb into what he has to say . . . as in music, unless you put on a consummate performance, you would be ridiculous, and you must either win the highest praise or be a laughingstock."[19] Erasmus's elegant colloquy, "The Godly Feast," models just such a "consummate performance," in which proverbs, many of them from his *Adages*, spark discussion among friends at a garden luncheon, conversation that ranges from lightly witty to deeply serious. When Chaucer's quasi-authorial "I" states that he places his proverbs in such a way as "To enforce with th'effect of my mateere," the primary meaning of "enforce" here is 'to strengthen or support' (*MED*, s.v. "enforcen," 3d, citing this passage). "Th'effect" is the realization of the author's aims as manifested in the impact of some part of the work on its reader; Chaucer writes elsewhere of "th'effect" as "the fruyt of al, / Whi I have toold this story" (*Legend of Good Women*, 1160–61).

In courtroom language that goes back to Albertanus, the lawyer and judge, *enforcen* as used in *Melibee* also means 'to provide support for one's claims', as when a wise old man seeks to "enforcen his tale by *resons* ['reasons, evidence']" (VII.1043). It can suggest undue pressure, as when the resisting Melibeus ruefully acknowledges the forcefulness of Prudence's argumentation, "I se wel that ye enforce yow muchel by wordes to overcome me" (1427). The *MED* testifies that the senses of *enforcen* include 'to force' as well as 'to reinforce', and, given the power wielded by proverbs in his culture, a hint of this secondary meaning may also lurk behind Chaucer's choice of the verb. I will return in my conclusion to this problematic aspect of the proverb, its potential to *enforcen*, in the sense of 'discipline' or 'constrain', the carefully crafted multiple meanings of Chaucer's fictions.

By calling attention in advance to *Melibee*'s abundance of proverbs and by implying that such an abundance may be problematic as well as advantageous, Chaucer prepares his reader for the thoroughly nonnaturalistic addition of a large and highly learned proverb collection to a fictional tale-telling contest. In its own way, *Melibee* is as unexpected as the pilgrim narrator's first tale. Chaucer introduces his "litel thing in prose" as an extreme response to the Host's rejection of the ignorance ("lewednesse") and the "rym dogerel" of *Sir Thopas*, a send-up of tales like *Guy of Warwick* and *Bevis of Hampton* in which *solaas* far outweighs *sentence*. Although many Middle English romances tell splendid stories, they generally lack the ambitious features Chaucer found in his reading of classical and continental European poetry, including their confident use of the verbal forms Chaucer calls *auctoritees, sentences,* or *proverbes*.[20] In the final lines of the *Thopas-Melibee* link, Chaucer repeats the keyword *sentence* five times, hinting that what *Sir Thopas* lacks, *Melibee* will supply in abundance.

What makes "sentences and proverbes" important enough to play such a conspicuous role in the contrast between the two tales Chaucer assigns to his fictional narrator at a critical juncture in the work? Relative to their prominence in his poetry, their role in Chaucer's poetic making has received surprisingly little attention from modern critics. A focus on proverbs at this key moment should be no surprise, however, if we consider the literacy education of the poet and his premodern readers, described in chapter 1. As we know, facility with proverbs, including the ability to apply a proverb to a story as its *moralite*, was beaten into premodern schoolchildren, all too literally. The more receptive these young pupils were to their early experiences with language, literature, and interpretive practices, the more likely that their corporeally enforced early lessons would continue to shape them as mature readers and writers, leaving them far more disposed than we are to consider the use of proverbs as an element of a poet's art.

READING *MELIBEE* AS A PROVERB COLLECTION

The choice to include the *Tale of Melibee* in a fiction about face-to-face storytelling has proved more puzzling than Chaucer's inclusion of any other tale. Its treatment in the 2002 volume *Sources and Analogues of the "Canterbury Tales"* indicates its exceptional closeness to its model and minimal adaptation to the *Tales*. While the usual practice in this work is to provide English translations of Chaucer's non-English sources, William Askins declines to translate Renaud's French: "in the case of this particular text, such a translation seemed pointless, an exercise which would involve little more than producing a modernized version of Chaucer's English."[21] Earlier, Severs reached a similar conclusion: with few exceptions Chaucer's work is "a straight translation of the *Mellibee*, reflecting in virtually every sentence the wording and phrasing of its source."[22]

As we have seen, nearly all the proverbs in Chaucer's *Melibee* are translated directly from Renaud, and the most alienating feature of Chaucer's tale for most modern readers is the seeming interruption of its narrative by two hundred and more of these expressions. In addition, rather than attempting to integrate them more subtly into the narrative, Chaucer follows his source and his own practice elsewhere by calling attention to them as *proverbes* or *sentences* or as the wise words of a named *auctoritee* such as Solomon or Seneca, thus making them all the more intrusive to the modern readers who regard them as superfluous. The generations of Chaucer's readers introduced to *Melibee* by the *Riverside Chaucer* are told, for example, that "though we conduct our political discussions without long lists of 'auctoritees' and sententiae, we have our own clichés, equally boring and much less learned."[23] The assumption is that the "political discussion" between Prudence and Melibeus is the point and the *proverbes* are expendable.

Dismayed by having to "slog through the proverbs of Prudence," one critic asks how medieval readers could possibly have enjoyed this work and "still belong to the same species" as we do.[24] Enjoy, or at least appreciate, *Melibee* premodern readers clearly did: testimony to its importance includes its distinctively elaborate decoration in the Ellesmere Manuscript, its special treatment in William Caxton's early printed text, and the ample marginalia it attracted in the early Chaucer editions examined by Alison Wiggins.[25] If only because Prudence offers another example of wifely patience to contrast with his own spouse, even Chaucer's fictional Host praises this tale (VII.1893–96), despite his consistent preference for mirth over seriousness. The challenge for moderns in reading *Melibee* is real, but a seeming excess of proverbs is hardly surprising in a "tale" initially assembled as a proverb collection. As such, *Melibee* is the greatest casualty among Chaucer's works of the historical shift to a post-romantic literary culture with a love of originality and little relish for the "sayings of dead wise-acres," as one early twentieth-century scholar memorably described its proverbs.[26]

As the premodern passion for proverbs subsided over the course of the eighteenth century, the point of Albertanus's original labors in collecting them became less evident and the treasures in *Melibee*'s storehouse declined dramatically in value. In 1783, the Italian critic Girolamo Tiraboschi wrote of Albertanus's *Liber consolationis*, "From this author, we must not expect method in treating his subject, nor force of reasoning nor precision of ideas. He almost contents himself with joining together passages from the Scripture, and from many sacred and profane authors, on the matter he discusses." Responding to Tiraboschi, Thor Sundby, nineteenth-century editor of Albertanus's book, acknowledges that it was the product of "an age of compilation" with a "relish for moral sentences."[27] But rather than pointing out that "joining together passages" from other sources was the proverb compiler's primary aim, Sundby responds with a tepid defense of the work's formal unity, holding that the *Liber consolationis*, "though largely woven from the sayings of different authors by no means deserves the name of a mere patchwork."[28]

Wisely, as it turns out, Erasmus prefaced the *Adages* with a theoretical statement about the value and function of proverbs and an explanation of how and why he collected them, but he chose not to frame them—hundreds at first and ultimately thousands—as Albertanus did with an allegory about learning to heed them, a story that might in later centuries have been mistaken in some quarters for the point of his labors. The presence of a first-person speaker in a proverb collection causes little trouble; such collections frequently include some suggestion of a narrating voice, often addressing a younger person or pupil. The Solomonic voice of the wisdom books is a compelling example, as are the imaginary peasant speakers of the proverb collections mentioned in chapter 2. The voice of Erasmus's engaging speaker ties together the *Adages*. Encountering a narrating voice in a proverb collection is not unusual but reading such a collection as a narrative, as a *story*, is likely to result in frustrated expectations.

The perils of reading *Melibee* as a story interrupted by an outrageous number of proverbs, rather than as a proverb collection wrapped in a slender story, are well-illustrated by the argument forwarded by some twentieth-century Chaucer critics that, like *Sir Thopas*, *Melibee* must be some kind of joke. According to this view, the pilgrim narrator tells a deliberately stultifying tale as a comic act of revenge on the Host for his interruption of *Sir Thopas*. In a pioneering effort in the 1970s to compare Chaucer's text to Renaud's, an article still useful in other ways, Dolores Palomo describes *Melibee* as "a very subtle stylistic parody," revealed in part by "the sheer excessiveness" of Prudence's "endless extrapolations on an arsenal of borrowed sententiae."[29] Few, if any, Chaucerians now read *Melibee* as a stylistic parody or a prank played on the Host, the world's longest and least funny joke, but the underlying premise—that the "sheer excessiveness" of its proverbs must be parodic—reveals the misleading assumption that the story is paramount and the proverbs of secondary importance. For the original collector of *Melibee*'s wisdom expressions, it seems clear that the reverse was true. That Albertanus valued his proverbs above the consistency of his allegory is a neglected but important point for readers of Chaucer's *Melibee*. It is hardly a surprise, yet it is surprisingly under-acknowledged by critics of *Melibee* over many decades, that the fortunes of a work that originated as a proverb collection have risen and fallen with the fortunes of the proverb itself.

Recognizing that Albertanus not only subordinated his story to his collected proverbs but also constructed that story largely *out of* those proverbs helps to explain many of *Melibee*'s now-frustrating features. While Renaud handled Albertanus's text with considerable freedom in that he cut it dramatically, what he did not excise, he generally translated quite faithfully, the main alterations consisting of substituted sententiae of his own.[30] Chaucer, for his part, translated faithfully from Renaud. Thus, most of the major decisions about *Melibee*'s form and method were made by Albertanus, the original compiler of its proverbs, and a look at his goals for his work will help to illuminate some important aspects of *Melibee*. A lawyer and judge in the northern Italian city of Brescia, Albertanus directed a substantial work of advice to each of his three sons. The preface to his *Liber consolationis* is addressed to his son John (Johannes), in training to be a physician. Albertanus advises his son that his future profession is likely to require ministering not just to bodily ailments but also to troubled souls, who will benefit from the consolation provided by the counsels in his book. That the counsels of the wise could provide comfort and alleviate suffering was an established belief of the time. Along with food, clothing, shelter, and care for the body after death, Chaucer's Parson includes "good conseil" among the necessities that must be provided as acts of Christian charity to the sorely distressed (X.1030–31).

At the close of his preface, Albertanus urges his son to read his work (*legas*) but to study (*perlegas*) its *auctoritates*—its collected sayings—"with attention and the greatest of zeal" (*attente ac studiosissime*).[31] These instructions could easily have come from Erasmus, and they are of course meant for all readers of the work. Some of the manuscripts annotated by Albertanus survive, attesting to the labor that went into collecting his proverbs, both from other proverb collections and directly from the works of learned authors.[32] His misattribution of quotations from certain of his sources reflects the challenges faced by readers of manuscripts prior to the consistent use of titles and author attributions. But the access to classical and Christian *auctoritees* it provides helps to explain the lasting respect the *Liber consolationis* garnered throughout medieval Europe from the thirteenth to the sixteenth centuries, as evidenced by abundant manuscript copies and vernacular translations.[33] Its assiduously collected proverbs are its primary *raison d'être*, and the same remains true for its abbreviated translation into Renaud's French and then into Chaucer's English.

Albertanus framed his large collection of sayings with a simple and somewhat tenuous allegory in which a feminine wisdom figure, literally Melibeus's wife and figuratively the cardinal virtue of prudence, schools Melibeus in the importance of seeking, approaching critically, and actively choosing from among wise counsels. His work, in other words, not only contains a wealth of "sentences and proverbes," it also instructs its reader in how to use them. As an example of how Albertanus privileges his collected proverbs over his framing story, in a section omitted by Renaud and thus by Chaucer, Prudentia instructs her husband, a local magnate, at length in the importance of disciplined study, deep reflection, carefully selected reading, and training of the memory. Its quoted *auctors* include Cicero, Seneca, the *Disticha Catonis*, Cassiodorus, Hugh of Saint Victor, and Innocent III.[34] Albertanus's primary investment is clearly in his *proverbes* as a path to deep learning, not in the plot of a framing tale in which a wife makes these lengthy and erudite recommendations as part of her effort to calm an infuriated husband vowing violent revenge against the enemies who have broken into his house and injured his wife and daughter. As a wealthy magnate, Melibeus is not the likeliest candidate for this rigorous course of study even in the best of times, but at this moment, their daughter lies close to death and his murderous enemies, for all the reader knows until well into the work, might be fleeing justice or plotting a return to wreak more havoc on their violated household. At one point in this section, Albertanus seems to abandon even the pretext that this extended discourse on study is spoken by a recently injured wife to her enraged husband. In the course of a speech ostensibly spoken by Prudentia to Melibeus, Albertanus addresses his son directly, recommending another of his own works, *De forma vitae*, "which I directed to your brother Vincent."[35] The author's casual treatment of his fictional frame indicates its subordinate status to the authoritative quotations he urges his son to ponder zealously.

Albertanus not only valued his collected proverbs above his story; to a notable extent he fashioned the story, such as it is, directly out of them. Sundby observes that Albertanus found "the name of Melibeus, the outline of his person, and the first sketch of the whole narrative" in a distich from Godfrey of Winchester's *Liber proverbiorum*:

> Consilio juvenum fidis, Melibee; ruinam
> Expectare potes, dum sine consilio es.
> [You trust in the counsel of the young, Melibeus; ruin
> is what you can expect so long as you are without (wise) counsel.]
> (chap. 25, 53.9–10)[36]

Similarly, Sundby notes that Prudentia's name and "the general idea of her character" derive from a saying by the late Roman writer Cassiodorus:

> Et certe prudentia expedita est et infatigabilis, et superat cuncta. Ait enim
>   Cassiodorus: "Superavit cuncta infatigabilis et expedita prudentia."
> [And certainly, prudence is agile and indefatigable, and overcomes
>   all things. As Cassiodorus says, "Agile and indefatigable prudence
>   overcame all things."]
> (chap. 6, 20.10–13)[37]

The first sentence of this last quotation also illustrates the way in which Albertanus's own prose at times derives directly from of the language of his quoted maxims.

As another example of the way in which Albertanus's story develops out of his proverbs, Chaucer scholars have placed importance on the moment in *Melibee* when Prudence, who otherwise remains patient and gracious despite her husband's recalcitrance, takes on "semblant of wratthe," the appearance of anger, as a successful means of breaking through to Melibeus (VII.1687).[38] The inspiration for using "semblant of wratthe" in dealing with someone who is acting foolishly comes directly from a proverb from Ecclesiastes that Albertanus gives to his Prudentia (chap. 49, 113.5–7).[39] In Chaucer's translation,

> "For Salomon seith, ☞ 'He is *moore worth that* ['more worthy who'] repreveth or chideth a fool for his folye, shewynge hym semblant of wratthe, / than he that supporteth hym and preyseth hym in his mysdoynge and laugheth at his folye.'" (1707–8)

Rather than interrupting his story, Albertanus's collected proverbs played a role in *generating* it.

As a translation of a framed proverb collection, Chaucer's *Melibee* also inherits from Albertanus an active defense of its own value as a source of wise counsels, many of them drawn from the most revered literature of the day, and it offers valuable instruction in how this wisdom can best be used. It does so at a substantial cost to its story, a point by no means lost on the English translator who paired it with *Thopas* as one of two contrastive ways in which a story can fall short of the balance implied by "best sentence and moost solaas." Nevertheless, what might be called the raw materials from which *Thopas* and *Melibee* were crafted, English romances and international proverbs, offered resources of great value to an ambitious and inventive author working out for himself how stories can best fulfill both their ancient functions, to teach *and* to delight.

That the work begins with its protagonist failing to heed one of the best-known of all medieval proverbs and ends when he finally agrees to be guided by it is a feature of its structure made more explicit in Chaucer's translation than in Renaud or Albertanus. As it appears in *Melibee*,

> "Salomon seith, ☞ '*Werk alle thy thynges by conseil* ['Always follow wise counsel'], and thou shalt never repente.'" (VII.1003)[40]

Middle English *conseil* or *counseil* has a variety of meanings, all employed in the course of *Melibee*: a body of advisers (a council), an individual adviser (a counselor), and, in the sense used in the Solomonic proverb, the advice itself (a counsel).[41] Only when Melibeus has finally "assented fully" to *werken* after the counsels of his prudential faculty as personified by his wife (1870–73) does the *Tale of Melibee* achieve closure, some two hundred and more wise counsels later. The self-validating quality of this central proverb gives it a somewhat authoritarian sound: a wise counsel that urges one to act always and only on wise counsel. But the Solomon of *Melibee* is a more genuine wisdom figure than the domineering antagonist of peasants and women we met in chapters 2 and 3, and for Albertanus and his later adapters, in the end his proverb steers Melibeus away from acting on his emotions and toward rational deliberation.

Moved in the end by the sincerity of Prudence's motivation ("hir trewe entente"), Melibeus's heart inclines to her will, but what he promises to abide by in future is not her will but her *conseil*: "Whanne Melibee hadde herd the grete *skiles* ['arguments'] and resouns of dame Prudence, and hire wise informaciouns and techynges, / his herte *gan enclyne* ['inclined'] to the wil of his wif, considerynge hir trewe entente, / and conformed hym anon and *assented fully to werken after hir conseil*, / and thonked God . . . that hym sente a wyf of so greet discrecioun" (VII.1870–73, my emphasis). This final echo of the Solomonic proverb, "Werk alle thy thynges by conseil," is absent from Renaud; in Albertanus at this point, Melibeus cites a different Solomonic proverb praising the sweetness of the good counsels of a friend (Proverbs 27:9), and what he agrees to act upon is Prudentia's will ("volo . . . in omnibus et per omnia tuam facere voluntatem").[42] Chaucer, however, makes a distinction between the inclination of Melibeus's *herte* toward Prudence's will (an expression of marital love?) and his full assent to govern his actions by her *conseil*. As we will see, the *conseil* that Melibeus eventually commits to *werken* by involves an active and critical process of deliberation, not blind adherence to *auctoritees*, which is impossible in any case because of the conflicting advice they offer.

Solomon's advice about heeding wise counsel is never far from the reader's mind as Melibeus slowly learns what it means. Early on, he raises objections to Prudence's advice, telling her, "I purpose nat . . . to *werke by thy conseil*, for many causes and resouns" (VII.1055, my emphasis). Not long after, he echoes the Solomonic proverb again in a premature claim that her wisdom and the sweetness of her words have persuaded him not to act in anger: "I wol governe me by thy conseil in alle thyng" (1114). He quickly backslides, disregarding her advice by choosing all the wrong kinds of counselors—strangers, youths, flatterers, former enemies—thus providing the opportunity for Prudence to review her lesson with the help of more proverbs (1241–60). Any medieval reader (and any reader of Chaucer's *Monk's Tale*) would recognize that Melibeus is yet again on the wrong track when he proposes that perhaps he should try trusting in Fortune to determine his course of action. "Certes," Prudence replies emphatically, "if ye wol werke by my conseil, ye shul nat *assaye* ['test, try'] Fortune by no wey" (1447).

In the vernacular translations, Albertanus's original focus on the usefulness of his collected *auctoritees* in promoting rational deliberation and upholding the rule of law comes through clearly in the many counsels that advise against violent acts committed in the heat of anger. As James Powell has shown, the threat of violence among rival magnates in medieval Italian cities was of great concern to Albertanus, and the results of the selection principle that guided his collection live on in the "sentences and proverbes" of *Melibee*. As a lawyer and judge who deplored the disruption of Italian civil society by the entrenched practice of vendetta, he believed deeply in nonviolent conflict resolution, and many of his selected proverbs reflect that commitment, counseling patience, moderation, rational deliberation, and clemency toward penitent wrongdoers.[43] Despite the artificiality of the story that places these *proverbes* within an ill-timed spousal lecture, there is something lifelike about Melibeus's erratic veering between affirming and rejecting the counsels of Prudence, especially her central Solomonic advice about reflecting on wise counsel before acting. Patient listening, especially to those with whom one disagrees, rational deliberation, and a willingness to adopt new precepts when circumstances change are not habits achieved once and possessed for life. Rather, they are part of an ongoing process of self-governance subject to backsliding and in need of continual renegotiation.

Unless we recognize that Albertanus's primary aim in shaping his story was to frame the sayings in his vast collection, Prudence's *proverbes* can indeed seem "repetitive, contradictory, arbitrary, and fundamentally simple-minded," as Palomo protested long ago.[44] If Albertanus were simply offering sound advice about how a powerful individual should go about recruiting trustworthy advisers, would it even occur to him to warn against approaching either a fool or an inebriate? Yet his Prudentia offers such warnings, as does Prudence in Renaud and Chaucer, citing proverbs that derive from the Solomonic wisdom books. These very ancient writings abound in cautions against heeding the speech of fools, with the implication that much human speech falls into this category. The advice that Chaucer's Prudence inherits from Albertanus's Prudentia sounds simple-minded on its own: "ye shul eschue the conseillyng of fooles." But when she cites the proverb from which this advice derives, it turns out to offer some wisdom after all: "for Salomon seith, 'Taak no conseil of a fool, for he kan noght conseille *but after his owene lust and his affecioun* ['except according to his own pleasure and desire']" (VII.1173, C465). The proverb defines a foolish counselor as one who can offer only self-serving advice, and it cautions sensibly against choosing such an adviser.

Prudence's seemingly gratuitous warning against seeking the advice of someone who is drunk also derives from a Solomonic proverb: "Thou shalt also eschue the conseiling of folk that been dronkelewe, for they ne kan no conseil hyde. / For Salomon seith, 'Ther is *no privetee ther as regneth dronkenesse* ['no secrecy (in the sense of confidentiality) where drunkenness reigns']'" (VII.1194, D425). The proverb itself warns, reasonably enough, against trusting confidences to the indiscretion of a drunken person. From Albertanus on, the versions of *Melibee* are more concerned with preservation of the collected proverbs than with their fit into the framing story. "Sentences and proverbes" were treasured for their own sake by a culture in which even snippets of the wisdom of the ancients were much harder to come by and valued accordingly.

The longwindedness of *Melibee*'s feminine wisdom figure, another problematic feature for some modern readers, also becomes more understandable when we read the tale as a proverb collection. In Albertanus's *Liber consolationis*, this feminine figure is more easily recognized as a personification of one of the four cardinal virtues acknowledged by Christian patristic writers, gendered feminine in keeping with the Latin noun *prudentia*. In an exchange that occurs in a section omitted by Renaud and thus Chaucer, Albertanus plays quite openly with Prudentia's status as both wife and personification. Early in the work, as an antidote to his thirst for revenge, Melibeus's wife encourages him to acquire "prudentia." He assures her that he already has it—after all, he has her, and that is her name. She corrects him, "Non ego sum prudentia, sed sum prudentiae verba," implying that it is not in herself that the quality of prudence resides but in her words.[45] He does not yet have prudence; his lesson is only beginning, she seems to be telling him. Such overt indications of Prudentia's allegorical function work to alleviate some of the improbabilities of the work's literal level, including the length, breadth, and specialized learning of her speeches to her husband.

The fatigue modern readers of *Melibee* experience in response to the length of Prudence's speeches presumably results in large part from indifference to her *proverbes*, but her loquacity also poses a challenge for us as readers less accustomed to the rapidly shifting levels of premodern allegory. Prudence's speeches operate on at least three different levels: as communications from a human wife to her husband, as the teachings of an abstract wisdom figure representing the cardinal virtue of prudence, and as the promptings of a nascent prudential faculty within Melibeus himself. If heeded, this internal faculty has the capacity to guide him toward increased rationality, moderation, and—if he can master his anger and aggression—ultimately toward a modicum of wisdom. In one of Chaucer's relatively few significant changes to Renaud, in the tale's opening sentence he fortifies these allegorical levels by christening the couple's previously nameless daughter "Sophie," from the Greek word for wisdom. Prudence assures Melibeus from the beginning, that, despite the severity of Sophie's injuries, "Youre doghter, with the grace of God, shal *warisshe* ['recover'] and escape" (VII.982).

Melibeus can expect his "doghter," his badly debilitated wisdom, to recover if he can control his anger and heed Prudence's maxims: "sire, *if ye wol triste to my conseil*, I shal restoore yow youre doghter hool and sound" (VII.1110, my emphasis). This promised cure of Sophie's physical injuries by means of Melibeus's adherence to Prudence's *conseil* is possible only in the allegorical sense of remedying a deficiency of wisdom in Melibeus.[46] If the primary goal were an engaging fiction, a literal level with naturalistic characters and dialogue, Prudence's *auctoritees* would have to be judged wildly overabundant. But following the precedent initially set by Albertanus in compiling this work as a proverb collection, Chaucer's *Melibee* presents her *proverbes* as a viable path from unchecked emotion to a wisdom more nearly "hool and sound," a journey that the aggressive and potentially violent magnates represented by Melibeus are implicitly encouraged to undertake for themselves. Mary Carruthers describes prudence in medieval thought as an "intellectual virtue" that "directs and 'perfects' the emotional, desiring will."[47] This educative function of "sentences and proverbes," so pervasive in premodern writings, meets with skepticism today because it is so far from our own ideas about moral and intellectual development.

Renaud omits a passage from near the end of the work in which Albertanus reports that Melibeus's unnamed daughter is indeed recovering fully under the care of her doctors, who are urged by Melibeus to continue to attend carefully to her health.[48] For readers concerned about the gravely injured daughter on *Melibee*'s literal level, it is disappointing that, following Renaud, Chaucer does not confirm the recovery confidently predicted by Prudence from the beginning. On another level, where the daughter is identified with Melibeus's debilitated wisdom, the omission of reassurance about her full recovery helps to make clear that Melibeus is still progressing toward wisdom, and, given his penchant for backsliding, Chaucer's work offers no firm guarantee that he will retain the judiciousness he achieves at the end.

But the improbabilities on the literal level of this framing story remain. Most notably for our purposes, it places Melibeus's wife in the unenviable position of imparting the work's prolific stock of proverbial wisdom in the midst of a dire household emergency, a stock even more voluminous in Albertanus before Renaud's excisions. On the face of it, the reduction in the number of Prudence's proverbs initiated by Renaud would seem to make Albertanus's work more congenial to modern readers with little use for a vast collection of sententiae. But changes such as reducing the number of individual proverbs on the same theme have complicated the tale's modern reception by making *Melibee* less immediately recognizable as a proverb collection. Renaud's reductions in the breadth of topics covered by Prudentia's speeches have also influenced the modern reception of *Melibee* by making his and Chaucer's Prudence more believable on the literal level as Melibeus's wife. The counsels of Albertanus's Prudentia extend over an immense range of knowledge, from legalistic factors governing the declaration of war to abstract theological questions about the nature of God. Askins writes that as a result of Renaud's cuts to the expansive topics in Albertanus's text, "these political and intellectual considerations are dropped or muted and the general effect is to domesticate Prudence, to present her as someone concerned primarily with how her husband and his circle of advisors think."[49] Ironically, Renaud's success in making Albertanus's more obviously allegorical proverb-bearer into a "someone," a more lifelike female figure, opens her to criticisms more likely to be directed at a naturalistically portrayed fictional woman than at an allegorical wisdom figure.[50]

Chaucer critics have been sharply divided on this issue of whether Prudence's *proverbes* succeed in bringing about a change in Melibeus or whether he learns nothing at all.[51] Some of the hostility toward Prudence's instruction seems to me to result from reading a modern distaste for proverbs back into this premodern work. In an article of lasting value that moved discussion of *Melibee* forward in other important ways, Lee Patterson takes the negative view of Melibeus's progress, arguing that Prudence's *auctoritates* turn out to be useless because they "are not to be examined but memorized"; they are "epitomes of cultural wisdom that demand unquestioned obedience." As a result of her coercive instruction, "the meditative self-reflectiveness that is the goal of Prudence's pedagogy is foreclosed by the very means with which it is sought."[52] The idea that Prudence's proverbs demand "unquestioned obedience" runs counter to the work's central focus on using wise counsels as a means of active deliberation, as I will argue in this chapter's next section. A key piece of support for the argument that Prudence's pedagogy fails hinges on one last instance of backsliding by Melibeus. After a humble speech of contrition by the enemies he has at long last agreed to forgive, Melibeus unexpectedly declares that he will have them disinherited and exiled, a reversal that shocks Prudence, who calls it "a crueel sentence and muchel agayn resoun" (VII.1834–36). In a much-quoted judgment, Patterson labeled this "a devastating moment," one that proves Melibeus has "learned nothing" and that "Prudence's teaching has been largely useless, as she herself seems to acknowledge."[53]

Against the idea that Prudence acknowledges the uselessness of her *proverbes*, at this point in Chaucer's text she responds with nine more by Speght's count, reduced by Renaud from an even larger number in Albertanus, where Melibeus's final *volte face* first appears. The awkward lateness of this reversal in the vernacular versions seems to suggest that it is part of the work's closure, but its position so near the ending results from Renaud's substantial cuts to the two long chapters in Albertanus that follow Melibeus's last act of backsliding.[54] As the collector of the proverbs spoken by his Prudentia, Albertanus would not have introduced this last and most distressing reversal as a rejection of their value. In *Melibee* as in its predecesors, Prudence rebukes her husband for the cruelty of his temporary relapse, but what brings him to acknowledge his error is a final and powerfully climactic series of *proverbes*, as I argue below. In one of his rare deviations from his French model, Chaucer extends the terse final speech spoken by Renaud's Mellibee to his enemies. In so doing, he gives Melibeus his most compelling speech of the entire work, a plea on behalf of mercy and Christian forgiveness that testifies to how far he has come and brings Chaucer's work to a close.[55]

The proverbial wisdom imparted by Prudence would have seemed less overbearing to premodern readers accustomed to authoritative allegorical personifications gendered feminine. Ambrogio Lorenzetti's famous fourteenth-century murals in Siena's Palazzo Pubblico feature stately feminine figures that represent major civic virtues, with Prudentia joined by Justitia and Pax. In the most influential literary allegory circulating in the Middle Ages, Boethius's *Consolation of Philosophy*, another feminine wisdom figure, Lady Philosophy, is far more imperious in her manner than Prudence, but there the enlightening visitation happens within the half-sleeping, half-waking consciousness of the male protagonist. In Boethius's more carefully constructed allegory, also translated by Chaucer, the wisdom figure does not appear as the protagonist's wife in his waking world, and thus the modern reader has no cause to wonder how in practical terms a married woman in that culture would acquire the formidable authority and erudition possessed by Lady Philosophy. Similarly, as we saw in the last chapter, in the *City of Ladies*, Christine de Pizan's Lady Reason appears to Christine's dazed speaker in her study, waking her as if from sleep, and equips her with a combination of rational arguments and reinterpreted proverbs with which to resist the debilitating misogyny encountered in her reading. As with Boethius's Lady Philosophy, Christine's Lady Reason and her two accompanying personifications, Rectitude and Justice, appear to the protagonist in a vision so that they are more readily recognizable as externalizations of her *own* reason, moral sense, and religious values.

Renaud's decision to focus Albertanus's sprawling collection of Latin sententiae more sharply on the ability of a diplomatic female figure to intercede with a powerful man on behalf of peaceful solutions also had the effect of making Albertanus's thirteenth-century work more timely in the 1340s. The efficacy of women as potential checks on masculine aggression became an increasingly potent political idea in the fourteenth and fifteenth centuries, as is evident from the writings of Christine de Pizan and the work of scholars including David Wallace and Lynn Staley, as well as Carolyn P. Collette and Misty Schieberle.[56] We saw in chapter 3 an example of Prudence's diplomacy in approaching an angry magnate: when Melibeus assails her with a series of harsh antifeminist proverbs justifying his rejection of advice from a woman, Prudence listens "ful debonairly and with greet pacience" until she has heard "al that hir housbonde liked for to seye" before responding with counter-maxims in support of women's counsels (VII.1064). Prudence's positive traits carry over from the personified cardinal virtue to the virtuous and diplomatic woman and wife on the work's literal level. In Chaucer's translation, "this noble wyf" (976, 979), this "deere and benygne lady" (1743), is praised for her "grete goodnesse" (1744) and "noblesse" (1766), as well as her "grete skiles and resouns" and "wise informaciouns and techynges" (1870).

## HOW TO DO THINGS WITH PROVERBS

Although we are not accustomed to thinking of "sentences and proverbes" in this way, *Melibee* treats them as time-tested frameworks through which an individual could come to a decision or opposing parties could arrive at a resolution. When early in the work Melibeus frets about whether following her proverb-laden counsels will give his wife "maistrie" over him, Prudence's response emphasizes that, no matter where he seeks advice, he bears the ultimate responsibility for his decisions. Although a man "asketh conseil," Prudence replies, "yet hath he *free choys* wheither he wole werke by that conseil or noon" (VII.1083, my emphasis). When Melibeus first makes a facile, premature promise to be guided by her *conseil* in all things, rather than readily accepting this compliance as one might expect of a domineering figure bent on exacting obedience, Prudence instead urges him first to take "conseil" from God, and after that, to "taken conseil in yourself, and examyne wel youre thoghtes of swich thyng as yow thynketh that is best for youre *profit* ['benefit, well-being']" (1116, 1119). A proverb, she is telling him, is only as wise as its user, who must evaluate the circumstances to which it will be applied, and Melibeus's wisdom, his "Sophie," is still sadly debilitated. The ability to exercise "free choys" and to examine critically which of a variety of counsels best suits the requirements of the current situation are the driving forces of Prudence's pedagogy. She seeks to equip Melibeus with the tools he will need to exercise his "free choys" and his deliberative powers without her prompting.

Enamored of proverbs for their own sake, trained on allegory from their earliest literary encounters with fables, and accustomed to authoritative personifications gendered feminine, premodern readers would more readily recognize the instruction Melibeus receives as not just the teachings of his wife but on another level the counsels of his own prudence, guiding him away from the rash promptings of his emotions and toward conduct governed by reason, clemency, respect for law, and, above all, a willingness to reflect on and adopt wise counsels such as this work offers in such profusion. Readers too can learn how to use these counsels and foster these desirable traits in themselves. As Prudence instructs Melibeus, so *Melibee* offers training to the reader in how to "taken conseil in yourself," "examyne wel youre thoghtes," and exercise "free choys" in determining the best counsel and resultant course of action.

Melibeus's progress toward the rehabilitation of his "Sophie" proceeds by fits and starts, with each setback providing fresh opportunities not just for slotting in more proverbs but also for providing further instruction in how to interpret and apply them. This literary representation of Prudence's instruction is idealized, but useful nevertheless in helping us to understand the sway her wise counsels once held with the many readers of the versions of this work over several centuries. According to Cicero's *De inventione*, prudence has three parts, memory, intelligence, and foresight.[57] Because on one level Melibeus's wife represents his own prudential faculty—*his* memory, and his potential for intelligence and foresight—the wisdom expressions Prudence cites can also be thought of as arising from his own recollection and reading. Prudence's first instance of proverb use posits a direct pathway from retrieval from memory to action in the world, a process resembling the one we saw imagined in the *Cook's Tale*, where a master victualer releases a misbehaving apprentice after "hym bithoughte / . . . of a proverbe" advising that it is better to remove a bad apple than to let it spoil the whole hoard (I.4403–7). Seeing her husband's sorrow and anger over their daughter's injuries, Prudence "remembred hire upon the sentence of Ovide," a "sentence" that advises allowing an afflicted person time to grieve before attempting comfort. Called up from memory, it provides the "resoun" for Prudence's decision to delay her consolation: "For which resoun this noble wyf Prudence *suffred* ['allowed'] hir housbonde for to wepe and crie as for a certein space." She soon introduces another proverb with "Remembre yow that Jhesus Syrak seith" (VII.976–79, 995).

Contemporary testimony to the way *auctoritates* memorized in youth continue to spring to mind in adult life comes from a letter from Petrarch to Boccaccio in 1359, in which Petrarch describes his recollection of memorized sayings and admonitions:

> I swallowed as a boy what I would ruminate upon as an older man. I have thoroughly absorbed these writings . . . implanting them not only in my memory but in my marrow. . . . If at times out of habit they return to the memory, it often happens that to the preoccupied mind . . . they seem not only to be yours but to your surprise, new and original. . . . I grant that I like to embellish my life with sayings and admonitions [*dictis ac monitis*] from others, but not my writings unless I acknowledge the author or make some

significant change in arriving at my own concept from many and varied sources in imitation of the bees.[58]

By this account, proverbs come almost involuntarily to the minds of premodern writers, and for Petrarch it takes restraint not to use them in formal writing without some twist of his own. As they do for Erasmus, proverbs provide pleasure: Petrarch likes to use them to "embellish" [*ornare*] his daily life. Memorized in youth, bred in the marrow, and ruminated upon in maturity, they could also prove problematic for ambitious writers, as Petrarch's concerns about attribution and originality in their use imply. We will see evidence of Chaucer's reservations about their use in my conclusion, but the present point is that step one in using "sentences and proverbes" is often envisioned as retrieval from memory.

Since it is not an activity in which we now engage, we might ask how exactly one would go about the next step, deliberating deeply on a proverb remembered or read, as recommended by Albertanus in his preface to the *Liber consolationis*. *Melibee* suggests some methods, all of which involve seeking out a variety of counsels and choosing intelligently among them. Prudence shows Melibeus how to examine what he has been told by various types of advisers such as physicians and lawyers, but her methods apply also to examining the "sentences and proverbes" in which their advice is couched. She advises him to pause to imagine the outcome of each recommended course of action, after which "thou shalt chese the beste and *weyve* ['avoid'] alle othere thynges" (VII.1207–8). A metaphor amplifies this recommendation: consider from what "roote" the counsel springs and thus what "fruyt" it is most likely to bear (1209). Consider also whether the recommended course of action is within your power, whether "thou mayst *parfourne* ['perform'] it and maken of it a good ende" (1212).

Prudence also teaches Melibeus, and *Melibee* teaches its reader, that responsible and critical use of *proverbes* involves attending very closely to their language, taking care not to distort the meanings of a proverb's words to produce the advice one wishes to hear. A group of physicians advises Melibeus with the medical proverb "oon contrarie is warisshed by another contrarie" ('one contrary is cured by another contrary', VII.1276), in which *contrary* means 'the opposite, antithesis, or reverse of something', as when cold is used to alleviate heat. But driven by his impulse toward violent revenge, Melibeus willfully adopts a secondary meaning of *contrary*, 'a hostile act, violation', and thus he interprets the proverb as advocating the return of one hostile act for another (1279–82).⁵⁹ "Lo, lo" exclaims Prudence in response, "how *lightly* ['easily'] is every man enclined to his owene desir and to his owene pleasaunce!" (1283). She shows him how to parse the proverb's wording more responsibly: the "contrary" that alleviates violence is not more violence, but peace and accord.

Prudence's most important lesson in proverb use emphasizes the need for flexibility and a willingness to adopt new counsels as circumstances change. Early on, Melibeus wants to adhere stubbornly to his decision to pursue vengeance lest he be thought a fool for changing his *conseil*. Prudence challenges his rigidity: "For I seye that it is no folie to chaunge conseil whan the thyng is chaunged, or elles whan the thyng semeth ootherweyes than it was biforn" (VII.1065). Returning to this point later, she puts it more forcefully: "And take this for a general reule, that every conseil that is affermed so strongly that it may nat be chaunged *for no condicioun that may bityde* ['for any circumstances that might arise'], I seye that *thilke* ['that same'] conseil is wikked" (1231). When circumstances change or appear in a new light upon reflection, adhering to a given precept out of stubbornness or fear of appearing irresolute to others is not just foolish but "wikked."

This emphasis on assembling a variety of counsels in order to determine the one that best fits the occasion and on changing one's *conseil* when circumstances change also helps us to see why premodern writers from Albertanus to Erasmus were never disturbed by the existence of contradictory proverbs. Contradictory proverbs are only a problem if we think of each one as an order to be obeyed. The proverbs in *Melibee* derive from sources of great temporal and ideological diversity: the Hebrew scriptures, rival schools of ancient philosophy, the secular literature of ancient Rome, Christian writings from late antiquity onward, medieval proverb collections and school texts, and anonymous sayings in oral circulation.⁶⁰ Conflicting counsels are inevitable, and the reader is meant to select from among them; their diversity is a strength. The *proverbes* on offer in *Melibee* are far from monologic, and they speak from a variety of perspectives on questions both practical and moral. Moderns sometimes equate proverbs with moralistic warnings, but by no means do all the sayings in *Melibee* admonish the reader; some, for example, extend the "consolation" of Albertanus's title to the "troubled souls" mentioned in his preface. Rather than commanding obedience, these sayings encourage the afflicted to keep their equanimity in a harsh world and to accept the unavoidable with grace, or at least resignation, and with faith in future happiness. Among the work's "sentences and proverbes," Speght marks "the joye of God . . . is . . . everelastynge" (VII.1510) and Job's words in accepting his many losses, still echoed in the Christian burial service, "Oure Lord hath *yeve* ['given'] it me; oure Lord hath *biraft it me* ['taken it away from me'] . . . blessed be the name of oure Lord!" (1000).

In addition to teaching how to deliberate on proverbs, Prudence models how to use them effectively in speech and writing. Her response to Melibeus's last instance of backsliding illustrates a technique for using proverbs persuasively: presenting them to the listener or reader in climactic order. Of the nine "sentences and proverbes" elicited by Melibeus's unexpected resolve to exile his repentant enemies (VII.1836–69), the first two warn against the covetousness in his implicit plan to appropriate their wealth. The next warns of damage to his reputation, followed by one against misuse of the power his subjects have granted him. Two more advocate courtesy and humility in wielding power, another promotes self-restraint, and the penultimate *proverbe* recommends avoiding the regret that would follow this misuse of his victory. Devoted mainly to practical concerns of this world and citing as its named sources the pagan authors Seneca and Cicero, this series ends with a climactic final bid for clemency in the form of an important Christian quotation.

Prudence's final *proverbe*, the last of this series and also the last of the *Tale of Melibee*, raises the stakes by addressing the fate of Melibeus's immortal soul:

> "Wherfore I pray yow, lat mercy been in your herte, / to th'effect and entente that God Almighty have mercy on yow in his laste juggement. / For Seint Jame seith in his Epistle: ☞ 'Juggement withouten mercy shal be doon to hym that hath no mercy of another *wight* ['being']." (VII.1867–69, James 2:13)

Those who extend to others only strict justice and show no mercy cannot expect mercy themselves when they are judged for their own sins. Addressed to his enemies, Melibeus's final speech echoes the emphasis on mercy in the tale's very last *proverbe*, revealing its efficacy in moving him to choose clemency over vengeance at long last: "yet for as muche as I see and biholde youre grete humylitee / and that ye been sory and repentant of youre giltes, / it constreyneth me to doon yow grace and mercy. / Wherfore

I receyve yow to my grace / and *foryeve* ['forgive'] yow *outrely* ['entirely'] . . . to this effect and to this ende, that God of his endelees mercy / wole at the tyme of oure diynge foryeven us oure giltes that we han trespassed to hym in this wrecched world" (1878–84). As well as illustrating the strategic benefit of climactic order in presenting a series of proverbs, the pivotal role of Prudence's final *proverbe* in bringing about the tale's resolution demonstrates once again the centrality to *Melibee* of its "sentences and proverbes."

Chaucer's narrator attributes Melibeus's eventual embrace of clemency and nonviolent conflict resolution directly to Prudence's instruction. While Renaud condenses Albertanus's laudatory language at the work's end, reporting more briefly that Melibeus praises Prudence's words and her wise teachings ("les paroles . . . et ses sages enseignemens"), Chaucer amplifies, adding praise for her "grete skiles and resouns" and "wise informaciouns."[61] Directly after Prudence's final, climactic series of proverbs, *Melibee* moves toward closure. Chaucer reports that Melibeus has finally "assented fully to werken after hir counseil," returning to the Solomonic proverb that governs the whole (1872, cf. 1003). Prudence's counsel, as we have seen, is that he restrain his anger and rash haste in order to remember and deliberate on the advice most likely to produce the results that will benefit him and others in the long term. Successfully schooled by the "sentences and proverbes" of a feminine wisdom figure, at least for the time being Melibeus has learned to rein in his emotions and heed the counsels of his own prudence. Rather than interrupting the story, proverbs and their uses *are* the story.

### WHY INCLUDE A PROVERB COLLECTION IN A STORYTELLING CONTEST?

If, as this book argues, one of the artistic issues Chaucer explores over the course of the *Canterbury Tales* is the relation of proverb to story, the discussion in this chapter should suggest the importance of *Melibee* to that exploration. Read strictly as a story, it is arguably as problematic as *Sir Thopas* in the thinness and improbability of its plot and its tilt toward an excess of *sentence*. As an exploration of the powers of the proverb, however, *Melibee* testifies to the riches of the international proverb tradition, that great unsung source for Chaucer's poetry. It imports into the *Canterbury Tales* a trove of "sentences and proverbes" ripe for skillful reapplication elsewhere, both in parody and in earnest.[62] It is a source unsung by modern readers, that is, not by Chaucer himself, who translated *Melibee* into English and positioned it prominently in his most ambitious work. Chaucer's *proverbes* were not unsung by the scribes who wrote phrases like *nota proverbium* in the margins of his texts, nor by Speght who marked some 776 of them in the *Canterbury Tales*, not by the contemporaries who praised Chaucer's proverb use, and not by the premodern readers who annotated the proverbs in *Melibee* in their own copies of his works.

The inverted reading of *Melibee* offered here, with its treasury of *proverbes* to the fore and its framing allegory only secondary, may also help to explain why Chaucer was content to offer a very close translation of Renaud, rather than freely altering the story to suit his own purposes, as he does with the plots and characterization of his other tales. If Chaucer's primary interest was in *Melibee* as a learned compendium of international proverbs, his best energies may have gone into rendering them from Renaud's French into English equivalents, an effort little recognized by modern readers. Chaucer did not need Albertanus or Renaud to introduce him to the best-known proverbs of his day, and a substantial number of the sources from which they drew proverbs, Chaucer had likely read for himself. It is nevertheless striking how often proverbs from *Melibee*'s abundant store emerge at key moments elsewhere in the *Canterbury Tales*, as though this proverb collection served Chaucer as an *aide-mémoire*, a prompt, or a rift of raw materials awaiting creative refashioning. As Mann observes, "Proverbs are part of a rich body of social wisdom" in the *Tales*, and "Chaucer's own Tale of Melibee—often passed over by modern readers—plays a central role as representative of this body of collective wisdom."[63] When Chaucer redeploys *Melibee*'s proverbs in new contexts elsewhere in the *Tales*, they function in unexpected new ways.

To conclude this chapter with a few of the most striking examples of this creative reuse, we saw in chapter 2 the clerk Nicholas's cynical repurposing of *Melibee*'s governing proverb, as he urges the unsuspecting carpenter to "Werk al by conseil, and thou shalt nat rewe" (I.3530). There, the "conseil" in question is Nicholas's own self-serving advice that leads to the carpenter's absenting himself from his marriage bed so that Nicholas can replace him. In contrast to *Melibee*'s claim that the path to wisdom lies in reflecting upon pertinent counsels and deciding which are most applicable to a particular situation, Nicholas heads off any agency that John might contemplate: "Thou mayst nat werken after thyn owene heed" (I.3528). In the *Merchant's Tale*, as part of an attempt to ingratiate himself with his lord,

January's flattering counselor Placebo ('I will please') reverses *Melibee*'s signature proverb. The elderly January wishes to be advised that, after a lifetime of sexual license, he can find wedded bliss with a much younger woman and, by confining his appetite to marriage, save his soul in the bargain. This fawning courtier first praises his lord for seeking advice, thereby heeding "the word of Salomon"—"Wirk alle thyng by conseil . . . / And thanne shaltow nat repente thee" (IV.1479–86). He then urges January to fly in the face of this proverbial wisdom and indulge his own will and appetites. For Solomon's dictum, Placebo substitutes a spurious counter-maxim ill-suited to January's obvious bent toward self-indulgence: "youre owene conseil is the beste" (IV.1490). In one sycophantic line, Placebo reverses all Prudence's advocacy for mindful deliberation in choosing and applying *proverbes*.

Another of Prudence's sayings, and another of the best known of medieval proverbs, serves as the central text for the Pardoner's preaching and drives his entire performance. When Melibeus threatens to exile his enemies with the implication that he will appropriate their property, Prudence warns him against the sin of covetousness, citing an expression still heard today: "The love of money is the root of all evil." Its source is 1 Timothy 6:10, and Prudence's version is "ye moste dryve coveitise out of your herte / For the Apostle seith that coveitise is roote of alle harmes" (VII.1129–30, cf. 1840, C491). Chaucer's Pardoner is cynically devoted to the same scriptural text, so effective in encouraging his victims to avoid deadly sin by giving what they have to him: "My theme is alwey *oon* ['one'], and evere was—/ "*Radix malorum est Cupiditas*" (VI.333–34). He repeats the Latin proverb and reaffirms its centrality to his preaching in lines 425–26. A malign inversion of the Parson, who favors *sentence* undiluted by story, the Pardoner recognizes that his proverb works best when upheld by engaging fictions:

| | |
|---|---|
| Thanne telle I hem *ensamples* many oon | *exempla, illustrative narratives* |
| Of olde stories longe tyme agoon. | |
| For *lewed* peple loven tales olde; | *uneducated* |
| Swiche thynges kan they wel reporte and holde. | |
| (VI.435–38) | |

In this uneasy moment, Chaucer's arch-hypocrite boasts about the effectiveness of the proverb-story partnership in separating an audience from its goods and money, another prompt to the reader to reflect on proverb and story in the poet's own "tales olde." The Pardoner's monologic devotion to preaching on his one saying—"My theme is alwey oon, and evere was"—warns against the use of a proverb to constrain a story to a single explicit moral. As a false and corrupted clerical figure, the Pardoner hopes that his listeners will accept the authority of his one proverb and act upon it without question or thought, the opposite of the approach taught by *Melibee*.

A final example of a significant proverb shared with *Melibee*, one with resonance for the *Canterbury Tales* as a whole, comes from the *Nun's Priest's Prologue*. A scene from early in *Melibee* offers some striking proverbs when an "olde wise man" attempts to persuade Melibeus and other young hotheads to undertake "greet conseil and greet deliberacion" before declaring war on their enemies (VII.1035, 1042). The old man's proverbs include a version of the adage upon which Erasmus would write his most extensive commentary: "Dulce bellum inexpertis" ('War is sweet for those who have not tried it,' IV.i.1). In Chaucer's version, "ther is ful many a man that crieth, 'Werre, werre!' that *woot* ['knows'] ful litel what werre amounteth" (1037).[64] The young men match proverb with proverb, using an expression still heard today: "whil that iren is hoot men sholden smyte" (1036, I60). As the old man prepares "to enforcen his tale by resons"—to support it with further arguments and more proverbial wisdom—the young men "rise for to breken his tale" and urge him "his wordes for to *abregge* ['abridge']" (1043). Recognizing that he has lost his audience, the old man quotes one last proverb before stepping down: "For Salomon seith: 'Ther as thou ne mayst have noon audience, enforce thee nat to speke'" (1046).

When it reappears in the *Nun's Priest's Prologue*, Solomon's proverb on the futility of speaking to unwilling listeners rises to a kind of metacommentary on proverbial wisdom in the *Canterbury Tales*. This prologue follows directly upon the gloomy sententiousness of the interrupted *Monk's Tale*, and its proverb stressing the importance of audience awareness serves as a counterweight or qualifier to *Melibee*'s central proverb with its all-out advocacy for Solomonic wisdom: "Werk alle thy thynges by conseil" (1003). Rephrased to fit the verse form, the old man's proverb, now spoken by the Host, employs as a rhyme word Chaucer's polysemous keyword *sentence*:

"For certeinly, as that thise clerkes seyn,
☞ Whereas a man may have noon audience,
Noght helpeth it to tellen his sentence."
(VII.2800–2802)

This proverb's original context in Ecclesiasticus 32:5–7 illuminates its special relevance to the *Canterbury Tales*. There it cautions a speaker at a feast against untimely sententiousness while the wine flows and the music plays: "do not hinder the music; where there is no hearing, do not pour out words, and do not exhibit your wisdom at the wrong time. A concert of music in a banquet with wine is as a gem set in gold."[65] This injunction speaks to judicious timing and thoughtfulness in proverb use, an insight that transcends the limited acumen of its fictional speaker, the Host.[66] Strategically placed before the *Nun's Priest's Tale*, the central text of my conclusion, it warns not against "sentences and proverbes" themselves but against losing one's audience—as Chaucer's Monk does—through a joyless and monologic wisdom, an excess of *sentence* that impinges on life's *solaas*—including music, wine, feasting, and, in this instance, the many pleasures of storytelling.

CONCLUSION

*Putting Proverbs in Their Places*

Manye smale maken a greet
—*Parson's Tale*, x.362

For the reasons presented in my introduction and opening chapter, I depart in this book from most modern critical practice by treating the proverb as a verbal form central to Chaucer's poetic art in the *Canterbury Tales*. Thomas Speght's annotated Chaucer edition of 1602 has served as a guide to identifying "sentences and proverbes" in Chaucer's work; its many hundreds of little pointing hands provide visual reminders of the lost practice of reading proverbially. In chapter 2, we saw one pattern that emerges from a proverb-conscious reading: the poet uses proverbs as a medium of exchange between clerks and ordinary people, serving both to uphold and to challenge the clerical claim to a monopoly on wisdom. Another pattern emerges in the third chapter, where we see the proverb depicted in the *Wife of Bath's Prologue* as an efficient weapon for attacking women; in the tale that follows, the wise old woman models a more constructive form of proverb use, substituting moral instruction for verbal assault. Chapter 4 explores the most overt discussion of proverb use in the *Canterbury Tales*; it reads *Melibee* as a treasure house of proverbs framed by a slender story, a story designed to instruct protagonist and reader in the effective and ethical use of *proverbes*.

My aim in this conclusion is to tease out what I can about the role of proverbs in the implicit *ars poetica* built into the *Canterbury Tales*. We have seen proverbs fueling contests over whose wisdom matters and whose will prevail, and I want to turn now to what Chaucer's last and most ambitious work tells us about the use of proverbs in storytelling. I will argue that one compositional question posed by this large and variegated work is how a poet, keenly aware of the power of proverbs, can draw on them to strengthen and support his "mateere" while also preventing these powerful little forms from supplanting or foreclosing the reader's own reception of a passage or tale. I begin with some observations drawn from the final pairing in the *Tales* as we have it, the tales of the Manciple and Parson, and then devote the remainder of this conclusion to the *Monk's Tale* and *Nun's Priest's Tale*, the pairing most revelatory of Chaucer's ideas about how to put proverbs in their places.

As we have seen, because premodern proverbs enjoyed a much greater cultural authority than their equivalents today, their transformational powers could make them volatile additions to fictions. Just before the Parson takes the *Canterbury Tales* toward a conclusion in which Chaucer's readers are asked to examine their own lives and consciences, the ending of the *Manciple's Tale* provides a conspicuous reminder that saddling a story with a single, explicit, proverb-enforced moral can be the enemy of a reader's or listener's freedom and pleasure. We know that premodern poets and their readers were well schooled in relating proverbs to stories: their early education included matching a fable with a *moralite* (Latin *moralitas*), which often took the form of a preexisting proverb, or conversely, the *moralite* became proverbial because of its attachment to a well-known fable.[1] To pause for a moment over this important word, in Chaucer's vocabulary, *moralite* and *sentence* are not synonymous, and the latter is closer to our idea of "meaning" in literature, but the two are closer than *moral* is to *meaning* in our current literary vocabulary. The glossary in the *Riverside Chaucer* captures the overlap by defining Chaucer's *moralite* as 'the moral significance (of a tale)' and *sentence* more generally as 'meaning', or 'significance'. Because Middle English *sentence* (Latin *sententia*) also alternates with *proverbe* as a term for a wisdom expression, it was easy to associate the *sentence* of a literary text with the individual maxims or *sentences* that appear within it. The *moralite* attached to the *Manciple's Tale*, an overt effort to supplant rather than support the reader's apprehension of the story's *sentence*, focuses attention on the potential threat the proverb can pose to a story.

The Manciple ends his Ovidian fable of the tell-tale crow with an obsessive recitation of remembered proverbs (IX.309–62). In fifty-three lines of verse, Chaucer offers a series of garrulous and repetitious—and thus ironic—injunctions against too much talk. Speght marks eight "sentences and proverbes" in this speech, all of which reiterate the need to hold one's tongue.[2] The passage is almost painful to read; Warren Ginsberg rightly associates "the hammer-beat bombardment of precept after precept" with a memory of the "educational drubbing" medieval children sustained as they were "pummeled by the blunt instrument" of such "lore."[3] The reigning king of proverbs in the *Tales*, Solomon, leads his fellow *auctoritees* in a series that sounds like a send-up of *Melibee*: "Daun Salomon, as wise clerkes seyn, / Techeth a man to keepen his tonge weel" (314–15); "Reed Salomon, so wys and honurable; / Reed David . . . ; reed Senekke" (344–45); "The Flemyng seith. . . ." (349). As spoken by the Manciple, this lengthy and over-authorized *moralite* leaves the impression of a speaker desperately trying to control the meaning of his tale.

As Ginsberg's reference to pedagogy suggests, the proverb-laden outburst Chaucer gives his fictional Manciple might be thought of as one of Jeff Dolven's "scenes of instruction," passages in which premodern writers show themselves haunted by the proverb-based instruction they received as schoolchildren. Trained on fables in which "a sententious moral typically provides both narrative closure and an account of what the tale meant," the early modern writers in Dolven's study return in their mature work to trouble the relationship between the immediate "paradigmatic understanding" conveyed by a maxim and the "narrative understanding" built up gradually over the length of a story. For premodern writers, the "paradigmatic understanding" conveyed by the maxim is "powerful, useful, and deserves sympathetic recognition," but it nevertheless arouses resistance, in part because of its association with the coercion of the schoolroom, but also because it "abstracts its object from time" by treating a narrative as already read, interpreted, and understood.[4] Stories can only unfold over time, and even the simplest narrative introduces potentially disruptive detail that can send readers or listeners in different interpretive directions, questing after what matters to them. By pronouncing with authoritative brevity upon what the story *means*, the proverb threatens to master it, wresting other potential meanings away from both author and reader.

Not only is the Manciple's extended *moralite* overly repetitious and insistent in a way that invites comparison to the authorial discomfort with proverbs revealed in Dolven's scenes of instruction, many readers also find its admonition, "Kepe wel thy tonge and thenk upon the crowe," a mismatch with the fable itself (IX.362).[5] The crow that we are enjoined to "thenk upon," and thus remember to hold our tongues, is punished by his master for speaking an unwelcome truth about the infidelity of the master's wife, whom his master then kills without allowing her a word. The crow's truth-telling does unnecessary harm, but the master's slaying of his wife and his permanent silencing of the messenger (and all crows ever after) are surely more grievous than the bird's failure to hold its tongue. The opening description of the mistreated crow depicts him as a Chaucerian author figure: he knows how to "*countrefete* ['imitate'] the speche of every man / ... whan he sholde tell a tale" (134–35). This harsh punishment of a truth-telling dependent by a seigneurial master, one who is allegedly "fulfild of gentilesse, / Of honour, and of parfit worthynesse," reflects ruefully on Chaucer's own experience of aristocratic patronage (123–24). The mismatch of this last of the fictional tales with a *moralite* hammered home by eight "sentences and proverbes" reminds the reader one last time of Chaucer's resistance to pinning a story to a single *moralite*, despite the ubiquity of the practice in premodern culture, from schoolroom to pulpit.

In the highly contrastive "tale" that follows, the Parson's avowed anti-fable, an abundance of disparate proverbs provides the reader with the diversity of counsels needed to support what *Melibee* calls "free choys." According to Speght's markings, the Parson's 168 "sentences and proverbes" make it the runner-up to *Melibee*. Although the *Parson's Tale* imparts an orthodox Christian view of sin and penitence that allows for very little deviation from its doctrinal position, its proverbs serve as part of the equipment the tale provides for active self-examination. A supply this ample, drawn from divergent sources and traditions, inevitably offers contradictory counsels. The tale's Speght-marked *proverbes* make competing claims about which sins do more harm than all the others. Even the fundamental worldviews that inform them can conflict. As an example, a *proverbe* from Aristotle that Chaucer found in Boethius holds that "A man is a *quyk* ['living'] thyng, by nature *debonaire* ['gracious'] and *tretable* ['amenable'] to goodnesse" (X.658). This view of humanity as by nature inclined toward the good departs from the worldview that informs the many sentences derived from Christian patristic writers, who assume that humans are born to original sin.[6] Just as the tale's readers are expected to identify in themselves the sinful behaviors that apply from among the many presented, so they must also negotiate its array of "sentences and proverbes," deliberating on those most applicable to their own spiritual state. Even in this most didactic and least fictive of "tales," we find a form of proverb use that resembles that of *Melibee* and contrasts with the Manciple's self-defeating efforts to enforce a single *moralite* onto a work of fiction.

## MANY SMALLS MAKE A GREAT

Before going further, I want to flesh out my claim that a proverb can attempt—never, I think, with full success—to challenge, overshadow, discipline, or replace in the reader's mind the possible meanings of a story. In the *Parson's Prologue*, the tensions I have been describing between stories and forms of explicit moralizing come to the surface. After so many pilgrims have readily complied with the Host's request for a tale, the Parson's flat refusal comes as a surprise: "Thou getest fable noon ytold for me." Saint Paul warns us against lying, this last of the pilgrim speakers continues, and thus, "Why sholde I sowen *draf* ['chaff'] out of my *fest* ['fist'], / Whan I may sowen whete, *if that me lest* ['if I wish']?" (X.31, 35–36). Why should he sow the grain's sterile outer husks, when he can avoid "fable" (here in its wider sense of 'fiction') and sow in his listeners fruitful kernels instead? Why not skip the fable and go straight to the *moralite*? Within the Parson's long and overtly nonfictional contribution to the tale-telling contest lurks what may be the most rigorously didactic and artistically slight story in the whole of the *Canterbury Tales*, paired with the seemingly innocuous proverb, "Manye smale maken a *greet* ['great']" (362). Yet even so underdeveloped and over-moralized a fiction retains a capacity to resist the lesson the teller seeks to impose upon it. Despite the Parson's readiness to do it for them, readers have a stubborn habit of separating *whete* from *draf* for themselves.

In keeping with the Parson's resolution to abstain from fiction and adhere to truth, his detailed taxonomy of sin and guide to penitence alludes only glancingly to some well-known biblical narratives and recounts the events of Adam and Eve's fall. For medieval audiences these were instances of sacred history, not fiction. The teller, however, does not quite fulfill his stated aim. A few brief exempla appear in his tale, including an account of a philosopher humbled by the young pupil he was about to thrash in a moment of uncontrolled anger (X.670–73) and a barebones little story of mariners drowned at sea, the latter accompanied by a proverb to drive home its lesson (361–65). Reversing the usual order by which the *moralite* follows the narrative, the Parson puts the fruitful grain of wisdom first: "the proverbe seith that 'Manye smale maken a greet'" (362). Although I have used *proverb* in this book in the very broad sense of Chaucer's *proverbe*, a term that includes what Whiting calls "sententious remarks"—sayings often attributed to specific sources and not infrequently quite verbose by our standards—this expression happens to be a proverb of the sort most moderns associate with the term. A short, easily remembered, anonymous, and broadly applicable piece of shared wisdom, it is attested in English in the early fourteenth century in words nearly identical to Chaucer's. Its close Latin equivalent, "Levia multa faciunt unum grande," was cited by Saint Augustine, and a member of the Paston family used the English proverb in a letter in 1465.[7] As with many proverbs, its literal proposition could hardly be more self-evident: many small insinuations make a great lie, many small building stones make a great cathedral, and, if well used, many small proverbs support "th'effect" of a great poem.

As he often does, Chaucer names the two microgenres in question, *proverbe* and *ensample*, noting that "the proverbe seith that 'Manye smale maken a greet'" and enjoining the reader or listener to "herkne this ensample" (*MED*, s.v. "exaumple," 3, 'a story which teaches a lesson'). Proverb and story appear in a discussion of venial sins, transgressions that may be small in themselves but are subject to dangerous accumulation if not confessed. Many small drops can inflict the damage of a great wave:

> A greet wawe of the see comth som tyme with so greet a violence that it drencheth the ship. And the same harm doon som tyme the smale dropes of water, that entren thurgh a litel crevace into the thurrok, and in the botme of the ship, if men be so necligent that they ne descharge hem nat by tyme. And therfore, although ther be a difference bitwixe thise two causes of drenchynge, algates the ship is dreynt. (X.363–64).

> [A great wave of the sea comes sometimes with such great violence that it sinks the ship. And sometimes the small drops of water that enter though a little crevice into the bilge, and into the bottom of the ship, do the same harm if men are so negligent that they do not discharge them in time. And therefore, although there may be a difference between these two causes of sinking, in any event the ship is sunk.]

Barely more than an analogy, the temporal scheme of this narrative is present tense and iterative: these two events happen, and will continue to happen, over time. Its language borrows directly from the moralizing that precedes it, and thus it is hard to imagine a fiction trained more precisely upon the lesson intended by its teller. Warning that unconfessed venial sins can lead to those that are deadly, the Parson urges, "lat us nat be necligent to deschargen us of venial synnes" (362). In the exemplum, the sailors are "so necligent that they ne descharge" the accumulating drops of water. The story's language also echoes the proverb: the single wave that sinks the first ship is "greet" in size and violence while the many drops that sink the second are "smale," but the results are the same. Could a teller do more to direct a reader toward the meaning of a fiction?

Yet even this scrap of story offers some arresting features, just enough, I would argue, to risk unsettling the lesson on which it is so forcibly trained. It presumably passes unremarked by most modern readers, but if, like proverb-conscious readers, we follow Speght's manicule and pause for a moment over the proverb and accompanying story, we might note that the story is not utterly devoid of imaginative power. The inundating wave that sinks the first ship with "so greet a violence" provides some drama; the leak that dooms the second is concretely rendered: "a litel crevace" lets water seep into its "thurrok" or bilge. The story includes morally culpable agents, those "necligent" sailors on the second ship who fail to discharge the bilge water. Despite its sharp, proverb-driven focus on the single lesson it sets out to teach, this brief lapse into story nevertheless provides some little crevices through which readerly subjectivity, doubt, and imagination can seep in.

How could the negligent sailors not notice the accumulation of water sufficient to swamp their ship? Why would they neglect to bail it out when their lives were at stake? On a higher plane, why does God's benevolent providence consign the apparently innocent mariners on the first ship, helpless against a sudden great wave, to the same fate as the crew who bring disaster on themselves by neglecting their duty? If Chaucer had brought his full fictional powers to bear on retelling this seemingly unpromising exemplum, amplifying it with a few individualized characters and a harrowing account of their drowning, instead of resolving to confess their venial sins at regular intervals, some members of the Parson's audience might instead have come away sorrowing over the loss of innocent lives on the first ship. To press the point to its limit, given the final emphasis on the identical fates of the two crews, a believer might even be prompted to a brief moment of religious doubt by the drowning of the blameless along with the culpable, though nothing could be further from the teller's intent.

Chaucer's Parson, in other words, is right to be leery of fiction as a means of teaching a single lesson to all comers, though his proposed solution, skipping the tale in favor of the *moralite*, is obviously not one his creator would support. After many decades of theorizing about reader response to literary texts, to us it now seems obvious that readers and listeners respond to stories in subjective ways based on the beliefs and experiences they bring to them. Such subjectivity was far from widely acknowledged in Chaucer's era when confidence in the didactic power of moral exempla was very strong.[8] The quadruple repetition in the *Tales* of the expression "Diverse folk, diversely they seyde" (I.3857), discussed in chapter 2, and the lively disagreements Chaucer creates among the Canterbury pilgrims reveal the pull of this insight on the poet's imagination.

As an example of Chaucer's interest in diverse responses to the same narrative, the Petrarchan *moralite* the Clerk attaches to his tale urges *all* Christians ("every wight, in his degree") to give to God the steadfast obedience Griselda gives to her husband (IV.1142–51). Yet in the work as we have it, two different pilgrim husbands understand the tale as morally binding—not on themselves as Christians but on wives they consider insufficiently obedient, not to God but to them. Chaucer may have intended to eliminate one instance of this duplication of husbandly subjectivity, but that he wrote it into the *Tales* in two different ways suggests its importance. The Host's fervent wish is not that he were more obedient to God but that his wife had heard the tale (1212b–d), and the Merchant responds with a general observation that Speght marks as a *proverbe*: "We wedded men liven in sorwe and care" (1228). As a response to the cruelty inflicted on the peasant girl Griselda by her aristocratic husband, this *moralite* from the Merchant about the universal suffering of wedded men is subjective to the point of perversity. He follows up this dubious wisdom with one of the work's most tellingly subjective, if not solipsistic, remarks: "I *trowe* ['believe'] that it be so, / For wel I *woot* ['know'] it fareth so with me" (1216–17). The proposition that husbands suffer ill-treatment from their wives appears to him to be universally true because it is true of him. We will see another example below of divergent responses to the same tale in the reactions of the Knight and Host to the *Monk's Tale*.

What these divergent responses imply is that fiction is too pliant, too rich in potential meanings, to convey a single explicit moral to all readers and listeners: "diverse folk" will respond to it diversely. In the minds of readers and listeners, stories will wrestle free of the meanings that "sentences and proverbes" often work to inculcate. If even in the Parson's quintessentially didactic fable of the mariners, the teller's meaning can give way to the reader's, the same is even truer of the tales that Chaucer endows with his considerable poetic powers and his capacity to layer signification upon signification. Proverbs can be a poet's potent allies; used well, they can summon what Dolven calls the immediate "paradigmatic understanding" that stories necessarily forfeit in favor of increased particularity, contingency, and the space to unfold over time. Given too much hegemony, however, small proverbs can inflict damage, though not as severe as that done by the great wave or the leaking bilges of the Parson's exemplum. Proverbs can restrain or direct a reader's impulse to make meaning, but they cannot drown it.

### PROVERBS AND TRAGEDY, PROVERBS AND POULTRY

By pairing *Sir Thopas*, the only tale with no proverbial wisdom at all, with *Melibee*, the most proverb-heavy "tale" in the whole work, Chaucer suggests the shortcomings of each in balancing "best sentence" with "moost solaas." The two tales that follow that pairing, the *Monk's Tale* and *Nun's Priest's Tale*, are as contrastive as *Thopas* and *Melibee*, not in the sheer number of proverbs this time but in how they are used. As it happens, Speght distributes his manicules with near equality between these two tales of roughly comparable length, eleven pointing hands to the *Monk's Tale* and ten to the the *Nun's Priest Tale*.[9] The *Monk's Tale* seems much longer, but it exceeds the tale of Chauntecleer by only 150 lines. Although some of the Monk's tragedies are arresting in their own right—the story of Zenobia, queen of Palmyra, and the so-called modern instances in particular—its seventeen repetitions of a single story pattern constitute generic overkill, and its proverb use is nearly as unvaried and doleful as the tragedies themselves. In the *Nun's Priest's Tale*, by contrast, proverbs are spoken (and crowed and clucked) in a rousing cacophony of voices, their advice very often in direct contradiction. As many Chaucerians have said in different ways, the tale's conflicting morals compete to supply the story with an ultimate *moralite*, and in that way they leave the making of meaning to the reader. What has not received attention is how the exuberant abundance of proverbs in this tale caps Chaucer's exploration of the role of proverbs in fiction.

In identifying eleven "sentences and proverbes" in the Monk's Tale, Speght contents himself with marking six versions of essentially the same warning against the vagaries of Fortune. The five expressions he marks on other topics, equally gloomy, address the inability of women to keep secrets (VII.2092), the value of the self-knowledge that one of his tragic figures sadly lacks (2139), the shame visited on wives who engage in marital relations when conception is not the goal (2293), the horrific results when great power is joined to cruelty (2493), and the misuse of power to force religious conversion (2559). The remaining six Speght-marked expressions use different words to convey the same caution to those temporarily favored by Fortune: once Fortune abandons him, no man can withstand her desertion (1995); she is certain to leave the powerful bereft of their reign, their wealth, and their friends (2239); her seemingly sweet honey conceals bitter gall (2347); she turns one's highest throw of the dice into the lowest (2661); no one can trust her favor long (2724); she assails the reign of the proud with an unanticipated blow (2763). Apparently regarding these six *proverbes* as sufficient opportunity for the reader to ponder Fortune's capricious ways, Speght passes over two additional and equally sententious versions of the same admonition: "Lo, who may truste on Fortune any *throwe* ['amount of time'] / For hym that folweth *al this world of prees* ['this deceptive world'] / *Er* ['before'] he be war, is ofte *yleyd* ['laid'] full lowe" (2136–38) and "Thus kan Fortune hir wheel governe and *gye* ['guide'], / And out of joye brynge men to sorwe" (2397–98).[10]

By repeating the same *moralite* in eight different verbal forms, the *Monk's Tale* attempts to force a single *sentence* on his succession of tragedies: early or late, Fortune will abandon those she has favored, and the results will be devastating. The tale's harping on this one note not only banishes any suspense about where an individual plot might go, more importantly, it works to exclude the audience from any role in deciding what the stories mean. A reader would have to read *very* hard against the grain to conclude that some of these adventurous lives of wealth and power might have been well worth living while they lasted. Despite the Monk's eight proverbial admonitions, might a resisting female reader of the *Tales* not have preferred the fate of Zenobia, the warrior queen taken captive after leading a revolt against the Roman imperial army, to the exemplary life of Griselda, reconciled to her Walter in the end? Might readers very determined to bring their own lived experience to their reading persevere in the belief that Fortune's favor is not *inevitably* the prelude to utter misery?

After all, some Fortune-favored individuals die, not in agony like Hercules, whose poisoned shirt "made his flessh al from his bones falle" (2126), but peacefully in their beds.

In the prologue that links the *Monk's Tale* to the *Nun's Priest's Tale*, Chaucer dramatizes the way in which the subjectivity of listeners and readers works against heavy-handed attempts to discipline a story to a single *moralite*. In keeping with Chaucer's observation that "diverse folk" respond diversely, the falls from high places in the *Monk's Tale* plunge the Fortune-favored, philosophical Knight into deep sorrow but leave the lower-placed and unreflective Host so detached that he complains of fighting off sleep (VII.2767–802). Despite the contrastive responses of these "diverse folk," both Knight and Host agree that, whether too sorrowful or too soporific, enough of one note is enough. After the Knight reminds the Monk that sorrow also has its "contrarie"—"joye and greet solas"—the Host utters the proverbial admonition discussed in the last chapter: a speaker with no audience offers his *sentence* in vain (2774, 2801–2). He pins his hopes for a tale of mirth and *solaas* on the Nun's Priest: "Telle us swich thyng as may oure hertes glade. / Be blithe . . . / Looke that thyn herte be murie evermo" (2811–15). This plea ushers in the tale of Chauntecleer—a name that embeds the poet's own, as many have noted—and a story that has gladdened readers' hearts for centuries.

Sharing the widespread view of the tale as "one of Chaucer's finest poetic achievements," Peter Travis describes it as Chaucer's "signature *ars poetica*: a fable wherein he contextualizes, critiques, deepens, and refunctions the most pressing concerns of a humanist poet writing in the late fourteenth century in England."[11] Its many echoes of previous tales signal that with the *Nun's Priest's Tale*, Chaucer begins to move gradually toward closure. For our purposes, what matters most among the "pressing concerns of a humanist poet" mentioned by Travis is that, far from banishing *proverbes*, the tale as *ars poetica* places them at the center of the interpretive possibilities extended to its readers. Although by Speght's count the *Nun's Priest's Tale* enjoys nearly the same number of "sentences and proverbs" as the Monk's, its proverb use contrasts sharply with the Monk's one-note determinism. No single *proverbe* prevails as the tale's *moralite*, and the conflicts among those on offer require the reader to weigh one against another in order to arrive at a satisfying *sentence*.

A miniature debate in proverbs launches the plot: as soon as Chauntecleer and Pertelote are introduced, they initiate a learned disputation marked by dueling *auctoritees*. When Chauntecleer reports his frightening dream of being menaced by a houndlike predator, reddish in color with black-tipped ears and tail, Pertelote assures him, on the authority of "so wys a man" as "Catoun," the supposed author of the *Disticha Catonis*, that he should put no faith in the prophetic power of dreams (VII.2949–50). Pertelote's dismissal of his dream and of his fear incites Chauntecleer to assert the existence of "many a man moore of auctorite / Than evere Caton was . . . / That al the revers *seyn* ['say'] of this sentence." The "revers" of the "sentence" cited by Pertelote holds that, on the contrary, dreams are "significaciouns / As wel of joye as of tribulaciouns / That folk enduren in this lif present" (2975–81).[12] Chauntecleer carries on with his demonstration that the best *auctoritees* are on his side, their dialogue a comic reworking of the more staid debates in proverbs between human marital partners in *Melibee* and a reprisal also of their role in sparking domestic conflict between the Wife of Bath and Jankyn.

Like an avian Monk, Chauntecleer attempts to drive home a single *sentence* with three stories, repetitive in genre, three "ensamples olde" coerced into demonstrating that "many a dreem ful soore is for to drede" (VII.3106, 3109). Along the way, the distractable rooster wanders into another possible *moralite*, 'Mordre wol out' (3052, 3057), a viable proverb to judge by its persistence to this day in connection with detective fiction, but one with only indirect bearing on his dispute with Pertelote about whether dreams possess prophetic power. Each exemplum tells of an individual undone by ignoring a dream, and each is reinforced with a single moral: "Hym thoughte his dreem *nas but a vanitee* ['was only an empty illusion']," but "truste wel, his dreem he foond ful trewe" (3011, 3024); "Heere may men seen that dremes *been* ['are'] to drede" (3063). He drives his point home to "faire Pertelote" once more: "By swiche ensamples olde *maistow leere* ['you may learn'] / That no man sholde been to *recchelees* ['heedless'] / Of dremes" (3106–9). Although Speght marks as a *proverbe* only the first assertion in 2979 that dreams are prophetic and not all these repetitions of the same warning, Chaucer's point is made. By representing his rooster as using *proverbes* to force the meaning of his three cautionary tales, Chaucer parodies the generic repetition of the preceding Monk's Tale and its attempt to yoke its stories to a single, totalizing *moralite*.

Leaving the role of an avian Monk seeking to constrain the meanings of his stories and taking up the part of an avian Melibeus distrusting his wife's *conseil*, Chauntecleer shifts the ground of his dispute with

Pertelote to an *ad feminam* proverb: "In principio / Mulier est hominis confusio" ('In the beginning, woman is man's ruin,' VII.3163-64). The narrating Nun's Priest supports his rooster's antifeminist position: "My tale is of a cok . . . / That tok his conseil of his wyf, *with sorwe* ['to his sorrow']" (3252-53). He clinches the point with a proverb attested in English as early as the mid-thirteenth century *Proverbs of Alfred*: "Wommennes conseils been ['are'] ful ofte colde" (3256, R66), with *colde* meaning 'ill-omened' or 'unfortunate', the Nun's Priest's example being the outcome of Eve's recommendation to Adam that he eat the forbidden fruit.

Despite the Nun's Priest's proverbial defamation of "wommennes conseils," what lures Chauntecleer to the ground is not a reasoned decision that Pertelote's *auctoritee* was right after all about the inability of dreams to predict the future, but in fact his own susceptibility to the "beautee" of her face and his recollection of perching by her "softe syde" at night. Filled with "joye" and "solas" by these amorous thoughts, Chauntecleer throws his *auctoritees* to the wind and flies down from his perch (VII.3160-71). He is the roosterly equivalent of Melibeus at the beginning of his schooling: he uses his proverbs more for show and contentiousness with his wife than as potential guides to appropriate action. Once again, we see that a *proverbe* is only as wise as its user. With the humor that everywhere enlivens this implicit *ars poetica*, Chauntecleer's special admiration of the scarlet red around Pertelote's eyes comically reasserts the birdness of his beloved amid all the erudition passing between them (3161). The fictional teller's pointed attribution of Pertelote's position to the masculine *auctoritee* Cato undermines his ominous proverb about the coldness of women's counsels, as does the amorous rooster's actual motivation for endangering himself. Comic mismatches such as these subvert the capacity of the tale's proverbs to predetermine its *sentence*.

Chauntecleer's notorious mistranslation of the Speght-marked antifeminist proverb that identifies woman as man's ruin, "Mulier est hominis confusio," draws special attention to the tale's weighing of the value and validity of "sentences and proverbes" and the conflicting counsels they offer. "Madame," he solemnly intones, "the sentence of this Latyn is, / 'Womman is mannes joye and al his blis'" (VII.3165-66). Chaucer here very likely plays on the meaning of a "Latyn," the name for a sentence or proverb set to schoolchildren as an elementary translation exercise. Among the set sentences in a workbook of circa 1427 is the memorable lament, "A hard latyn to make, my face *wexyth blakke* ['is turning black']," duly translated as "difficilem latinitatem composituri, facies mea nigrescit."[13] This memorable moment in the *Nun's Priest's Tale*, in which contradictory positions are attributed to a single "Latyn"—a single *proverbe* on one of the great debates of the *Canterbury Tales* and of the era—has inspired an appropriately diverse array of modern critical interpretations. To give a sampling, Chauntecleer's mistranslated proverb reveals the uncertain grip on Latin possessed by a rooster vain of his learning; it is meant to flatter Pertelote in keeping with his desire to "feather" her; it condemns the transitory "joy and bliss" afforded by women at the possible cost of a man's salvation; it parodies clerical "glossing" or allegorizing by rendering the proverb's *sentence* as the exact opposite of its literal meaning; and—my suggestion from chapter 3—it speaks to the disadvantage to women of not knowing Latin, the language in which they could be slandered with impunity, not just behind their backs but to their faces, as here.[14] All this and more from one small *proverbe*—spoken by a rooster.

In direct defiance of the dismal outcomes demonstrated by the Monk's tragedies and enforced by his eight monologic *proverbes*, the *Nun's Priest's Tale* ends with the narrow escape of Chaucer's resplendent rooster from the jaws of the fox. Although Chaucer alludes to the one-note *moralite* of the *Monk's Tale* by including the dour proverb "*evere* ['always'] the latter end of joy is wo" (VII.3205), experience tells us that "the latter ende of joye" is not invariably "wo," and so does the outcome of this tale. Its conflicting *moralites*, its high-spirited comedy, and the happy survival of its protagonist leave readers free to draw their own conclusions. Told by a clerk whose skinny horse suggests material poverty like two of the work's more sympathetic clerics, the Oxford Clerk and the humble Parson, the *Nun's Priest's Tale* begins the movement toward the moment when, late in the day, with the sun low in the sky, the Host will declare his plan "almoost fulfild," and entrust the ending to the Parson: "Thou sholdest knytte up wel a greet mateere" (X.19, 28).

As a miniature framing tale that embeds many genres, the *Nun's Priest's Tale* invites the reader to contemplate the extraordinary generic variety of the whole, just as the generic sameness of the Monk's framed tragedies shows up the larger work's variety by contrast. Thus we might add the framing tale to one scholar's already long list of the generic affiliations of the *Nun's Priest's Tale*: beast-fable, epic, burlesque, parody, tragedy, dream vision, debate, romance, and allegory.[15] Similarly, the tale's exuberant approach to proverbial wisdom displays in miniature the variety in Chaucer's proverb use across the whole work and reprises the role of proverbs in proposing meanings that readers and hearers are free to accept, discard, or modify to suit their own situated readings. Travis aptly describes the tale's ending, "Taketh the moralite . . . / Taketh the fruyt, and lat the chaf be stille," as offering "a *moralitas* that graciously empowers readers to discover for themselves the essence of the *Tale*'s meaning."[16] This gracious empowerment owes much to the tale's abundant, varied, and conflicting "sentences and proverbes."

We have already seen that the tale's *auctoritees* contradict one another on the prophetic power of dreams, and that a single proverb serves to define woman as man's curse and as his bliss. The restoration to happiness of the hero at the end contradicts the proverb "evere the latter ende of joye is wo" (VII.3205). To these instances may be added the tale's comically conflicting wisdom about flattery. Just as Chauntecleer succumbs to the fox's flattering invitation to show off his singing voice, closing his eyes and stretching out his neck for easy grabbing, a Speght-marked *proverbe* warns sternly against fawning courtiers who win favor with flattery instead of giving their lords honest counsels (3325). Spoken as an aside addressed to "ye lordes," this *moralite* seems slightly askew as applied to the tale, given that the flattering fox is an interloper who, rather than serving as Chauntecleer's courtier or adviser, has only the night before broken through the farmyard's hedges to await the right moment to seize him (3215–20).

Like a comic version of Prudence, who recommends to Melibeus a stiff course of deliberation on the words of various *auctoritees* while their daughter lies near death and her assailants remain at large, the Nun's Priest interrupts this moment of high drama to recommend that his addressees "Redeth Ecclesiaste of flaterye" and learn to beware its treachery (VII.3329–30).[17] Despite the dire warnings against it, however, flattery is arguably the key to Chauntecleer's survival. He encourages the fox to make a speech to his pursuers, boasting of his success in seizing his prey. Flattered, the fox opens his mouth to speak and releases the rooster, who eludes his captor and lives to crow another day. The tale ends with a final surge of potential *moralites*. First, Chauntecleer vows never again to be blinded by flattery, "For he that wynketh, whan he sholde see, / Al willfully, God lat him nevere *thee* ['thrive']!" (3431–32). Next, even the fox takes the opportunity to assert his own rival wisdom. He disputes the rooster's proffered *moralite*—"'Nay,' quod the fox,"—and substitutes his own instead, warning against speaking when one should hold one's peace (3433–35). Finally, the teller reasserts the warning against flattery and then provides the third *proverbe* in a row, his famous injunction, "Taketh the fruyt, and lat the chaf be stille." (3443, C428).

With so many earnest and vexatious issues raised by the words and deeds of the widow's prize poultry, nothing in this tale is safe from laughter: the nature of dreams, the nature of women, the workings of fortune, the meaning and measurement of time, the constraint of predestination on free will, and human pretension. All come within the tale's expansive purview. To these far-reaching concerns, we can perhaps add the poet's laughter at his own protracted search for a workable relation between proverb and story. Given the culminating advice to readers to "Taketh the fruyt, and lat the chaf be stille," it is amusing to notice the earlier passage in which, with a roosterly "chuk," the sound we call a "cluck," Chantecleer expresses his satisfaction at finding a "corn," a fruitful kernel of grain, in the farmyard. Separating the "corn" from the chaff is the more common proverbial form in English of Chaucer's "fruyt" and "chaf" expression, as in the Man of Law's Tale: "*Me list nat* ['I do not wish'] *of the chaf. . . / [to] Maken so long a tale as of the corn*" (II.701–2).[18] Chaucer or his speaker enjoys the joke so much that it is repeated a few lines later: "He chukketh when he hath a corn yfounde" (VII.3175, 3182). This comic juxtaposition of high moral wisdom and farmyard practicality resembles one of Marcolf's replies to Solomon in their proverb contest. The patriarch intones that he who sows wickedness will reap evil, and Marcolf replies, "He that sowyth chaf shal porely mowe."[19]

With the audacity that is everywhere in this tale, the closing lines urging the reader to choose the nourishing grain and leave the dry husks behind redirect an eschatological metaphor from the gospels to the interpretation of secular fiction. Early Christian writers interpreted the biblical image as figuring the separation of damned from saved souls at the Last Judgment, when Jesus will "gather his wheat into the barn, but the chaff he will burn with unquenchable fire" (Matthew 3:12, Luke 3:17). By joining this resonant image of sorting out what is fruitful to an injunction to "Taketh the moralite," Chaucer recommends to the reader of his fiction a version of Prudence's central advice to Melibeus about how to use "sentences and proverbes": a person confronted with a particular proverbial counsel can deliberate on it, and "yet hath he free choys wheither he wole werke by that conseil or noon" (VII.1083). As we have seen, despite its limitations as a story, *Melibee* offers not only a treasury of potentially fruitful kernels but also guidance about what to do with multiple and conflicting counsels: "taken conseil in youreself and examyne wel youre thoghtes of swich thyng as yow thynketh that is best for youre profit" (1119). To return to Kenneth Burke's phrase, proverbs were a significant part of the "equipment for living" that humanist poets provided to their readers, and it is no surprise that Chaucer places them so prominently in his implicit *ars poetica*, a brilliant tale in which real controversies and real proverbs are heatedly debated by fictional chickens.

The invitation at the end of the *Nun's Priest's Tale* to take the fruit and leave the chaff can be extended to many of the hundreds of "sentences and proverbes" strategically placed throughout the *Canterbury Tales*. Whether they reinforce one another or conflict, whether they bear out the narrative action, contradict it, or seem comically irrelevant to it, Thomas Speght's 1602 Chaucer edition marks them with the same neutral pointing finger, unintentionally giving graphic form to Chaucer's injunction at the end of the *Nun's Priest's Tale* to let the reader decide which if any of a tale's proverbs lead toward its *fruyt*, *sentence*, or *moralite*. Speght's manicules bear witness to a proverb-conscious reading practice, alien to us but thoroughly alive for premodern audiences, a reading practice I have tried to recover some part of in this book. Proverbs serve as a medium of exchange between members of different classes in a highly stratified society, and as weapons in combats between clerics and ordinary people and between clerics and women. An absence of manicules emphasizes that *Sir Thopas* is all too wisdom-free, and the presence of two hundred and more makes it hard to miss that, as a story, *Melibee* suffers from proverbial overload. The manicules that point to the Monk's admonitions about Fortune's instability make their repetitious insistence even more obvious, as do those that alert readers to the Manciple's ironically loquacious *moralite* about holding one's tongue. The *Nun's Priest's Tale* seems even funnier with its abundant, exuberant, and wildly contradictory proverbial wisdom solemnly marked out with pointing index fingers for the reader's deliberation and delectation. The tale's proverb use demonstrates by comic example Chaucer's resistance to the Monk's single-note insistence, imitated in Chauntecleer's repetitious exempla about dreams, and his resistance also to the Manciple's efforts to use the considerable authority inherent in proverbs to enforce a single *moralite*.

One of the tenets of Chaucer's poetic practice—a key aspect of his mature *ars poetica*—is that a story succeeds best when, in the words of *Melibee*, it allows readers to exercise "free choys," to "examyne wel" their own thoughts, and to pause over those *proverbes* that offer most help in mediating between past wisdom and individual lived experience. For Chaucer, who finds occasion for many hundreds of proverbs in the *Canterbury Tales*, it is not proverb use but proverb misuse that undermines the success of a story. By putting proverbs in their places, by leaving readers free to choose the kernels of wisdom they find most fruitful and pass over what for them is useless chaff, tellers like Chaucer and his many pilgrim speakers meet some of the challenges posed by the subjectivity of the "diverse folk" who hear or read their stories.

# NOTES

## INTRODUCTION

1. Both Speght editions, 1598 and 1602, have been digitized by Early English Books Online (EEBO). The 1598 edition is STC [2nd ed.] nos. 5077, 5078, 5079. The revised edition cited here is STC no. 5080, *The Workes of our Ancient and Lerned English Poet, Geffrey Chaucer, Newly Printed* (London: Printed by Adam Islip, 1602). STC 5081 is a variant of 5080 with the imprint "impensis Geor. Bishop." Both EEBO scans of the 1602 edition, 5080 and 5081, are made from copies held by the Huntington Library. A publication of 1687 is essentially a reprint of Speght's 1602 edition with the marginal manicules replaced by asterisks placed within the text block at the head of the line. I have also consulted the physical copy of the 1602 edition, STC 5080, "printed by Adam Islip," in the Mortimer Rare Book Collection at Smith College, Northampton, MA, from the Judith and Robert R. Raymo Chaucer Collection.

2. In this and subsequent quotations of the useful premodern formulation "Sentences and Prouerbes" from the title page of Speght's 1602 edition, I substitute lower case letters and modernize the *u* to *v* in "proverbs." I discuss terminology in chapter 1.

3. The title *Rival Wisdoms* is adapted from the title of an article I wrote in 2008 ("Rival Wisdom") that is not about Chaucer but about proverbial wisdom; for this book I chose the plural, *Wisdoms*, rare in modern English, after I found it used in Middle English, as I note in chapter 2.

4. All references to Speght's manicules in this study derive from those present in the Huntington Library copy of the 1602 edition, STC [2nd ed.] 5080 ("printed by Adam Islip"), scanned on EEBO. It is important to note that these marginal indicators sometimes print very faintly or not at all so that in some instances, a manicule present in one copy is undetectable in another. For example, in the Huntington copy on EEBO, STC 5080, the faintly printed manicules present at lines I.1799, 1811, and 1838 (very faint) of the *Knight's Tale* are undetectable in the Raymo copy at Smith College, also STC 5080 ("printed by Adam Islip"). The observations in this book are based on the manicules in the Huntington copy specified above; their failure to print in some other copies has no effect on those points.

5. My modernization of John Trevisa's translation of *Bartholomaeus Anglicus On the Properties of Things*, as cited by the *Middle English Dictionary* (*MED*), s.v. "index," n. 1: "The secoun [finger] hatte index . . . with hym we greteth & schewith & techith al thing" (thorn rendered as *th*).

6. For a history of premodern use marks, see Sherman, *Used Books*.

7. Hunter, "Marking of *Sententiae*"; Lesser and Stallybrass, "First Literary *Hamlet*."

8. Dane, "Fists and Filiations"; Dane, *Out of Sorts*, 106–17.

9. Barker, *Adages of Erasmus*, 15–16. I cite the *Adages* from this accessible introduction to Erasmus's sprawling and much-revised work, providing page numbers from this one-volume selection from the *Adages* and also, for individual adages, citations (i.e., I.ii.39) from the Latin text in *Opera Omnia*, edited by van Poll-van de Lisdonk, Phillips, and Robinson. Barker's single volume of 2001 includes Erasmus's introduction to the 1508 edition, all the long essays, and selected adages in English translation, about 119 of Erasmus's eventual 4,151 (see Barker, *Adages of Erasmus*, xl). Its translations, annotations, and notes are drawn from the *Collected Works of Erasmus*,

vols. 30–36, assembled and introduced by William Barker.

10. David Wallace writes that the terms "medieval" and "Renaissance" are in themselves "generally resistant to thoughts of historical transition" and "might be assigned to the trash can of historiography" (*Chaucerian Polity*, xv, 11). James Simpson argues for historical research that does not make England's break with the papacy in 1534 an insurmountable endpoint ("Diachronic History").

11. Stock, *Listening for the Text*, 69.

12. In the introduction to their wide-ranging handbook *Further Reading*, Matthew Rubery and Leah Price call for more studies of reading itself, rather than subordinating reading to other disciplines such as the history of the book; the volume provides a wealth of current bibliography on reading practices.

13. For an introduction to literary manuscript studies with attention to premodern readers and special attention to Chaucer, see Kerby-Fulton, Hilmo, and Olson, *Opening Up Middle English Manuscripts*. Two historical overviews of reading practices are Manguel, *History of Reading*, and Cavallo and Chartier, *History of Reading in the West*. On use marks, see Sherman, *Used Books*, and its many references.

14. A significant early precursor to this argument is Parkes, "Influence of the Concepts"; it has been usefully extended by Dagenais, *Ethics of Reading*, quotation at 27, and Bahr, *Fragments and Assemblages*, quotation at 69, cf. 3.

15. Whiting, *Chaucer's Use of Proverbs*, 4.

16. Praiseworthy exceptions appear in the notes to this book, but I mention here the important pioneering article by Karla Taylor, "Proverbs and the Authentication of Convention"; also strong on proverb use in *Troilus* is Lori Ann Garner ("Role of Proverbs"). Stephen D. Winick ("Proverbial Strategy and Proverbial Wisdom") shares the emphasis on proverb *use* adopted here, though my thought is shaped by the subsequent work of Roger Chartier, *Forms and Meanings*. Alliterative proverbs are not a major force in Chaucer but an informed study is Deskis, *Alliterative Proverbs*; an extensive knowledge of proverbs informs Bowden, *Wife of Bath in Afterlife*; Kramer, "Proverbial Wisdom"; the essays in Chichon and Liu, *Proverbia*; and Cannon, "Proverbs and the Wisdom of Literature." Still useful for locating primary sources and earlier scholarship is Louis, "Proverbs, Precepts."

17. Gray, *Simple Forms*, 173–74; quotations from a characteristically learned and insightful chapter on Middle English proverbs.

18. Gibson, *Figures of Speech*, 5.

19. All Chaucer quotations are from Chaucer, *Riverside Chaucer*, ed. L. Benson et al.; I cite the *Canterbury Tales* by fragment number (Roman) followed by line number (Arabic), as in VII.1083. Except where it might cause confusion, if multiple Chaucer citations in a paragraph all derive from the same fragment, I use only line numbers after the first. An excellent and more readily available edition of the *Canterbury Tales* in paperback is edited by Jill Mann; an accessible companion with current bibliography is Grady, *Cambridge Companion to "The Canterbury Tales"*; a companion for literature scholars is Fein and Raybin, *Chaucer*.

20. My glosses are indebted to the *Riverside Chaucer* and Mann's edition of the *Canterbury Tales*, as well as the *Middle English Dictionary*.

CHAPTER 1

1. Frost, "Mending Wall," cited by line number from Lathem, ed., *Poetry of Robert Frost*. Wolfgang Mieder discusses the evidence for the proverb's circulation prior to and after Frost's poem in "Good Fences Make Good Neighbours."

2. Bakhtin, "Problem of Speech Genres"; Benjamin, "On Proverbs"; Burke, "Literature as Equipment."

3. I follow the trajectory of the proverb's reception as outlined by Obelkevich, "Proverbs and Social History," with its zenith of popularity in the second half of the sixteenth and the early seventeenth centuries and its waning in the later seventeenth and early eighteenth (57). As an

example of modernist hostility to cliché, George Orwell's famous 1948 essay "Politics and the English Language" gives as rule number 1 for writers, "Never use a metaphor, simile or other figure of speech which you are used to seeing in print," 365, advice that would have astonished Chaucer, even if "in print" were "in writing."

4. For the flourishing of proverb use today, see Mieder, *Proverbs*; Lau, Tokofsky, and Winick, *What Goes Around Comes Around*.

5. For proverbs in Old English, see Deskis, "*Beowulf.*" On proverbs and schooling, see Orme, *Medieval Schools*; Cannon, "Proverbs." On premodern pedagogy and reading practices, see Cannon, "In the Classroom."

6. Proverbs from Orme, *Education and Society*, 83, nos. 6, 7, 11, and 12, reproduced by Orme from the "Lincoln Sentences" of ca. 1425–50 in Beinecke Library MS 3 (34).

7. Wheatley, *Mastering Aesop*; Dolven, *Scenes of Instruction*.

8. For the trilingual culture of medieval England, see Wogan-Browne, *Language and Culture*; Butterfield, *Familiar Enemy*.

9. Whiting (*Chaucer's Use of Proverbs*, 5) collects praise for Chaucer's proverbs, which I cite here from more recent editions. Lydgate, *Siege of Thebes*, ed. Edwards, Prologus, line 51; Metham, *Amoryus and Cleopes*, ed. Page, lines 2191–92.

10. The quotation from Caxton's "Prohemye" appears on the opening page of his 1483 edition of the *Canterbury Tales*; Brathwait, *Comments*, ed. Spurgeon, 92, 92n. See Bowden, *Wife of Bath in Afterlife*, 51–52.

11. Boffey, "Proverbial Chaucer."

12. Barker, *Adages of Erasmus*, 3.

13. Arpad Steiner's list of crossover proverbs, "Vernacular Proverb," is still useful.

14. As cited by Barker, *Adages of Erasmus*, ix, xxxviii–xxxix.

15. Barker, *Adages of Erasmus*, xxxvi–xxxviii.

16. Quotations in this paragraph are cited by page number from Barker, *Adages of Erasmus*.

17. The classic study of Erasmus's publishing career is Jardine, *Erasmus, Man of Letters*.

18. Respectively, "Nosce teipsum," "Festina lente," and "Dulce bellum inexpertis." These extended essays appear in Barker, *Adages of Erasmus*, 96–98, 132–53, and 317–56.

19. Barker, *Adages of Erasmus*, 5; Erasmus's text reads "pariter et translationis pigmento delectent et sententiae prosint vtilitate." *Adagiorum Chilias Prima*, in *Opera Omnia*, ed. Van Poll-van de Lisdonk, Phillips, and Robinson, quotation at 46, lines 39–40.

20. Horace's dictum "Aut prodesse volunt aut delectare poetae" describes poets as aiming either for profit or pleasure, but the two are firmly joined in the line that follows: a poet's words should be "at once pleasing and helpful to life" ("aut simul et iucunda et idonea dicere vitae"), lines 333–34; Quintus Horatius Flaccus, *Satires, Epistles, and Ars Poetica*.

21. Barker, *Adages of Erasmus*, xxxii.

22. Moss, *Printed Commonplace-Books*; see 24–27 for *florilegia*.

23. Vine, *Miscellaneous Order*, 238.

24. Barker, *Adages of Erasmus*, 27n16.

25. Barker, *Adages of Erasmus*, 149. Erasmus mistook the anonymous *Suda* for the work of an author named Suidas.

26. Obelkevich, "Proverbs and Social History," 57; Jones, "Depiction of Proverbs."

27. For the proverbs and other wall texts at Leconfield and Wressle recorded in the mid-fifteenth century in British Library MS Royal 18.D.ii, see Blatt, "Mapping the Readable Household."

28. McCutcheon, *Sir Nicholas Bacon's Great House Sententiae*.

29. Erasmus, *Institutio Principis Christiani*, *Collected Works* 27:210, as cited by Dolven, *Scenes of Instruction*, 112n32.

30. See Jones, "Depiction of Proverbs," 206–7, 218n6. An image appears on the museum's website: https://www.gardnermuseum.org/experience/collection/11959.

31. As cited by Gibson, *Figures of Speech*, 5.

32. Whiting was of course aware of Speght's annotations, mentioning them in

*Chaucer's Use of Proverbs* (5), and he presumably drew upon them. Where possible, the entries in the Whitings' 1968 index provide multiple attestations of an expression, but it also includes many found only once in Chaucer. The volume's selection principle includes a compiler's "sense of recognition, a pricking of the thumbs, which says that a statement is proverbial" (xiii–xiv).

33. Chapter and verse in biblical citations are those of the Latin Vulgate Bible. Unless otherwise indicated (as here where I cite Chaucer's rendering of the biblical texts), English translations follow the Douay-Rheims version.

34. The *Riverside Chaucer* suggests that X.127 may be a version of Proverbs 28:13 and that X.155–57 is Proverbs 11:22. Speght marks only the latter: he is of necessity more selective in indicating "sentences and proverbes" in *Melibee* and the *Parson's Tale*, where the sententiousness of the prose could almost result in more of the text marked than not. Louis, "Concept of the Proverb," offers a more comprehensive survey of the meaning of *proverbe* with essentially the same results.

35. Whiting, *Chaucer's Use of Proverbs*, viii.

36. Whiting, "Nature of the Proverb," 302.

37. Whiting, *Chaucer's Use of Proverbs*, 4; "pawky" here means 'shrewd' or 'wry'. Whiting also collected expressions in a third category, the "proverbial phrase" ("not worth a bean"); these are often delightful in Chaucer but are not addressed in this study.

38. Whiting, *Chaucer's Use of Proverbs*, 4.

39. Whiting, *Chaucer's Use of Proverbs*, 18, 75.

40. A. Taylor, *Proverb*, 4–5; Jerome's version is "Noli (ut vulgare est proverbium) equi dentes inspicere donati." If the expression's present-day familiarity derives primarily from a "learned" source, Erasmus's *Adages* (IV.v.24) is more likely than Jerome as a conduit (the proverb appears in Barker, *Adages of Erasmus*, xxxix). Winick ("Proverbial Strategy") also critiques Whiting's 1934 effort to separate proverbs from sententious remarks, citing Taylor's 1931 dismissal.

41. For the spade, see Barker, *Adages of Erasmus*, 170 (II.iii.5); for the change from jar to box, see Barker, *Adages of Erasmus*, 32–33 (I.i.31).

42. Whiting, *Proverbs, Sentences, and Proverbial Phrases*, xv–xvi. Like Kittredge, Whiting was a legendary figure at Harvard; an apocryphal story held that he was recruited as a Harvard undergraduate by a vacationing university president who spotted him reading Aristophanes in Greek by the side of a country road in Maine. See L. Benson, foreword to *Modern Proverbs and Proverbial Sayings*, v.

43. Chartier, *Forms and Meanings*, 89.

44. Chartier, *Forms and Meanings*, 88–89.

45. Mieder gives a brief history of attempted definitions and sides with those who continue to stipulate that to be a proverb, an expression must be "in circulation," "handed down from generation to generation" (*Proverbs*, 1–31, esp. 2–5, with bibliography).

46. Arora, "Perception of Proverbiality," 6.

47. Shippey, "Proverbs and Proverbiousness," 128.

48. Honeck, *Proverb in Mind*. I discuss Honeck's research in "Transforming Experience into Tradition."

49. Foley, *Singer of Tales in Performance*, 47–49.

50. Dolven, *Scenes of Instruction*, 39.

51. Still useful on proverb form are Dundes, "On the Structure of the Proverb"; Abrahams and Babcock, "Literary Use of Proverbs."

52. On numerical sayings, see Nel, *Structure and Ethos*, 11–12.

53. Burke, "Literature as Equipment," 293, 296, 298.

54. Paulhan, "Experience of the Proverb," 8, 27.

55. Paulhan, "Experience of the Proverb," 26, and for the two Malagasy proverbs, 18, 8. As he reports them in French, "Un morceau de pierre est pierre"; "La voix de la cigale couvre les champs, mais son corps entier tient dans la main"; see Paulhan, "Expérience du proverbe," 184, 188.

56. Paulhan, "Experience of the Proverb," 26–27.
57. Noted by Hannah Arendt in her introduction to Benjamin, *Illuminations*, xxiii–xxiv.
58. Benjamin, "On Proverbs," 582. He concludes the fragment by citing Paulhan's name and the title of his essay, "*Expérience du proverbe*."
59. Benjamin, "On Proverbs," 582.
60. Benjamin, "Storyteller," 48, 73.
61. Honeck's definition of the proverb follows from his theory: "A proverb can be regarded as a discourse deviant, relatively concrete, present (nonpast) tense statement that uses characteristic linguistic markers to arouse cognitive ideals that serve to categorize topics in order to make a pragmatic point about them" (*Proverb in Mind*, 18).
62. Stewart, "Teaching Complex Ethical Thinking," 241.
63. I use this example in my article "Proverb as Embedded Microgenre," 67–68.
64. In block quotations only, I reproduce Speght's manicules to give a sense of what it is like to encounter proverbs in his edition; see the frontispiece to this book for a page from the *Wife of Bath's Tale*.
65. See K. Taylor, "Proverbs," on the thematic role of proverbs in *Troilus*.
66. Kempe, *Book of Margery Kempe*, ed. Windeatt, 415–17 (book 2, chap. 9).
67. Krug, *Margery Kempe and the Lonely Reader*, 133.
68. Blake, "Proverbs of Hell," line 44, from *Marriage of Heaven and Hell*, 37. Paul Miner cites evidence for the influence on Blake of proverbs from the Hebrew scriptures in "Blake's 'Proverbs of Hell.'"
69. For this proverb's popularity, see Mieder, *Proverbs*, 131. Whiting includes this expression in *Modern Proverbs*, B379; his first citation, interestingly, comes from James Joyce's *Ulysses*.
70. Barker, *Adages of Erasmus*, 15–16.
71. For Speght's refusal and this comment on it by F. N. Robinson, see the note to the *Merchant's Tale*, IV.1424, in the *Riverside Chaucer*. Wade is also mentioned in *Troilus* 3.614.
72. Pearsall, "Thomas Speght," 91.
73. Pearsall, "Thomas Speght," 83.
74. Pearsall, "Thomas Speght," 82; see "Tabard" in Speght's alphabetical glossary, found near the end of his 1602 edition. For the Tabard as an historical inn, see the *Riverside Chaucer*'s note to the *General Prologue*, I.20, and for Herry Bailly's living namesake, Henri Bayliff ostlyer (innkeeper), see the *Riverside* note to the portrait of the Host on p. 825.
75. On Speght's editorial work and the front matter to his editions, in addition to Pearsall, see Machan, "Speght's *Works*"; Trigg, *Congenial Souls*, 129–43; Cook, *The Poet and the Antiquaries*, 100–129.
76. Pearsall, "Thomas Speght," 74–75, 86; Cook, *The Poet and the Antiquaries*, 115–23.
77. See the discussion in Cook, *The Poet and the Antiquaries*, 120–21.
78. Moss, *Printed Commonplace-Books*, 106.
79. III.361 (B116), 386 (H530); 487 (G443).
80. Pearsall, "Thomas Speght," 86; Kinney, "Thomas Speght's Renaissance Chaucer," 75.
81. Moss, *Printed Commonplace-Books*, 27.
82. Kinney, "Thomas Speght's Renaissance Chaucer," 68; see also Bahr, *Fragments and Assemblages*; Dolven, *Scenes of Instruction*, esp. 29–59.
83. *Oxford Dictionary of National Biography*, s.v. "Thomas Speght." An extract from Rachel Speght's *Muzzle* appears in Aughterson, *Renaissance Woman*, 270–77.
84. Wiggins, "What Did Renaissance Readers Write?," 16 and 16n37.
85. Bowden, *Wife of Bath in Afterlife*, 40–41 and 41n16.
86. V. Burke, "Ann Bowyer's Commonplace Book"; see also Cook, *The Poet and the Antiquaries*, 5.
87. The contents of Painter's book are transcribed and annotated by Bowden in "*Chaucer New Painted*."
88. Wright, "William Painter," 166.
89. See Orgel, *Reader in the Book*, on the challenges of historicizing reading practices (1–29), the premodern practice of reading for use (esp. 50–83), and the value of studying contemporary responses to

premodern literature; for "compilational" reading and interpretation, see Bahr, *Fragments and Assemblages*, 1–49 and esp. 155–207 on the *Canterbury Tales*.

90. The explanatory notes to the *Riverside Chaucer* cite a wealth of borrowed proverbs; favored sources include the Bible, Jean de Meun's continuation of the *Romance of the Rose*, and Boethius's *Consolation*. In chapter 4, I discuss Chaucer's use elsewhere in the *Tales* of proverbs also found in *Melibee*.

91. This section incorporates points and examples from my article, "Proverb as Embedded Microgenre."

92. Jauss, "Alterity and Modernity," 218, and "Aphorism" in the appendix, 228.

93. Colie, *Resources of Kind*, 33, 34, 115.

94. Hernadi, *Beyond Genre*, 180–81.

95. As a rough indicator, the twelve non-Chaucerian expressions quoted by the *MED* to illustrate the meaning of *proverbe* range from three to fourteen words and average about eight. The eighteen expressions explicitly labeled as *proverbes* by Chaucer range from five to twenty-five words (both extremes occur in the *Parson's Tale*, X.155–56 and 362), about twelve words on average.

96. Bakhtin, "Problem of Speech Genres," esp. 75–79, quotation in the previous sentence at 61. This essay is especially useful for medievalists because here Bakhtin lets go his earlier claims for the modern novel as virtually the sole site of dialogic effects. I examine this theory in detail in "Proverb as Microgenre."

97. Barker, *Adages of Erasmus*, 18, 12.

98. Bakhtin describes the boundaries around an embedded utterance as "clear-cut" (93), signaled by the change in speaking subject; he writes, "Intonation that isolates others' speech (in written speech designated by quotation marks) is a special phenomenon. . . . The *boundaries* created by this change are weakened here and of a special sort: the speaker's expression penetrates through these boundaries and spreads to the other's speech" (92, emphasis in original).

99. Bakhtin, "Problem of Speech Genres," 91.

100. Bakhtin, "Problem of Speech Genres," 76, 74, 72.

101. Barker, *Adages of Erasmus*, 18.

102. Although his assessment of the proverbial wisdom in this tale is different from my own, Thomas H. Luxon acknowledges its prominence and the importance of active reflection in applying proverbs in "'Sentence' and 'Solaas.'"

CHAPTER 2

1. Once again, letter and number combinations such as C291 refer to the indexing by the Whitings in *Proverbs, Sentences, and Proverbial Phrases*.

2. *MED*, s.v. "clerk." Ann W. Astell discusses Chaucer's uses of this term in *Chaucer and the Universe of Learning*, 32–60.

3. Quotations from Pecock's *Folewer*, ed. Hitchcock, are cited parenthetically in the text by page and line number, separated by a period; "presumptuose" at 60.9. I have lightly modernized Pecock's spelling, substituting modern for obsolete letters and using *thee* instead of *the* and *I* instead of *y* for the pronouns in question.

4. A widely influential though contested study of the three estates as ideology is Duby, *Three Orders*; the seminal work on Chaucer and the three estates is Mann, *Chaucer and Medieval Estates Satire*.

5. Barker, *Adages of Erasmus*, 15.

6. Carruthers, *Book of Memory*, 246. Betsy Bowden argues that proverbs are ideally suited to retention in memory in "Modest Proposal."

7. Barker, *Adages of Erasmus*, 132–53 (II.i.1); *Melibee* VII.1054; *Troilus* 1.956; Whiting H171.

8. The refutation of the "greatest clerks" proverb appears in *Folewer*, ed. Hitchcock, 57.28–61.9. On Pecock's life and writings, see Scase, *Reginald Pecock*, and Campbell, *Call to Read*.

9. For Pecock's outreach to lay readers, see Gayk, *Image, Text, and Religious Reform*, 155–88.

10. Two studies of the Protestant Reformation, very different, but both with attention to continuity as well as rupture

and with more sympathetic views of medieval religious practice than was common in earlier scholarship, are Duffy, *Stripping of the Altars*, and Simpson, *Reform and Cultural Revolution*.

11. Douglas Gray describes a related effect in Chaucer, "revivifying" a proverb by cleverly rewording it or deepening its meanings (*Simple Forms*, 174).

12. For the scholarly and theological background to Symkyn's mockery, see Woods, "Symkyn's Place."

13. The poem, item 4076 in the *Digital Index of Middle English Verse*, begins "O thou most noble pastour chosen by God"; its nineteenth-century editor, Thomas Crofton Croker, describes its source (now lost) as a book of texts and fragments ca. 1600 in the Dublin "State Paper Office" (*Popular Songs of Ireland*, 293–312, quoted stanza at 310–11). Gordon Smith reviews possible identities for this young pretender in "Lambert Simnel and the King"; Michael J. Bennett prints the relevant sources, including extracts from this poem, as an appendix to *Lambert Simnel*, 121–38.

14. For the sources of the fable of the wolf and the mare, see Mann, *From Aesop to Renard*, 266n12.

15. See Baum, "The Mare and the Wolf." *Canterbury Tales*, ed. Mann, note to I.4055, cites an Old French version involving a mare and wolf, as in Chaucer, with the moral "Now I see clearly that learning [*clergie*] is a waste of time."

16. On the medieval reception of Solomon, see Bose, "From Exegesis to Appropriation"; Hansen, *Solomon Complex*.

17. In dealing with the representation of peasant speech in this section, I draw upon three previously published essays, only the last of which concerns Chaucer: "Rival Wisdom"; "Representations of Peasant Speech"; and "Proverb as Embedded Microgenre." The first of these includes copious citation of previous scholarship on the Latin *Dialogue*.

18. Justice, *Writing and Rebellion*; Crane, "Writing Lesson of 1381."

19. I quote Gower, *Major Latin Works*, trans. Stockton, 67–68.

20. Translation of Walsingham's Latin from *St Albans Chronicle*, ed. and trans. Taylor, Childs, and Watkiss, 426–27.

21. Freedman, *Images of the Medieval Peasant*.

22. Aristotle, *Rhetoric* 2.21, trans. Freese, 282–83. Aristotle disapproves of the citing of maxims by young men and "rustics"; they are best spoken by experienced elders.

23. As cited in *Oxford Latin Dictionary*, s.v. "proverbium": "'Minime sis,' inquit, 'cantherium in fossa,' quae vox in rusticum inde prouerbium prodita est."

24. Cited from Isidore's definition of the proverb or *paroemia* in *Etymologies* 1.37.28, trans. Barney, Lewis, et al., 63. John Trevisa's translation of Bartholomaeus, *De proprietatibus rerum* 2.14–19, as cited by Whiting W475: "Churles spekyth of hym and meanyth that a man lesyth his voys yf the wulf seeth hym fyrste. Therfore to a man that is sodenly stylle and levyth to speke, it is sayde (*Lupus est in fabula*) the wulfe is in the tale."

25. A. Taylor, *Proverb*, 87. Collections of proverbs attributed to peasants are discussed in a seminal essay by Davis, "Proverbial Wisdom and Popular Errors," esp. 230–44. See also *Li Proverbe au Vilain*, ed. Bednar; Goddard, "Marcabru"; and B. Taylor, "Medieval Proverb Collections," esp. 30–31.

26. For the Latin text with English translation and extensive notes, see *Solomon and Marcolf*, ed. Ziolkowski; the Latin text there reproduced was edited by Walter Benary in 1914. Quotations from the Middle English text, lightly modernized, are from *Dialogue*, ed. Bradbury and Bradbury, cited by page number followed by parenthetical chapter and line number separated by a period, i.e., 27 (2.4).

27. "The Debate of the Horse, Goose, and Sheep," in Lydgate, *Minor Poems*, ed. MacCracken, 2:604–11.

28. Richard Firth Green cites English references to Marcolf in "Marcolf the Fool"; see also Schieberle, "Proverbial Fools and Rival Wisdom." (Schieberle attributes the second element of her title to my article "Rival Wisdom," from which I adapted the

title of this book.) For Audelay's poems, see Audelay, *Poems and Carols*.

29. Cooper, "Sources and Analogues," 203. I outline the work's five verbal contests in "Rival Wisdom."

30. The internationally circulating proverbs assigned to Marcolf have been studied by Singer, *Sprichwörter des Mittelalters*, 1:33–61; see also Bradbury, "Rival Wisdom," 347–55; introduction to *Dialogue*, ed. Bradbury and Bradbury, 5–8.

31. I cite the Middle English translation (ca. 1492) of the proverb contest by exchange number, followed by *a* for Solomon's contributions, *b* for Marcolf's, from *Dialogue*, ed. Bradbury and Bradbury, 29–41 (4.1a–4.91b).

32. Davis, "Proverbial Wisdom," 231–32.

33. I discuss Roger Chartier's recommended shift from seeking popular origins to examining popular cultural uses in the previous chapter.

34. Davis, "Proverbial Wisdom," 227.

35. *Dialogue*, ed. Bradbury and Bradbury, 102 (appendix); *Solomon and Marcolf*, ed. Ziolkowski, 72–73.

36. See Bradbury, "Rival Wisdom," 342–45; introduction to *Dialogue*, ed. Bradbury and Bradbury, 3–8, for the longstanding assumption of clerical authorship for at least part of this work; Ziolkowski describes its "protean existence," including clerical authorship, in *Solomon and Marcolf*, ed. Ziolkowski, 9–12. For proverbs in circulation, Singer, *Sprichwörter*, 1:33–61. For the estimate that about a fifth of the exchanges in the longest versions involve direct scriptural parody, see Bradbury, "Rival Wisdom," 348 and 348n55.

37. Bakhtin, *Rabelais and His World*, 20.

38. Bakhtin, "Response to a Question," 7.

39. The Latin word for *proverb* here is *parabola*.

40. Saint Jerome attributed Proverbs, Ecclesiastes, and The Song of Songs to Solomon; medieval authors sometimes also attribute all or parts of Wisdom and Ecclesiasticus (Sirach) to him as well. See B. Taylor, "Medieval Proverb Collections," 24–25. The eleven tales are those of the Knight, Miller, Cook, *Melibee*, Wife of Bath, Clerk, Merchant, Squire, Canon's Yeoman, Manciple, and Parson.

41. Whiting C470 records about twenty examples in English of Ecclesiasticus 32:24, "Work all by counsel," and T88 lists a similar number for Ecclesiastes 3:1, "All things have their season, and in their times all things pass under heaven," with variations on the wording "All thing (everything) has time."

42. Pandarus also cites "Everything has its time" to Criseyde, with better effect, in 3.855. Douglas Gray discusses the anti-sententious strain in Chaucer's proverb use in "Lat be thyne olde ensaumples."

43. The Whitings include in their index Middle English expressions that are referred to as, or sound like, proverbs but are recorded nowhere else (as noted in the volume's introduction, xiii–xiv). Where other attestations are listed, users of their index can examine them for evidence of prior circulation, but the use of a Chaucerian proverb post-Chaucer is less conclusive: it could testify to the poet's influence on his successors rather than to independent circulation.

44. For the proverb (W645) as a Chaucerian comment on the opacity of language and its inevitable ambiguity, see P. Taylor, "Chaucer's *Cosyn to the Dede*"; Turner, *Chaucerian Conflict*, 134–36.

45. For a detailed discussion and further references on these northernisms, see the explanatory note to line I.4022ff. of the *Reeve's Tale* in Mann's edition of the *Tales*.

46. For the complexity of "narrators" and "speakers" in premodern works, see Spearing, *Textual Subjectivity*. Spearing describes the term *narrator* as "a shorthand expression for an enormously diffuse process of subjectivization" (130). David Lawton argues for the value of thinking in terms of voice and speaker rather than a narrating character in *Voice in Later Medieval Literature*. For an historical overview of varying ideas of authorship in Chaucer's era, see Edwards, *Invention and Authorship*.

47. As cited by Duffy, *Stripping of the Altars*, 583, from John White's *Way to the True Church*, preface to the reader.

Questions about the destination of a journey feature in some of the most widespread charms: "Where are you going?" Jesus asks "the three good brothers" in a charm found in all three languages of medieval England; see Roper, *English Verbal Charms*, 127. Saint Peter is the patient healed in a widespread charm against toothache, "Super petram," collected in England from the tenth to the nineteenth centuries (Roper, *English Verbal Charms*, 122–25).

48. Grosseteste refers to "incantationes que Gallice dicunter *charmes*" (incantations that are called *charmes* in French), see Wenzel, "Two Notes."

49. Quoted by Duffy, *Stripping of the Altars*, 277, from fol. 4v. For healing charms, in addition to Roper, *English Verbal Charms*; Forbes, "Verbal Charms"; and Duffy, *Stripping of the Altars*, 266–98; see Olsan, "Charms and Prayers," and Olsan, "Corpus of Charms," both with extensive bibliography. Clerics expressed disapproval but also participated in charm rituals; see Skemer, *Binding Words*, 47–73.

50. For Frydeswyde's role as patron saint of Oxford, see the explanatory note to I.3449 in the *Riverside Chaucer*.

51. Fletcher, "Faith of a Simple Man," 101.

52. My modernization of the quotation, as cited by Fletcher, "Faith of a Simple Man," 99: "it is inougth to the to beleven as holychurche techeth the and lat the clerkes alone with the argumentes" (modern letters substituted for *thorn* and *yogh*).

53. My modernization of the passage as cited by Fletcher, "Faith of a Simple Man," 100, from Oxford Bodleian Library, MS Laud Misc. 706, fol. 160v: "For now euery lewde man is becomen a clerke and talkys in his termys. Who, I pray yow, is more bolde to talke of the mysteri of the priuyte that is conteynet in the holy sacrament of the auter, more bolde to dispute of the hy mater of desteny and forknowyng of almyghty God? Who entermetes hym more of the sacramentis and deuowt obseruawns of Holy Chirche then dose a lewde webster, a taylioure or a carpenter? And yet truliche to talke the truthe in playne termes, hit semes no better then a kow to bere a sedul." (Modern letters substituted for *thorn* and *yogh*.)

54. *Dialogue*, ed. Bradbury and Bradbury, 39 (4.79ab). For a cow in a saddle, see Whiting C501; for a sow, see S533; for Marcolf's version with a dog, D311.

55. I discuss the central role played by this proverb in the *Tale of Melibee* in chapter 4. Its source is Ecclesiasticus (Sirach) 32:24, "Fili, sine consilio nihil facias, et post factum non paeniteberis"; in the Douay-Rheims translation, "My son, do thou nothing without counsel, and thou shalt not repent when thou hast done." This proverb was regularly attributed to Solomon by medieval writers, as here. Whiting C470 cites about 20 instances in English, six that attribute it to Solomon, two of those in Chaucer.

56. For the other three versions of "diverse folk," see II.211, IV.1469, V.202–3, with only V.203 marked by Speght. See Whiting F370, H230, and M202 for numerous English examples of V.203, "As many heddes, as manye wittes," going back to ca. 900. In his brief but generative remarks on proverbs in the *Canterbury Tales*, Gray notes that they "tend to cluster around favourite ideas or topics" and that "ironies . . . can be woven around them" (*Simple Forms*, 177); his examples include "diverse folk," "werk al by conseil" (discussed above and in chapter 4), and "men shal nat maken ernest of game" (I.3186).

57. Barker, *Adages of Erasmus*, 63–64 (I.iii.7). For the Latin expression, "Quot homines, tot sententiae," see Walther and Schmidt, *Proverbia sententiaeque latinitatis medii aevi*, no. 26216. Whiting H230 gives another Latin version, attributed to Terence, "Tot capita tot sensus."

58. *Melibee* VII.1524–25, cf. 1528; Whiting O56, F491.

59. Matthew 7:1–5; Whiting M710.

60. The usual expression for the first is "Need has no law," with numerous examples at Whiting N51; Chaucer's "Need has no peer" is the sole instance of this wording at N52 and may reflect his revision for a rhyme with "heer" in I.4025.

61. *The Taill of Rauf Coilyear*, ed. Bawcutt and Riddy, lines 70–71. I support this point about the proverbs in *Rauf Coilyear* in "Representations of Peasant Speech."

62. In the friar's speech, Speght marks "sentences and proverbes" in lines III.1973, 1989–91, 2001–3, 2009, 2015–16, 2049–50, 2051–52, 2054–55, 2074, 2086–88.

63. The "workman" proverb in III.1973 is Whiting W655. For the controversy over the use of Luke 10:1–12 to justify the begging of friars, see Szittya, *Antifraternal Tradition*, esp. 41–54 and 239–46.

64. The Solomonic proverbs occur in lines III.1989–91 (Ecclesiasticus 4:35), 2001–3 (Ecclesiasticus 25:22–23), and 2085–88 (Proverbs 22:24–25).

65. Lightly modernized from *Dialogue*, ed. Bradbury and Bradbury, 39 (4.70, 71, 81).

66. Speght marks the prologue and tale with twenty-two manicules; one, the marked proverb in VIII.688–89, is spoken by Chaucer's first-person narrator; the rest belong to the represented speech of the Yeoman.

67. Still the most powerful reading of the imagery in this tale in my view is Charles Muscatine, *Chaucer and the French Tradition*, 213–221.

68. In this series, I would include the Speght-marked proverbs in VIII.645–46, 648–49, 740–41, 874, 947–48, 962–63, 964–65, 967–68, 995, 996–97, 1388–89, 1400–1401, 1410, 1413–14, 1422–24, 1476–78, a sampling of which I discuss below.

69. Both the *Riverside Chaucer* and *Canterbury Tales* (ed. Mann) associate the Yeoman's proverb in VIII.644–46 with a complex of expressions about avoiding excess (see Whiting E199, E200, E203). Whiting indexes this proverb as a sole example at O63 and cross-references it with another about avoiding excess, M463; T86 also cites some early examples of proverbs warning against things that are overdone. The context makes clear this proverb's affinity with the large complex of expressions that warn against excesses of wisdom and cleverness.

70. Quotation from the Middle English *Dialogue*, ed. Bradbury and Bradbury, 43 (7.7–8). For responses in the Latin *Dialogue* that in some way undermine Solomon's claim to transcendent wisdom, see *Solomon and Marcolf*, ed. Ziolkowski, 52–74, exchanges nos. 6, 19, 24, 70, 85, 89, 90, 101, 126, and 139. In the truncated proverb contest in the Middle English text, seven exchanges concern wisdom and foolishness; see *Dialogue*, ed. Bradbury and Bradbury, 28–41 (exchanges 4.6, 16, 19, 51, 62, 79, 88).

71. Modern editors follow the Ellesmere MS in placing the incipit for the tale after line 719. But the autobiographical narrative in lines VIII.720–971 (the present prologue plus "part one" of the tale as scribally rubricated in Ellesmere) resembles the "confessio" prologues given to the Wife of Bath and Pardoner. The Yeoman's "tale proper," which introduces a canon demonized to the point of an allegory for the devil, would then begin after lines 970–71, in which the Yeoman refers to what his listeners will hear or learn before he leaves them, "er that I fro yow wende." That a teller will "part" or "go" from an audience at the end of a tale is a conventional opening remark in Middle English storytelling, as in *Troilus* (1.5) and the tales of the Cook (I.4362), Wife (III.171), and Friar (III.841).

72. Barker, *Adages of Erasmus*, 14.

CHAPTER 3

1. Barker, *Adages of Erasmus*, 16.

2. For a summary of early scholarship, see Hanna and Lawler, *Jankyn's Book of Wikked Wives*, 1:2–8. An analysis of the *Wife's Prologue* contextualized with its primary sources is Desmond, *Ovid's Art*.

3. An exception is Bowden, *Wife of Bath in Afterlife*, which addresses Chaucer's proverbs and their handling by later adapters of the tale.

4. For antagonism and desire between clerks and wives, and between Chaucer's Clerk and Wife, see Scala, *Desire*, esp. 123–31. An important historical analysis of these relations is Farmer, "Persuasive Voices."

5. John Ray, *A Collection of English Proverbs*, 1678, as quoted in Aughterson, *Renaissance Women*, 103.

6. Whiting, *Proverbs, Sentences, and Proverbial Phrases*, xiv. As Whiting also notes, "Medieval writers . . . did not give heed to such definitions and distinctions, and they used the same words and phrases for what we regard as proverbs and for what, once we have set up the two categories, we can only consider sentences" (xiv).

7. The *Wife's Prologue* and *Tale* appear on fols. 31–37 of Speght's 1602 edition.

8. For *parable* in the sense of 'proverb . . . wise saying', see *MED*, s.v. "parable," noun 2b, citing this passage.

9. Two important sources for the proverbs in the *Wife's Prologue* are Jerome, *Adversus Jovinianum*, and Jean de Meun, *Le Roman de la Rose*. Relevant extracts are printed and translated in Hanna and Lawler, "Wife of Bath's Prologue," 2:361–78. Many proverbs borrowed from these and other sources are identified in the notes to the *Riverside Chaucer* and the *Canterbury Tales*, ed. Mann.

10. The number of "sentences and proverbes" will of course vary by the definitions applied: Whiting's 1934 monograph counts thirty-nine proverbs and "sententious remarks" in the *Wife's Prologue* and nine in the *Tale*.

11. Blamires, *Woman Defamed*, 6–7. This anthology provides valuable commentary, translated sources, and references to original language editions of antifeminist works. For sources in their original languages, see Hanna and Lawler, *Jankyn's Book*.

12. Christine de Pizan, *Book of the City of Ladies*, trans. Richards, 4–5; Christine de Pizan, "Livre de la Cité," ed. Curnow, 2:619.

13. Giovanni Boccaccio, *Il Corbaccio* (ca. 1355), trans. Anthony K. Cassell, excerpted in Blamires, *Woman Defamed*, 166–76, at 167; the same passage refers to woman's "foul" and "abominable" passions and to uncleanness worse than that of a pig.

14. Boccaccio, *Corbaccio*, in Blamires, *Woman Defamed*, 167; Andreas Capellanus, *De Amore* (ca. 1185), trans. P. G. Walsh, in Blamires, *Woman Defamed*, 114–24, at 122.

15. In addition to Desmond, *Ovid's Art*, see L. Patterson, "'For the Wyves Love of Bathe'"; Fein, "'Thyng Wommen Loven Moost.'"

16. For the manuscript glosses, see the explanatory notes to the *Wife's Prologue* in the *Riverside Chaucer*, 864–72; Caie, "Significance of the Early Chaucer Manuscript Glosses"; Partridge, "*Canterbury Tales* Glosses"; and, to see the glosses *in situ*, Woodward and Stevens, *New Ellesmere Chaucer Monochromatic Facsimile*, and the Huntington Digital Library, https://hdl.huntington.org/digital/collection/p15150coll7/id/2838.

17. The proverbs quoted in III.180–82 and 326–27 derive from a list of sayings attributed to Ptolemy in a medieval preface attached to a Latin translation of the *Almageste*; see Young, "Chaucer's Aphorisms."

18. This language derives from Bakhtin's "Problem of Speech Genres," as discussed in chapter 1. The proverb is "Inter altos altior est qui non curat in cuius manu sit mundus"; Young, "Chaucer's Aphorisms," 6.

19. Despite the conviction of Jerome, translator of the Latin Vulgate Bible, that neither Wisdom nor Ecclesiasticus were of Solomonic authorship, medieval writers frequently attribute to him quotations from these and the other wisdom books. See B. Taylor, "Medieval Proverb Collections," 24. Lawrence Besserman notes this practice in Chaucer and other Middle English writers in *Chaucer's Biblical Poetics*, 72–73, 245–46, 246n22.

20. Blamires includes relevant extracts from both sources in English translation in *Woman Defamed*, 63–74, 148–59.

21. The most relevant of these misuses are noted below; see Besserman, *Chaucer's Biblical Poetics*, 126–77. Besserman also gives a lucid account of the debates over Chaucer's familiarity with the Vulgate Bible and his biblical reading practices with reference to the *Wife's Prologue*, esp. 140–59. For Christine de Pizan's critique of the practice of distorting a source for antifeminist purposes, see J. Patterson, "Solomon *au feminin*."

22. For the Latin text, see *Solomon and Marcolf*, ed. Ziolkowski, 90–98; for the abbreviated Middle English version, see

*Dialogue*, ed. Bradbury and Bradbury, 53–61 (16.1–23.12).

23. *Queste del Saint Graal*, ed. Pauphilet, 220.

24. See Hanna and Lawler, "Wife of Bath's Prologue," 2:351–55, and Desmond, *Ovid's Art*.

25. *Dialogue*, ed. Bradbury and Bradbury, 27 (Prologue), 49 (12.20–21); for Marcolf's inventive wit (*ingenium*) in the Latin *Dialogue*, see Bradbury, "Rival Wisdom," 338–42.

26. Hanning, *Individual in Twelfth-Century Romance*, 105–6. See also Blamires, "Women and Creative Intelligence."

27. *Dialogue*, ed. Bradbury and Bradbury, 41 (5.1–4), 51 (13.5–8, 14.3).

28. In an influential article, Maria Corti writes of Marcolf's "dissent from a culture which persists in basing itself exclusively on the *auctoritates* of the past and in paying no heed to new aspects of work and technique" ("Models and Antimodels," 358).

29. For "Should one marry?" as a *quaestio* or disputation topic, see Hanna and Lawler, *Jankyn's Book*, 9–15.

30. Hasan-Rokem, "Proverb," 129.

31. *Dives*, ed. Barnum. Relevant excerpts are also modernized in Blamires, *Woman Defamed*, 260–70.

32. Blamires, *Woman Defamed*, 268; *Dives*, ed. Barnum, EETS o.s. 280, 88–90. Barnum notes the use of selective quotation in the explanatory note to lines 22–37, p. 89.

33. *Dives*, ed. Barnum, EETS o.s. 280, 89, spelling lightly modernized.

34. In-text citations of the English *Dialogue* in this and the following paragraph by chapter and line from *Dialogue*, ed. Bradbury and Bradbury, 55–61.

35. Andreas Capellanus, *De Amore (On Love)*, in Blamires, *Woman Defamed*, 114–24, at 122–24.

36. Jehan Le Fèvre, *The Lamentations of Matheolus*, trans. Karen Pratt, in Blamires, *Woman Defamed*, 177–97, at 193–94.

37. Le Fèvre, *Lamentations*, in Blamires, *Woman Defamed*, 194.

38. "Mulierem fortem quis inveniet procul et de ultimis finibus pretium eius." Jeanette Patterson points out the subtle shift from the Latin Vulgate's *inveniet* (future indicative) to Le Fèvre's *porroit* (conditional) ("Solomon *au feminin*," 364).

39. Jerome, *Against Jovinian*, trans. W. H. Fremantle, in Blamires, *Woman Defamed*, 63–82, at 68, emphasis in original; Latin text in Hanna and Lawler, *Jankyn's Book*, 187 (28.394–98).

40. Jerome, *Against Jovinian*, in Blamires, *Woman Defamed*, 67; Latin text, Jerome, *Adversus Jovinianum*, in Hanna and Lawler, *Jankyn's Book*, 187–89 (28.406–7).

41. Jerome, *Against Jovinian*, in Blamires, *Woman Defamed*, 67.

42. Blamires, *Woman Defamed*, 34n56.

43. Jean de Meun, *The Romance of the Rose (Le Roman de la rose)*, trans. Charles Dahlberg, in Blamires, *Woman Defamed*, 148–66, at 158.

44. Renaud de Louens, *Livre de Mellibee*, ed. Askins, 1:338–39.

45. Richard de Bury, *Philobiblon*, 43–45.

46. In *Chaucer and the Fictions of Gender*, Elaine Tuttle Hansen explores the reception of the *Wife of Bath's Prologue* and *Tale* "as a pro- or antifeminist document" (40), citing scholarship on both sides up to the time of her study, including David S. Reid's description of the *Prologue* as an "antifeminist gallimaufry" (39). Blamires suspends the *Wife's Prologue* between "antifeminism" and "responses to antifeminism," in part because Chaucer's character defends women "even in the process of submerging the reader in a welter of misogynistic quotations" (*Woman Defamed*, 198).

47. Bakhtin, "Problem of Speech Genres," 71–76, 91–93.

48. Robertson, *Preface to Chaucer*, 324.

49. Dinshaw, *Chaucer's Sexual Poetics*, 124–25.

50. Gray also makes this comparison: the *Wife's Prologue* "is almost in effect a proverb contest (similar in some ways to that of Solomon and Marcolphus)" (*Simple Forms*, 175).

51. Ben Parsons tracks the intriguing way in which Jankyn tries to administer both the sanctioned violence of a husband "correcting" his wife and that of a

schoolmaster disciplining a pupil in "Beaten for a Book."

52. In both the *Miller's Tale* (I.3529–30) and the *Merchant's Tale* (IV.1483–86), Chaucer attributes a well-known proverb from Ecclesiasticus to Solomon, as was the custom in his day. See Besserman, *Chaucer's Biblical Poetics*, 30.

53. In contrast to his usual thoroughness, Speght leaves unmarked the prohibition against wifely roaming in III.653, despite Chaucer's labeling it as a *proverbe*; he also omits the last proverb in the quoted passage, 784–85.

54. Lines III.775–77 from Ecclesiasticus 25:23; lines 778–79 from Proverbs 21:9–10, 25:24; lines 782–83, a nonbiblical proverb from Jerome, *Against Jovinian* 1.48; the unmarked expression in lines 784–85 is from Proverbs 11:22; the Latin text is quoted in the margin of the Ellesmere MS.

55. Christine de Pizan, *City of Ladies*, trans. Richards, 5.

56. For the Latin proverb, see Walther and Schmidt, *Proverbia sententiaeque Latinitatis medii aevi*, II/2:8751; for the English, Whiting D120 and cf. W537. *Canterbury Tales*, ed. Mann, note to III.401–2, points out that some Chaucer manuscripts add the Latin as a marginal gloss to the version in the *Wife's Prologue*.

57. The Richards translation of Christine cited here (27) translates *nere* in the Latin proverb as "sew," but as it usually refers to making thread or weaving it into cloth, I have substituted "spin," as in Chaucer's English rendering in III.401.

58. Christine de Pizan, *City of Ladies*, trans. Richards, 4–5 (I.1.1).

59. The evidence is summarized in the *Riverside Chaucer*, 910, and in more detail, in *Canterbury Tales*, ed. Mann, 875–77, both with references.

60. Green, *Elf Queens and Holy Friars*, 50.

61. Within the speech, Speght marks with manicules expressions that begin in lines III.1113, 1119, 1128, 1146, 1152, 1158, 1163, 1170, 1175, 1183, 1185, 1187, 1189, 1193, 1195, 1201, 1203, 1215; see fol. 36r-v of the 1602 edition and the frontispiece to this volume; what constitutes a single "remark" is of course a judgment call, and Whiting, *Chaucer's Use of Proverbs*, 99–100, counts seven sententious remarks, beginning in lines 1158, 1168, 1183, 1187, 1191, 1203, and 1215.

62. Dolven, *Scenes of Instruction*, 6.

63. Crane, *Gender and Romance*, 37. Peggy Knapp offers a reading of the ending similar to Crane's and mine: "Yet for all its seemingly traditional wisdom, embedded deep in this story is the untraditional idea that men must learn from women, that they must reconstitute their lore and their affections to include women as subjects . . . and partners" (*Chaucer and the Social Contest*, 127). In her engaging study, *The Wife of Bath: A Biography*, which I read as this book went to press, Marion Turner also shares this favorable view of the wise old woman's instruction, calling her "the ethical centre of the story" (43), "eloquent, reasonable, and ethical" (44), and arguing that "Part of Alison's project is to shine a light on the fact that there is usually no place in stories like this for reasonable older women" (44).

CHAPTER 4

1. C. D. Benson, "Their Telling Difference," 65. As in more recent criticism, attention to proverbs—their absence in one and their overwhelming of the narrative in the other—goes almost unnoted in this important essay.

2. In *Chaucer's Use of Proverbs*, Whiting observes, "Chaucer does not use any proverbs [or sententious remarks] in his own first tale, that of Thopas, . . . but in his account of Melibee . . . he brings forward many" (113). In a list of proverbial comparisons (as distinct from proverbs or sententious remarks), 155–77, Whiting includes phrases from *Thopas* such as "Whit . . . as payndemayn" and "rede as rose" (VII.725–6).

3. Examples of additional, unmarked proverbs include VII.1158–61, where he uses one mark for the first of 3 expressions, each separately attributed to Solomon; the unmarked injunction attributed to "Catoun" (the *Disticha Catonis*) in 1594 seems little

different from the flagged expressions that precede and follow it.

4. For *Melibee* as a proverb collection, and a different reading of the role of its proverbs, see Cannon, *From Literacy to Literature*, 211–29, and Cannon, "Proverbs and the Wisdom of Literature." See also Bowden, "Ubiquitous Format?" Another study fruitfully aware of the central role of proverbs in *Melibee* is Schieberle, *Feminized Counsel*. For a useful survey of the genre (though it does not include the versions of *Melibee*), see B. Taylor, "Medieval Proverb Collections." For collections of current proverbs, see Speake, *Oxford Dictionary of Proverbs*, and the extensive bibliography on modern proverb collections in many languages in Mieder, *Proverbs*, 266–78.

5. Severs, "Tale of Melibeus," 561–62.

6. An important source for the approach to genre employed in this chapter is Bakhtin's "Problem of Speech Genres." I argue for its relevance to reading the premodern proverb in "Proverb as Embedded Microgenre." For the consistent mixing of genres in Middle English works, see Hiatt, "Genre Without System."

7. For these labels, see Travis, *Disseminal Chaucer*, 29–30, and the references there given. For problems with the traditional division into fragments, see Meyer-Lee, "Abandon the Fragments."

8. On "narrators," "speakers," and "authors" in premodern works, see Spearing, *Textual Subjectivity*; Lawton, *Voice in Later Medieval Literature*; and Edwards, *Invention and Authorship*.

9. Thomas J. Farrell defends this identification in "Chaucer's Little Treatise."

10. Besserman, *Chaucer's Biblical Poetics*, 12.

11. Quotations from Albertanus's *Liber consolationis* are cited by chapter, page, and line number (chap. 7, p. 119, line 7) from Albertanus, *Liber consolationis*, ed. Thor Sundby. On Albertanus and his work, see Powell, *Albertanus of Brescia*.

12. See Askins, "Tale of Melibee." For readings in Chaucer that may derive directly from Albertanus, see Askins's notes to his composite text of Albertanus and Renaud, section 2.46 on p. 338 and sections 51.10 and 51.13, pp. 407–8. Sundby's introduction to his edition of the *Liber consolationis*, p. XX, recommends Albertanus as an important supplement and corrective to Renaud (whom he misidentifies as Jean de Meun) for the study of Chaucer's *Melibee*.

13. Severs, "Tale of Melibeus," 561–62.

14. On these additions and the subtraction, see *Canterbury Tales*, ed. Mann, 1001, and notes to *Melibee*, lines 1054, 1199, 1325–26.

15. On *Melibee*'s relation to Richard II, see Green, *Poets and Princepleasers*, 142–46, and Staley, *Languages of Power*, 190–91, 331–33.

16. *Canterbury Tales*, ed. Mann, 1001.

17. On the importance of *materia*, see Minnis and Scott, *Medieval Literary Theory and Criticism*, 2, and see *materia* in the index for many uses of the term in primary sources.

18. For a compelling account of Chaucer's movement out of the worldview of the court and into a broader social awareness, see Turner, *Chaucer*.

19. Barker, *Adages of Erasmus*, 18.

20. Two classic pieces on Chaucer's aspirations toward European poetry are Brewer, "Relationship of Chaucer," and Wetherbee, *Chaucer and the Poets*.

21. Askins, "Tale of Melibee," 327. Two arguments for subtle alterations in Chaucer's translation of Renaud are Palomo, "What Chaucer Really Did" (stylistic treatment), and J. Taylor, "Chaucer's *Tale of Melibee*" (changes in a small number of key words).

22. Severs discusses Renaud's main deviations from Albertanus ("Tale of Melibeus," 561–63); for the quotation about Chaucer's translation, see 566. As a measure of Renaud's general faithfulness, Askins ("Tale of Melibee") is able to slot back into Renaud's text the passages (in English translation) that Renaud excised from Albertanus, with little or no disruption to the flow of the work.

23. L. Benson, introduction to the *Canterbury Tales* in the *Riverside Chaucer*, ed. L. Benson et al., 17.

24. Foster, "Has Anyone Here Read 'Melibee'?," 399.

25. Maidie Hilmo describes the special treatment of *Melibee* in Chaucer manuscripts and in William Caxton's printed edition in Kerby-Fulton, Hilmo, and Olson, *Opening Up Middle English Manuscripts*, 250–54, 282–89; for annotation of *Melibee*, see Wiggins, "What Did Renaissance Readers Write?" Orgel, *Reader in the Book*, also notes the favorable attention to *Melibee* by a contemporary reader who "covered the margins . . . with enthusiastic notes" (29, cf. 109).

26. J. S. P. Tatlock, *The Development and Chronology of Chaucer's Works* (1907), as quoted by L. Patterson, "'What Man Artow?,'" 135n60.

27. Girolamo Tiraboschi, *Storia della letteratura italiana* (1783), as quoted by Sundby in the introduction to his edition of Albertanus, *Liber consolationis*, XIV.

28. Albertanus, *Liber consolationis*, ed. Sundby, XVIII.

29. Palomo, "What Chaucer Really Did," 306, 316–18. For the theory of revenge on the Host, see Gaylord, "*Sentence* and *Solaas*."

30. Both Severs, "Tale of Melibeus," and Askins, "Tale of Melibee," offer detailed accounts of these variations. Askins reproduces the text of Renaud's *Livre de Mellibee* essentially as edited by Severs. All references to Renaud's text are cited from Askins by page, chapter, and subsection, the latter two separated by a period (p. 349, 12.2). These chapter numbers (12 in this example) correspond to the chapters in the text of Albertanus, *Liber consolationis*, ed. Sundby.

31. Albertanus, *Liber consolationis*, ed. Sundby, Incipit, p. 1, lines 13–15: "Legas itaque similitudinem infra scriptam, et auctoritates in hoc libro notatas attente ac studiosissime perlegas."

32. On manuscripts of Seneca with Albertanus's autograph glosses, see Villa, "Tradizione delle 'Ad Lucilium.'"

33. For the circulation of Albertanus's work into the sixteenth century, see Powell, *Albertanus of Brescia*, 125, and Graham, "Albertanus of Brescia." For explanation of some of Albertanus's misattributions, see *Canterbury Tales*, ed. Mann, 1001.

34. Albertanus, *Liber consolationis*, ed. Sundby, chap. 10, p. 23, line 5, to p. 29, line 13, with quotations identified by Sundby; for the absence of this section from Renaud and provision of an English translation, see Askins, "Tale of Melibee," 344–47.

35. Askins, "Tale of Melibee," 344, note to section 10.2, points out this anomaly. See Albertanus, *Liber consolationis*, ed. Sundby, chap. 10, p. 23, lines 8–10: "plenius scriptum est in libro De Forma Vitae in principio, quem ad Vincentium fratrem tuum direxi." Melibeus asks Prudentia at the end of chap. 5 to explain how one becomes prudent, and her response apparently continues until Melibeus breaks in after this reference to Albertanus's son, midway through chap. 10. The full title of the work addressed to Vincent is *De amore et dilectione Dei et proximi et aliarum rerum et de forma vitae*.

36. Albertanus mistakenly attributes the quotation to the Roman writer Martial; Askins identifies Godfrey as its source, "Tale of Melibee," 360; translation is mine with "wise" added for clarification.

37. Albertanus, *Liber consolationis*, ed. Sundby, XVI, for his point about the origins of Melibeus and Prudence. Translation of the quotation about Prudence is mine, taking *expedita* as '[mentally] agile'.

38. This "crucial moment" is emphasized, for example, by Wallace in *Chaucerian Polity*, 243, which remains one of the most insightful discussions of *Melibee*, and one that is conscious of the importance of Albertanus's aims as the work's original author. More recent attention to Prudence's feigning of anger is Schieberle, *Feminized Counsel*, 115–18.

39. Ecclesiastes 7:4: "Melior est ira risu quia per tristitiam vultus corrigitur animus delinquentis."

40. Albertanus, *Liber consolationis*, ed. Sundby, chap. 2, p. 6, lines 11–12; Albertanus's version is "Omnia cum consilio fac, et non te poenitebit." The proverb derives from Ecclesiasticus 32:24, "Fili, sine consilio nihil facias et post factum non paeniteberis." Cf. *Canterbury Tales* I.3530, IV.1485–86;

Whiting C470 cites dozens of Middle English examples.

41. The *MED* (s.v. "conseil," noun 5d) translates the phrase "werken bi (with) counseil" as 'to follow advice, act after due consideration or consultation'.

42. Albertanus, *Liber consolationis*, ed. Sundby, chap. 51, p. 125, lines 5–7. See Askins, "Tale of Melibee," 404–8, esp. p. 407, section 51.11, for Renaud's substantial cuts to Albertanus's final chapters, 50 and 51, excising many proverbs and truncating Melibeus's praise of Prudentia's instruction.

43. "Much of his writing was an attempt either to explain violence or to find solutions for it," Powell, *Albertanus of Brescia*, 113.

44. Palomo, "What Chaucer Really Did," 306.

45. A compact treatment of these virtues and the main sources for thought about them is Carruthers, *Book of Memory*, 65–66.

46. For the identification of Sophie with Melibeus's wisdom, see Thundy, "Chaucer's Quest for Wisdom," and Staley, "Chaucer and the Postures of Sanctity," 230–31.

47. Carruthers, *Book of Memory*, 66, citing Cicero's *De inventione*, the anonymous *Rhetorica ad Herennium*, and the *Summa theologiae* of Thomas Aquinas.

48. Albertanus, *Liber consolationis*, ed. Sundby, chap. 49, p. 119, lines 9–13: "Cui dixerunt medici: Ecce filia tua quasi liberata est, nec de illius convalescentia te nullatenus dubitare oportet. Quos Melibeus copiose remuneravit, eosque rogavit, ut de filiae suae sanitate studiosissime procurarent." See Askins, "Tale of Melibee," 404, section 49.47, on the absence of the passage in Renaud.

49. Askins, "Tale of Melibee," 324.

50. As examples, Palomo speaks of Prudence as "a domineering albeit polite wife" who "argues her husband into acquiescence" ("What Chaucer Really Did," 316); L. Patterson, "What Man Artow?," 144, 158, presents Melibeus's eventual success in controlling his anger as a failure of his masculinity: in yielding to his wife's "overbearing pedagogy," he becomes "less the husband of a dutiful wife than the submissive son of a domineering mother."

51. For positive views of Prudence's instruction and Melibeus's learning, see Staley, "Chaucer and the Postures of Sanctity," 217–33; Collette, "Heeding the Counsel of Prudence"; and Schieberle, *Feminized Counsel*, 93–137; for a strong statement of the opposing position, see Turner, *Chaucerian Conflict*, 177–91, esp. 188–89. Although he takes a view more like my own, Stephen Yeager notes the continued currency of Lee Patterson's negative view of Prudence's instruction in "Chaucer's Prudent Poetics," 314n10. Another positive reading of Prudence's instruction, viewed as a route toward a new civic discourse, is K. Taylor, "Social Aesthetics."

52. L. Patterson, "What Man Artow?," 157–58.

53. L. Patterson, "What Man Artow?," 157–58.

54. For Melibeus's reversal of his promised clemency, Renaud, *Livre de Mellibee*, ed. Askins, p. 404, 49.59; Albertanus, *Liber consolationis*, ed. Sundby, chap. 49, p. 119, lines 19–21: "Volo illos bonis omnibus spoliare illisque praecipere, ut ad partes ultramarinas se transferant, ulterius huc non reversuri."

55. In Renaud, Melibeus's final speech corresponds to *Melibee* VII.1874–83 (see Askins, "Tale of Melibee," 406) while in Chaucer it continues through to 1887, nearly doubling in length.

56. Wallace, *Chaucerian Polity*, 234–46; Staley, *Following Chaucer*, 24–39; Collette, *Performing Polity* and "Heeding the Counsel of Prudence"; Schieberle, *Feminized Counsel*, esp. 93–137 on *Melibee*.

57. Cicero, *De inventione* 2.53.160, as cited by Carruthers, *Book of Memory*, 65; the three parts of *prudentia* are *memoria*, *intelligentia*, and *providentia*. Carruthers discusses the connections among prudence, memory, and wisdom in other ancient and medieval sources, including the capacity of prudence to channel the appetites and the "emotional, desiring will" (66).

58. As quoted by Carruthers, *Book of Memory*, 219.

59. For the primary meaning, see *MED*, s.v. "contrarie," noun 1; the secondary

meaning is *MED* noun 2a, citing this passage.

60. The sources of Albertanus's proverbs are identified by Sundby in his edition of Albertanus, *Liber consolationis*, supplemented by Askins, "Tale of Melibee"; those in Chaucer (nearly all translated from Renaud) are glossed in the notes to the *Riverside Chaucer* and in Mann's edition of the *Canterbury Tales*.

61. Even Renaud's abbreviated praise in 407, 51.10, applies the word *sage* ('wise') to Prudence twice. Askins, 407, 51.11, indicates the portion of Albertanus's praise omitted by Renaud, and cites Severs's judgment that in VII.1870–73, Chaucer's praise for Prudence "resembles the parallel passage in the Latin somewhat more than it does the French text." For Albertanus's text of this passage, see chap. 51, p. 125, lines 5–11.

62. In "Proverb Tradition as a Soft Source," I propose including proverbs among Chaucer's "soft" sources, defined as sources that need not be a single written text, but might include a pictorial image, cultural practice, oral tradition, or historical event, with the proviso that it leaves a distinct verbal imprint on the text in question to justify its status as source.

63. *Canterbury Tales*, ed. Mann, xxiv. Mann notes the multiple occurrences of "Werk al by conseil" discussed below.

64. Barker, *Adages of Erasmus*, 317–56 (IV.i.1). Albertanus gives, "Multi clamant 'sic, sic', qui vim verborum nesciunt et quod dicunt penitus ignorant" (chap. 2, 10.6–8); Renaud, "Moult de gens crient 'Guerre!' haultement qui ne scevent que guerre se monte" (ed. Askins 336, 2.38). In *Melibee*, instead of marking the initial "Werre, Werre," expression, Speght marks the follow-up saying, which observes that it is easier to get into a war than out of one.

65. Vulgate, Ecclesiasticus 32:5–7: "non inpedias musica / ubi auditus est non effundas sermonem / et inportune noli extolli in sapientia tua / gemmula carbunculi in ornamento auri / et conparatio musicorum in convivio vini." My translation is adapted from Douay-Rheims with the aid of the New Revised Standard version.

66. Throughout the *Tales*, the Host stands as a leading example of audience subjectivity. He is obsessed with his strong-willed wife, and he consistently weighs in heavily on the side of *solaas*: Chaucer introduces him in the *General Prologue* with ten forms of the words *merry*, *mirth*, *disport*, *play*, and *comfort*, as against a single mention of *sentence* when he pronounces the rules of the game (I.751–801); he expresses impatience with tellers who are too earnest to suit what he understands as a purely festive occasion, despite the pilgrimage's solemn destination.

CONCLUSION

1. Chaucer uses "moralite" in this sense in the *Nun's Priest's Tale*, VII.3440. Fables "had fully detachable *moralitates*, useful as maxims on their own or in relation to other texts," Wheatley, *Mastering Aesop*, 89–90. See also Cannon, *From Literacy to Literature*, esp. 85–124 and 159–220 for pedagogy and school texts in late medieval England with application to Chaucer.

2. Speght's manicules occur at IX.310, 319 (T373), 325, 335, 347, 350 (J13), 351, 359; Whiting numbers in parentheses.

3. Ginsberg, "Manciple's Tale," 336.

4. Dolven, *Scenes of Instruction*, 53–59, quotations at 58–59. Dolven attributes the distinction between "paradigmatic" and "narrative" understanding to Jerome Bruner.

5. Still valuable on the *Manciple's Tale* is Fradenburg, "Manciple's Serpent Tongue"; for the tale's generic affiliations with fable and other forms, see Wheatley, "Manciple's Tale."

6. Mann tracks the transmission of the Aristotelian proverb in the explanatory note to *Canterbury Tales* X.658. Her notes and those in the *Riverside Chaucer* identify the Parson's many quotations from Jerome and Augustine. The tale addresses original sin directly in X.333–35.

7. See Whiting S397 and the explanatory note to line X.362 in the *Riverside Chaucer*.

8. For many medievalists, the landmark work on reader response theory and genre

is Jauss, *Toward an Aesthetic of Reception*. The definitive study of the Middle English exemplum is Scanlon, *Narrative, Authority, and Power*.

9. Manicules in the *Monk's Tale* occur at lines VII.1995, 2092, 2139, 2239, 2293, 2347, 2493, 2559, 2661, 2724, 2763; in the *Nun's Priest's Tale*, at lines 2913, 2979, 3053, 3163, 3205, 3256, 3325, 3431, 3433, 3443.

10. For the proverbial nature of these two unmarked expressions, see Whiting F546, F506, and many similar observations about fortune, F502 to F549. In *Chaucer's Use of Proverbs*, 125, Whiting includes the second expression in his list of sententious remarks.

11. Travis, *Disseminal Chaucer*, 1, 14. The brief treatment of this "supremely Chaucerian" tale in Muscatine, *Chaucer and the French Tradition*, is the foundation for many modern readings, including my own, 237–43, quotation at 243.

12. Unsurprisingly, Speght does not mark every occurrence of the two opposing expressions that fuel this disputation. Unmarked is Pertelote's observation from the "wys" Cato about giving no credence to one's dreams (VII.2941), but its status as an attributed wisdom expression is clear: Chauntecleer refers to it as "this sentence" (2977). Speght marks the claim in 2975–80 that dreams are "significaciouns" to be taken seriously as warnings, but he does not mark Chauntecleer's repetition of the same point in 3106–9.

13. Orme, *Education and Society*, 104, no. 43; see also Cannon, *From Literacy to Literature*, with illuminating discussion of Chauntecleer's "Latyn," 138–44.

14. For these interpretations and others, see Derek Pearsall's still valuable *Nun's Priest's Tale*, 200–201, and also the discussion in Cannon, *From Literacy to Literature*, 138–44. Pearsall's "Survey of Criticism," 30–82, summarizes the foundations upon which most modern readings, including my own, are built.

15. Finlayson, "Reading Chaucer's *Nun's Priest's Tale*," 493.

16. Travis, *Disseminal Chaucer*, 2.

17. The biblical passage indicated by this reference to "Ecclesiaste" is disputed; see the note to VII.3329 in *Canterbury Tales*, ed. Mann.

18. Whiting C428 offers many examples of the corn and chaff image from Chaucer and other sources.

19. *Dialogue*, ed. Bradbury and Bradbury, 31 (4.15ab).

# BIBLIOGRAPHY

PRIMARY SOURCES

Albertanus of Brescia. *Albertani Brixiensis, Liber consolationis et consilii.* Edited by Thor Sundby. London: Trübner for the Chaucer Society, 1873.

Aristotle. *Art of Rhetoric.* Translated by J. H. Freese. Revised by Gisela Striker. Cambridge, MA: Harvard University Press, 2020.

Audelay, John the Blind. *Poems and Carols (Oxford, Bodleian Library MS Douce 302).* Edited by Susanna Fein. Kalamazoo, MI: Medieval Institute Publications, 2009.

Blake, William. "Proverbs of Hell," from *The Marriage of Heaven and Hell.* In *The Complete Poetry and Prose of William Blake,* edited by David V. Erdman, 35-38. Rev. ed. New York: Anchor, 1988.

Brathwait[e], Richard. *Comments, in 1665, upon Chaucer's Tales of the Miller and the Wife of Bath.* Edited by Caroline F. E. Spurgeon. London: Kegan Paul, Trench, and Trübner, 1901.

Chaucer, Geoffrey. *The Canterbury Tales.* Edited by Jill Mann. London: Penguin, 2005.

———. *The Riverside Chaucer.* Edited by Larry D. Benson et al. Boston: Houghton Mifflin, 1987.

———. *The Workes of our Antient and Lerned English Poet, Geffrey Chaucer, Newly Printed.* Edited by Thomas Speght. London: Adam Islip for George Bishop, 1598.

———. *The Workes of our Antient and Lerned English Poet, Geffrey Chaucer, Newly Printed.* Rev. ed. Edited by Thomas Speght. London: Adam Islip, 1602.

Christine de Pizan. *The Book of the City of Ladies.* Translated by Earl Jeffrey Richards. New York: Persea, 1982.

———. "The *Livre de la Cité des Dames* of Christine de Pisan: A Critical Edition." Edited by Maureen Cheney Curnow. 2 vols. PhD diss., Vanderbilt University, 1975.

Croker, Thomas Crofton. *Popular Songs of Ireland.* London: G. Routledge and Sons, 1886.

*The Dialogue of Solomon and Marcolf: A Dual-Language Edition from Latin and Middle English Printed Editions.* Edited by Nancy Mason Bradbury and Scott Bradbury. Kalamazoo, MI: Medieval Institute Publications, 2012.

*Dives and Pauper.* Edited by Priscilla Barnum. 3 vols. Early English Texts Society, o.s., 275, 280, 323. Oxford: Oxford University Press, 1976-2004.

Erasmus, Desiderius. *The Adages of Erasmus.* Selected by William Barker. Toronto: University of Toronto Press, 2001.

———. *Collected Works of Erasmus,* Vols. 30–36, *Adages.* Assembled and introduced by William Barker, translated and annotated by Margaret Mann Phillips, R.A.B. Mynors, Denis Drysdall, Betty Knott Sharpe, and John N. Grant. Toronto: University of Toronto Press, 1974-2017.

———. "The Godly Feast." In *Collected Works of Erasmus,* Vol. 39, *Colloquies.* Translated and annotated by Craig R. Thompson, 171-243. Toronto: University of Toronto Press, 1997.

———. *Opera Omnia Desiderii Erasmi Roterodami, Adagiorum Chilias Prima.* Edited by M. L. van Poll-van de Lisdonk, M. Mann Phillips, Chr. Robinson. Amsterdam: North-Holland, 1993.

Frost, Robert. "Mending Wall." From *North of Boston* (1914). In *The Poetry of Robert Frost,* edited by Edward

Connery Lathem, 33–34. New York: Holt, Rinehart and Winston, 1969.

Gower, John. *The Major Latin Works of John Gower.* Translated by Eric W. Stockton. Seattle: University of Washington Press, 1962.

Hanna, Ralph, III and Traugott Lawler, eds. *Jankyn's Book of Wikked Wives.* Vol. 1, *The Primary Texts.* Athens: University of Georgia Press, 1997.

———. "The Wife of Bath's Prologue." In *Sources and Analogues of the "Canterbury Tales,"* edited by Robert M. Correale and Mary Hamel, 2:351–403. Cambridge: D. S. Brewer, 2005.

[Horace] Quintus Horatius Flaccus. *Satires, Epistles, and Ars Poetica.* Edited and translated by Henry Rushton Fairclough. Cambridge, MA: Harvard University Press, 2014.

Isidore of Seville. *The "Etymologies" of Isidore of Seville.* Translated by Stephen Barney, W. J. Lewis, et al. Cambridge: Cambridge University Press, 2006.

Kempe, Margery. *The Book of Margery Kempe: Annotated Edition.* Edited by Barry Windeatt. Cambridge: D. S. Brewer, 2004.

Lydgate, John. *The Minor Poems of John Lydgate.* Vol. 2, *Secular Poems.* Edited by Henry Noble MacCracken. Early English Text Society, o.s., 192. London, 1934.

———. *The Siege of Thebes.* Edited by Robert R. Edwards. Kalamazoo, MI: Medieval Institute Publications, 2001.

Metham, John. *Amoryus and Cleopes.* Edited by Stephen F. Page. Kalamazoo, MI: Medieval Institute Publications, 1999.

Pecock, Reginald. *The Folewer to the Donet.* Edited by Elsie Vaughan Hitchcock. Early English Text Society, o.s., 164. London: Oxford University Press, 1924.

*Li Proverbe au Vilain: A Critical Edition.* Edited and translated by John Bednar. New Orleans: University Press of the South, 2000.

*Queste del Saint Graal.* Edited by Albert Pauphilet. Paris: Champion, 1923.

Renaud de Louens. *Livre de Mellibee.* Edited by William Askins, from the edition by J. Burke Severs. In *Sources and Analogues of the Canterbury Tales,* edited by Robert Correale and Mary Hamel, 1:321–408. Cambridge: D. S. Brewer, 2002.

Richard de Bury. *Philobiblon.* Edited by Michael Maclagan from the text and translation of E. C. Thomas. Oxford: Basil Blackwell for Shakespeare Head, 1960.

*Solomon and Marcolf.* Edited and translated by Jan M. Ziolkowski. Cambridge, MA: Harvard University Press, 2008.

*The Taill of Rauf Coilyear.* In *Longer Scottish Poems,* Vol. 1, *1375–1650,* edited by Patricia Bawcutt and Felicity Riddy, 94–133. Edinburgh: Scottish Academic Press, 1987.

Walsingham, Thomas. *The St. Albans Chronicle: The Chronica maiora of Thomas Walsingham.* Vol. 1, *1376–1394.* Edited and translated by John Taylor, Wendy R. Childs, and Leslie Watkiss. Oxford: Oxford University Press, 2003.

SECONDARY SOURCES

Abrahams, Roger D., and Barbara A. Babcock. "The Literary Use of Proverbs." In *Wise Words: Essays on the Proverb,* edited by Wolfgang Mieder, 415–37. New York: Garland, 1994.

Adams, Jenny, and Nancy Mason Bradbury, eds. *Medieval Women and Their Objects.* Ann Arbor: University of Michigan Press, 2017.

Amodio, Mark C., ed. *New Directions in Oral Theory.* Tempe: Arizona Center for Medieval and Renaissance Studies, 2005.

Arendt, Hannah. Introduction to *Illuminations: Essays and Reflections,* by Walter Benjamin, translated by Harry Zohn, edited by Hannah Arendt. 1968; repr., Boston: Houghton Mifflin Harcourt, 2019.

Arora, Shirley L. "The Perception of Proverbiality." In *Wise Words: Essays on the Proverb*, edited by Wolfgang Mieder, 3–29. New York: Garland, 1994.

Askins, William. "The Tale of Melibee." In *Sources and Analogues of the "Canterbury Tales,"* edited by Robert M. Correale and Mary Hamel, 1:321–408. Cambridge: D. S. Brewer, 2002.

Astell, Ann W. *Chaucer and the Universe of Learning*. Ithaca: Cornell University Press, 1996.

Aughterson, Kate, ed. *Renaissance Woman: Constructions of Femininity in England*. London: Routledge, 1995.

Bahr, Arthur. *Fragments and Assemblages: Forming Compilations of Medieval London*. Chicago: University of Chicago Press, 2013.

Bakhtin, Mikhail M. "The Problem of Speech Genres." In *Speech Genres and Other Late Essays*, translated by Vern W. McGee, edited by Caryl Emerson and Michael Holquist, 60–102. Austin: University of Texas Press, 1986.

———. *Rabelais and His World*. Translated by Hélène Iswolsky. Bloomington: Indiana University Press, 1984.

———. "Response to a Question from the *Novy Mir* Editorial Staff." In *Speech Genres and Other Late Essays*, translated by Vern W. McGee, edited by Caryl Emerson and Michael Holquist, 1–9. Austin: University of Texas Press, 1986.

Barker, William, ed. *The Adages of Erasmus*. Toronto: University of Toronto Press, 2001.

Barney, Stephen, ed. *Chaucer's "Troilus": Essays in Criticism*. Hamden: Archon, 1980.

Baum, Paull Franklin. "The Mare and the Wolf." *Modern Language Notes* 37 (1922): 350–53.

Bednar, John, ed. and trans. *Li Proverbe au Vilain: A Critical Edition*. New Orleans: University Press of the South, 2000.

Benjamin, Walter. "On Proverbs." In *Selected Writings*, Vol. 2, *1927–1934*. Translated by Rodney Livingstone et al., edited by Michael W. Jennings et al., 582. Cambridge, MA: Belknap of Harvard, 1999.

———. "The Storyteller: Reflections on the Work of Nikolai Leskov." In *The Storyteller Essays*, translated by Tess Lewis, edited by Samuel Titan, 48–73. New York: New York Review of Books, 2019.

Bennett, Michael. *Lambert Simnel and the Battle of Stoke*. New York: St. Martin's, 1987.

Benson, C. David. "Their Telling Difference: Chaucer the Pilgrim and His Two Contrasting Tales." *Chaucer Review* 18, no. 1 (1983): 61–76.

Benson, Larry D. Foreword to *Modern Proverbs and Proverbial Sayings*, edited by Bartlett Jere Whiting, v–ix. Cambridge, MA: Harvard University Press, 1989.

Benson, Larry D., et al., eds. *The Riverside Chaucer*. Boston: Houghton Mifflin, 1987.

Besserman, Lawrence. *Chaucer's Biblical Poetics*. Norman: University of Oklahoma Press, 1998.

Blamires, Alcuin. "Women and Creative Intelligence in Medieval Thought." In *Voices in Dialogue: Reading Women in the Middle Ages*, edited by Linda Olson and Kathryn Kerby-Fulton, 213–30. Notre Dame: University of Notre Dame Press, 2005.

Blamires, Alcuin, ed., with Karen Pratt and C. W. Marx. *Woman Defamed and Woman Defended: An Anthology of Medieval Texts*. Oxford: Oxford University Press, 1992.

Blatt, Heather. "Mapping the Readable Household." In *Spaces for Reading in Later Medieval England*, edited by Mary C. Flannery and Carrie Griffin, 165–81. London: Palgrave MacMillan, 2016.

Boffey, Julia. "Proverbial Chaucer and the Chaucer Canon." *Huntington Library Quarterly* 58, no. 1 (1995): 37–47.

Bose, Mishtooni. "From Exegesis to Appropriation: The Medieval Solomon." *Medium Aevum* 65 (1996): 187–210.

Bowden, Betsy. "*Chaucer New Painted* (1623): Three Hundred Proverbs in Performance Context." *Oral Tradition* 10 (1995): 304–58.

———. "A Modest Proposal, Relating Four Millennia of Proverb Collections to Chemistry within the Human Brain." *Journal of American Folklore* 109 (1996): 440–49.

———. "Ubiquitous Format? What Ubiquitous Format? Chaucer's *Tale of Melibee* as a Proverb Collection." *Oral Tradition* 17 (2002): 169–207.

———. *The Wife of Bath in Afterlife: Ballads to Blake*. Bethlehem, PA: Lehigh University Press, 2017.

Bradbury, Nancy Mason. "The Proverb as Embedded Microgenre in Chaucer and *The Dialogue of Solomon and Marcolf*." *Exemplaria* 27 (Spring/Summer 2015): 55–72.

———. "Proverb Tradition as a Soft Source for the *Canterbury Tales*." *Studies in the Age of Chaucer* 28 (2006): 237–42.

———. "Representations of Peasant Speech: Some Literary and Social Contexts for *The Taill of Rauf Coilyear*." In *Medieval Romance, Medieval Contexts*, edited by Rhiannon Purdie and Michael Cichon, 19–33. Cambridge: D. S. Brewer, 2011.

———. "Rival Wisdom in the Latin *Dialogue of Solomon and Marcolf*." *Speculum* 83 (2008): 331–65.

———. "Transforming Experience into Tradition: Two Theories of Proverb Use and Chaucer's Practice." *Oral Tradition* 17 (2002): 261–89.

Brewer, Derek. "The Relationship of Chaucer to the English and European Traditions." In *Chaucer and Chaucerians*, edited by D. S. Brewer, 1–38. Birmingham: University of Alabama Press, 1966.

Burke, Kenneth. "Literature as Equipment for Living." In *The Philosophy of Literary Form*, 3rd ed., 293–304. Berkeley: University of California Press, 1973.

Burke, Peter, and Roy Porter, eds. *The Social History of Language*. Cambridge: Cambridge University Press, 1987.

Burke, Victoria E. "Ann Bowyer's Commonplace Book (Bodleian Library Ashmole MS 51): Reading and Writing Among the 'Middling Sort.'" *Early Modern Literary Studies* 6 (2001): 1–28.

Butterfield, Ardis. *The Familiar Enemy: Chaucer, Language, and Nation in the Hundred Years War*. Oxford: Oxford University Press, 2009.

Caie, Graham D. "The Significance of the Early Chaucer Manuscript Glosses (with Special Reference to 'The Wife of Bath's Prologue')." *Chaucer Review* 10, no. 4 (1976): 350–60.

Campbell, Kirsty. *The Call to Read: Reginald Pecock's Books and Textual Communities*. Notre Dame: University of Notre Dame Press, 2010.

Cannon, Christopher. *From Literacy to Literature: England 1300–1400*. Oxford: Oxford University Press, 2016.

———. "In the Classroom." In *Further Reading*, edited by Matthew Rubery and Leah Price, 28–37. Oxford: Oxford University Press, 2020.

———. "Proverbs and the Wisdom of Literature: *The Proverbs of Alfred* and Chaucer's *Tale of Melibee*." *Textual Practice* 24 (2010): 407–34.

Carruthers, Mary. *The Book of Memory: A Study of Memory in Medieval Culture*. Cambridge: Cambridge University Press, 1990.

Cavallo, Guglielmo, and Roger Chartier. *A History of Reading in the West*. Translated by Lydia G. Cochrane. Amherst: University of Massachusetts Press, 1999.

Chartier, Roger. *Forms and Meanings*. Philadelphia: University of Pennsylvania Press, 1995.

Cichon, Michael, and Yin Liu, eds. *Proverbia Septentrionalia: Essays on Proverbs in Medieval Scandinavian* and *English Literature*. Tempe: Arizona Center for Medieval and Renaissance Studies, 2019.

Colie, Rosalie L. *The Resources of Kind: Genre-Theory in the Renaissance*. Edited by Barbara K. Lewalski. Berkeley: University of California Press, 1973.

Collette, Carolyn P. "Heeding the Counsel of Prudence: A Context for the *Melibee*." *Chaucer Review* 29 (1995): 416–33.

———. *Performing Polity: Women and Agency in the Anglo-French Tradition, 1385–1620*. Turnhout: Brepols, 2006.

Cook, Megan. *The Poet and the Antiquaries: Chaucerian Scholarship and the Rise of Literary History, 1532–1635*. Philadelphia: University of Pennsylvania Press, 2019.

Cooper, Helen. "Sources and Analogues of Chaucer's *Canterbury Tales*: Reviewing the Work." *Studies in the Age of Chaucer* 19 (1997): 183–210.

Corti, Maria. "Models and Antimodels in Medieval Culture." Translated by John Meddemmen. *New Literary History* 10 (1979): 339–66.

Crane, Susan. *Gender and Romance in Chaucer's "Canterbury Tales."* Princeton: Princeton University Press, 1994.

———. "The Writing Lesson of 1381." In *Chaucer's England: Literature in Historical Context*, edited by Barbara Hanawalt, 201–21. Minneapolis: University of Minnesota Press, 1992.

Dagenais, John. *The Ethics of Reading in Manuscript Culture: Glossing the "Libro de buen amor."* Princeton: Princeton University Press, 1994.

Dane, Joseph A. "Fists and Filiations in Early Chaucer Folios, 1532–1602." *Studies in Bibliography* 51 (1998): 48–62.

———. *Out of Sorts: On Typography and Print Culture*. Philadelphia: University of Pennsylvania Press, 2011.

Davis, Natalie Zemon. "Proverbial Wisdom and Popular Errors." In *Society and Culture in Early Modern France*, 227–67. Stanford: Stanford University Press, 1975.

Deskis, Susan E. *Alliterative Proverbs in Medieval England: Language Choice and Literary Meaning*. Columbus: Ohio State University Press, 2016.

———. *"Beowulf" and the Medieval Proverb Tradition*. Tempe: Medieval & Renaissance Texts and Studies, 1996.

Desmond, Marilynn. *Ovid's Art and the Wife of Bath: The Ethics of Erotic Violence*. Ithaca: Cornell University Press, 2006.

Dinshaw, Carolyn. *Chaucer's Sexual Poetics*. Madison: University of Wisconsin Press, 1989.

Dolven, Jeff. *Scenes of Instruction in Renaissance Romance*. Chicago: University of Chicago Press, 2007.

Duby, Georges. *The Three Orders: Feudal Society Imagined*. Translated by Arthur Goldhammer. Chicago: University of Chicago Press, 1980.

Duffy, Eamon. *The Stripping of the Altars: Traditional Religion in England 1400–1580*. 2nd ed. New Haven: Yale University Press, 2005.

Dundes, Alan. "On the Structure of the Proverb." In *The Wisdom of Many: Essays on the Proverb*, edited by Wolfgang Mieder and Alan Dundes, 43–64. New York: Garland, 1981.

Edwards, Robert R. *Invention and Authorship in Medieval England*. Columbus: Ohio State University Press, 2017.

Farmer, Sharon. "Persuasive Voices: Clerical Images of Medieval Wives." *Speculum* 61 (1986): 517–43.

Farrell, Thomas J. "Chaucer's Little Treatise, the *Melibee*." *Chaucer Review* 20 (1985): 61–67.

Fein, Susanna. "The 'Thyng Wommen Loven Moost': The Wife of Bath's Fabliau Answer." In *Medieval Women and Their Objects*, edited by Jenny Adams and Nancy Mason Bradbury, 15–38. Ann Arbor: University of Michigan Press, 2017.

Fein, Susanna, and David Raybin, eds. *Chaucer: Contemporary Approaches*.

University Park: Penn State University Press, 2010.

Finlayson, John. "Reading Chaucer's *Nun's Priest's Tale*: Mixed Genres and Multi-Layered Worlds of Illusion, *English Studies* 86, no. 6 (2005): 493–510.

Fletcher, Alan J. "The Faith of a Simple Man: Carpenter John's Creed in the *Miller's Tale*." *Medium Aevum* 61, no. 1 (1992): 96–105.

Foley, John Miles. *The Singer of Tales in Performance*. Bloomington: Indiana University Press, 1995.

Forbes, Thomas R. "Verbal Charms in British Folk Medicine." *Proceedings of the American Philosophical Society* 115, no. 4 (1971): 293–316.

Foster, Edward E. "Has Anyone Here Read 'Melibee'?" *Chaucer Review* 34, no. 4 (2000): 398–409.

Fradenburg, Louise. "The Manciple's Serpent Tongue: Politics and Poetry in the *Canterbury Tales*." *ELH* 52 (1985): 85–118.

Freedman, Paul. *Images of the Medieval Peasant*. Stanford: Stanford University Press, 1999.

Garner, Lori Ann. "The Role of Proverbs in Middle English Narrative." In *New Directions in Oral Theory*, edited by Mark C. Amodio, 255–77. Tempe: Arizona Center for Medieval and Renaissance Studies, 2005.

Gayk, Shannon. *Image, Text, and Religious Reform in Fifteenth-Century England*. Cambridge: Cambridge University Press, 2010.

Gaylord, Alan T. "*Sentence* and *Solaas* in Fragment VII of the *Canterbury Tales*: Harry Bailly as Horseback Editor." *PMLA* 82 (1967): 226–35.

Gibson, Walter S. *Figures of Speech: Picturing Proverbs in Renaissance Netherlands*. Berkeley: University of California Press, 2010.

Ginsberg, Warren. "The Manciple's Tale: Response." *Studies in the Age of Chaucer* 25 (2003): 331–37.

Goddard, R. N. B. "Marcabru, *Li Proverbe au Vilain*, and the Tradition of Rustic Proverbs." *Neuphilologische Mitteilungen* 88 (1987): 55–70.

Grady, Frank, ed. *The Cambridge Companion to "The Canterbury Tales."* Cambridge: Cambridge University Press, 2020.

Graham, Angus. "Albertanus of Brescia: A Preliminary Census of Vernacular Manuscripts." *Studi Medievali* 3, ser. 41 (December 2000): 891–924.

Gray, Douglas. "'Lat be thyne olde ensaumples': Chaucer and Proverbs." In *Interstices: Studies in Middle English and Anglo-Latin Texts in Honour of A.G. Rigg*, edited by Richard Firth Green and Linne R. Mooney, 122–36. Toronto: University of Toronto Press, 2004.

———. *Simple Forms: Essays on Medieval English Popular Literature*. Oxford: Oxford University Press, 2015.

Green, Richard Firth. *Elf Queens and Holy Friars: Fairy Beliefs and the Medieval Church*. Philadelphia: University of Pennsylvania Press, 2016.

———. "Marcolf the Fool and Blind John Audelay." In *Speaking Images: Essays in Honor of V. A. Kolve*, edited by R. F. Yeager and Charlotte C. Morse, 559–76. Asheville: Pegasus, 2001.

———. *Poets and Princepleasers: Literature and the English Court in the Late Middle Ages*. Toronto: University of Toronto Press, 1980.

Hanna, Ralph, III and Traugott Lawler, eds. *Jankyn's Book of Wikked Wives*. Vol. 1, *The Primary Texts*. Athens: University of Georgia Press, 1997.

———. "The Wife of Bath's Prologue." In *Sources and Analogues of the "Canterbury Tales*," edited by Robert M. Correale and Mary Hamel, 2:361–78. Cambridge: D. S. Brewer, 2005.

Hanning, Robert W. *The Individual in Twelfth-Century Romance*. New Haven: Yale University Press, 1977.

Hansen, Elaine Tuttle. *Chaucer and the Fictions of Gender*. Berkeley: University of California Press, 1992.

———. *The Solomon Complex: Reading Wisdom in Old English Poetry*.

Toronto: University of Toronto Press, 1988.
Hasan-Rokem, Galit. "Proverb." In *Folklore, Cultural Performances, and Popular Entertainments: A Communications-Centered Handbook*, edited by Richard Bauman, 128–33. Oxford: Oxford University Press, 1992.
Hernadi, Paul. *Beyond Genre: New Directions in Literary Classification*. Ithaca: Cornell University Press, 1972.
Hiatt, Alfred. "Genre Without System." In *Middle English: Oxford Twenty-First Century Approaches to Literature*, edited by Paul Strohm, 277–94. Oxford: Oxford University Press, 2007.
Honeck, Richard P. *A Proverb in Mind: The Cognitive Science of Proverbial Wit and Wisdom*. Mahwah, NJ: Erlbaum, 1997.
Hunter, G. K. "The Marking of *Sententiae* in Elizabethan Printed Plays, Poems, and Romances." *The Library*, 5th ser., 6, nos. 3–4 (1951): 171–88.
Jardine, Lisa. *Erasmus, Man of Letters: The Construction of Charisma in Print*. 1993; repr., Princeton: Princeton University Press, 2015.
Jauss, Hans Robert. "The Alterity and Modernity of Medieval Literature." Translated by Timothy Bahti. *New Literary History* 10 (1979): 181–229.
———. *Toward an Aesthetic of Reception*. Translated by Timothy Bahti. Minneapolis: University of Minnesota Press, 1982.
Jones, Malcolm. "The Depiction of Proverbs in Late Medieval Art." *Europhras 88: Actes du Colloque International*, edited by Gertrud Gréciano. 205-23. Strasbourg: Université des Sciences Humaines, 1989.
Justice, Steven. *Writing and Rebellion: England in 1381*. Berkeley: University of California Press, 1994.
Kerby-Fulton, Kathryn, Maidie Hilmo, and Linda Olson. *Opening Up Middle English Manuscripts: Literary and Visual Approaches*. Ithaca: Cornell University Press, 2012.
Kinney, Clare R. "Thomas Speght's Renaissance Chaucer and the *Solaas of Sentence* in *Troilus and Criseyde*." In *Refiguring Chaucer in the Renaissance*, edited by Theresa M. Krier, 66–84. Gainesville: University Press of Florida, 1998.
Knapp, Peggy. *Chaucer and the Social Contest*. New York and London: Routledge, 1990.
Kramer, Johanna. "Proverbial Wisdom and the Pursuit of Knowledge in the *Squire's Tale*." *Chaucer Review* 57 (2022): 68–100.
Krug, Rebecca. *Margery Kempe and the Lonely Reader*. Ithaca: Cornell University Press, 2017.
Lau, Kimberly J., Peter Tokofsky, and Stephen D. Winick, eds. *What Goes Around Comes Around: The Circulation of Proverbs in Contemporary Life*. Logan: Utah State University Press, 2004.
Lawton, David. *Voice in Later Medieval Literature: Public Interiorities*. Oxford: Oxford University Press, 2017.
Lesser, Zachary and Peter Stallybrass. "The First Literary *Hamlet* and the Commonplacing of Professional Plays." *Shakespeare Quarterly* 59 (2008): 371–420.
Louis, Cameron. "The Concept of the Proverb in Middle English." *Proverbium* 14 (1997): 173–85.
———. "Proverbs, Precepts, and Monitory Pieces." In *A Manual of the Writings in Middle English, 1050–1500*, edited by Albert E. Hartung, 9:2957–3048. New Haven: Connecticut Academy of Arts and Sciences, 1993.
Luxon, Thomas H. "'Sentence' and 'Solaas': Proverbs and Consolation in the *Knight's Tale*." *Chaucer Review* 22 (1987): 94–111.
Machan, Tim William. "Speght's *Works* and the Invention of Chaucer." *Text* 8 (1995): 145–70.
Manguel, Alberto. *A History of Reading*. New York: Penguin, 1996.

Mann, Jill, ed. *The Canterbury Tales by Geoffrey Chaucer*. London: Penguin, 2005.
———. *Chaucer and Medieval Estates Satire*. Cambridge: Cambridge University Press, 1973.
———. *From Aesop to Renard: Beast Literature in Medieval Britain*. Oxford: Oxford University Press, 2009.
McCutcheon, Elizabeth, ed. and trans. *Sir Nicholas Bacon's Great House Sententiae*. Amherst, MA: English Literary Renaissance, 1977.
Meyer-Lee, Robert John. "Abandon the Fragments." *Studies in the Age of Chaucer* 35 (2013): 47–83.
Mieder, Wolfgang. "'Good Fences Make Good Neighbours': History and Significance of an Ambiguous Proverb." *Folklore* 114 (2003): 155–79.
———. *Proverbs: A Handbook*. Westport, CT: Greenwood Press, 2004.
Mieder, Wolfgang, and Alan Dundes, eds. *The Wisdom of Many: Essays on the Proverb*. New York: Garland, 1981.
Miner, Paul. "Blake's 'Proverbs of Hell.'" *Notes and Queries* 59 (2012): 350–54.
Minnis, A. J., and A. B. Scott, eds., with David Wallace. *Medieval Literary Theory and Criticism, c. 1100–c. 1375: The Commentary Tradition*. Rev. ed. Oxford: Clarendon, 1991.
Moss, Ann. *Printed Commonplace-Books and the Structuring of Renaissance Thought*. Oxford: Clarendon, 1996.
Muscatine, Charles. *Chaucer and the French Tradition*. Berkeley: University of California Press, 1957.
Nel, Philip Johannes. *The Structure and Ethos of the Wisdom Admonitions in Proverbs*. Berlin: de Gruyter, 1982.
Obelkevich, James. "Proverbs and Social History." In *The Social History of Language*, edited by Peter Burke and Roy Porter, 43–72. Cambridge: Cambridge University Press, 1987.
Olsan, Lea T. "Charms and Prayers in Medieval Medical Theory and Practice." *Social History of Medicine* 16, no. 3 (2003): 343–66.
———. "The Corpus of Charms in the Middle English Leechcraft Remedy Books." In *Charms, Charmers and Charming*, edited by Jonathan Roper, 214–37. Houndsmills, Basingstoke: Palgrave Macmillan, 2009.
Orgel, Stephen. *The Reader in the Book: A Study of Spaces and Traces*. Oxford: Oxford University Press, 2015.
Orme, Nicholas. *Education and Society in Medieval and Renaissance England*. London: Hambledon, 1989.
———. *Medieval Schools: From Roman Britain to Renaissance England*. New Haven: Yale University Press, 2006.
Orwell, George. "Politics and the English Language." In *The Orwell Reader: Fiction, Essays, and Reportage*, 355–66. New York: Harcourt, 1956.
Palomo, Dolores. "What Chaucer Really Did to *Le Livre de Mellibee*." *Philological Quarterly* 53, no. 3 (1974): 304–20.
Parkes, Malcolm B. "The Influence of the Concepts of *Ordinatio* and *Compilatio* on the Development of the Book." In *Medieval Learning and Literature: Essays Presented to Richard William Hunt*, edited by J. J. G. Alexander and M. T. Gibson, 115–41. Oxford: Clarendon, 1976.
Parsons, Ben. "Beaten for a Book: Domestic and Pedagogic Violence in *The Wife of Bath's Prologue*." *Studies in the Age of Chaucer* 37 (2015): 163–94.
Partridge, Stephen. "The *Canterbury Tales* Glosses and Manuscript Groups." In *The Canterbury Tales Project Occasional Papers*, edited by Norman Blake and Peter Robinson, 1:85–94. Oxford: Office for Humanities Communication, 1993.
Patterson, Jeanette. "Solomon *au Feminin*: (Re)Translating Proverbs 31 in Christine de Pizan's *Cité des dames*." *Mediaevalia* 36/37 (2015–16): 353–92.
Patterson, Lee. "'For the Wyves Love of Bathe': Feminine Rhetoric and Poetic Resolution in the *Roman de la Rose* and the *Canterbury Tales*." *Speculum* 58 (1983): 656–95.

———. "'What Man Artow?': Authorial Self-Definition in *The Tale of Sir Thopas* and *The Tale of Melibee*." *Studies in the Age of Chaucer* 11 (1989): 117–75.

Paulhan, Jean. "*L'Expérience du proverbe*." In *Œuvres complètes II: L'Art de la contradiction*, edited by Bernard Baillaud, 169–94. Paris: Gallimard, 2009.

———. "The Experience of the Proverb." In *On Poetry and Politics*, translated by Eric Trudel, edited by Jennifer Bajorek and Eric Trudel, 5–27. Urbana: University of Illinois Press, 2008.

Pearsall, Derek. *The Nun's Priest's Tale*. Part 9 of *The Canterbury Tales*. Vol. 2 of *A Variorum Edition of the Works of Geoffrey Chaucer*. Norman: University of Oklahoma Press, 1984.

———. "Thomas Speght." In *Editing Chaucer: The Great Tradition*, edited by Paul G. Ruggiers, 71–92. Norman, OK: Pilgrim Books, 1984.

Powell, James M. *Albertanus of Brescia: The Pursuit of Happiness in the Early Thirteenth Century*. Philadelphia: University of Pennsylvania Press, 1992.

Robertson, D. W. *A Preface to Chaucer: Studies in Medieval Perspectives*. Princeton: Princeton University Press, 1962.

Roper, Jonathan. *English Verbal Charms*. Helsinki: FF Communications no. 288, Folklore Fellows, 2005.

Rubery, Matthew, and Leah Price. *Further Reading*. Oxford: Oxford University Press, 2020.

Scala, Elizabeth. *Desire in the "Canterbury Tales."* Columbus: Ohio State University Press, 2015.

Scanlon, Larry. *Narrative, Authority, and Power: The Medieval Exemplum and the Chaucerian Tradition*. Cambridge: Cambridge University Press, 1994.

Scase, Wendy. *Reginald Pecock*. Aldershot: Variorum, 1996.

Schieberle, Misty. *Feminized Counsel and the Literature of Advice in England, 1380–1500*. Turnhout: Brepols, 2014.

———. "Proverbial Fools and Rival Wisdom: Lydgate's *Order of Fools* and Marcolf*.*" *Chaucer Review* 49 (2014): 204–27.

Severs, J. Burke. "The Tale of Melibeus." In *Sources and Analogues of Chaucer's "Canterbury Tales*," edited by W. F. Bryan and Germaine Dempster, 560–614. Chicago: University of Chicago Press, 1941.

Sherman, William H. *Used Books: Marking Readers in Renaissance England*. Philadelphia: University of Pennsylvania Press, 2008.

Shippey, Tom. "Proverbs and Proverbiousness in Hrafnkels Saga Freysgoða." In *The Hero Recovered: Essays on Medieval Heroism in Honor of George Clark*, edited by Robin Waugh and James Weldon, 127–41. Kalamazoo, MI: Medieval Institute Publications, 2010.

Simpson, James. "Diachronic History and the Shortcomings of Medieval Studies." In *Reading the Medieval in Early Modern England*, edited by Gordon McMullan and David Matthews, 17–30. Cambridge: Cambridge University Press, 2007.

———. *Reform and Cultural Revolution*. Oxford: Oxford University Press, 2002.

Singer, Samuel. *Sprichwörter des Mittelalters*. 3 vols. Bern: H. Lang, 1944–47.

Skemer, Don C. *Binding Words: Textual Amulets in the Middle Ages*. University Park: Penn State University Press, 2006.

Smith, Gordon. "Lambert Simnel and the King from Dublin." *The Ricardian* 10 (1994–96): 498–536.

Speake, Jennifer, ed. *Oxford Dictionary of Proverbs*. 6th ed. Oxford: Oxford University Press, 2015.

Spearing, A. C. *Textual Subjectivity: The Encoding of Subjectivity in Medieval Narratives and Lyrics*. Oxford: Oxford University Press, 2005.

Staley, Lynn. "Chaucer and the Postures of Sanctity." In *The Powers of the Holy: Religion, Politics, and Gender in Late Medieval English Culture*, by David Aers and Lynn Staley, 217–33. University Park: Penn State University Press, 1996.

———. *Following Chaucer: Offices of the Active Life*. Ann Arbor: University of Michigan Press, 2020.

———. *Languages of Power in the Age of Richard II*. University Park: Penn State University Press, 2005.

Steiner, Arpad. "The Vernacular Proverb in Mediaeval Latin Prose." *American Journal of Philology* 65, no. 1 (1944): 37–68.

Stewart, Anne W. "Teaching Complex Ethical Thinking with Proverbs." In *The Cambridge Companion to the Hebrew Bible and Ethics*, edited by C. L. Crouch, 241–56. Cambridge: Cambridge University Press, 2021.

Stock, Brian. *Listening for the Text: On the Uses of the Past*. Baltimore: Johns Hopkins University Press, 1990.

Szittya, Penn R. *The Antifraternal Tradition in Medieval Literature*. Princeton: Princeton University Press, 1986.

Taylor, Archer. *The Proverb*. Cambridge, MA: Harvard University Press, 1931.

Taylor, Barry. "Medieval Proverb Collections: The West European Tradition." *Journal of the Warburg and Courtauld Institutes* 55 (1992): 19–35.

Taylor, Jamie. "Chaucer's *Tale of Melibee* and the Failure of Allegory." *Exemplaria* 21 (Spring 2009): 83–101.

Taylor, Karla. "Proverbs and the Authentication of Convention in *Troilus and Criseyde*." In *Chaucer's "Troilus": Essays in Criticism*, edited by Stephen Barney, 277–96. Hamden: Archon, 1980.

———. "Social Aesthetics and the Emergence of Civic Discourse from the *Shipman's Tale* to *Melibee*." *Chaucer Review* 39 (2005): 298–322.

Taylor, P. B. "Chaucer's *Cosyn to the Dede*." *Speculum* 57 (1982): 315–27.

Thundy, Zacharias. "Chaucer's Quest for Wisdom in *The Canterbury Tales*." *Neuphilologische Mitteilungen* 77 (1976): 582–98.

Travis, Peter W. *Disseminal Chaucer: Rereading the "Nun's Priest's Tale."* Notre Dame: University of Notre Dame Press, 2010.

Trigg, Stephanie. *Congenial Souls: Reading Chaucer from Medieval to Postmodern*. Minneapolis: University of Minnesota Press, 2002.

Turner, Marion. *Chaucer: A European Life*. Princeton: Princeton University Press, 2019.

———. *Chaucerian Conflict: Languages of Antagonism in Late Fourteenth-Century London*. Oxford; Clarendon, 2007.

———. *The Wife of Bath: A Biography*. Princeton: Princeton University Press, 2023.

Villa, Claudia. "La Tradizione delle 'Ad Lucilium' e la cultura di Brescia dall' età carolingia ad Albertano." *Italia medioevale e umanistica* 12 (1969): 9–51.

Vine, Angus. *Miscellaneous Order: Manuscript Culture and the Early Modern Organization of Knowledge*. Oxford: Oxford University Press, 2019.

Wallace, David. *Chaucerian Polity: Absolutist Lineages and Associational Forms in England and Italy*. Stanford: Stanford University Press, 1997.

Walther, Hans, and Paul Gerhard Schmidt, eds. *Proverbia sententiaeque latinitatis medii aevi*. 9 vols. Göttingen: Vandenhoeck & Ruprecht, 1963–86.

Wenzel, Siegfried, "Two Notes on Chaucer and Grosseteste." *Notes and Queries* 17, no. 12 (1970): 449–51.

Wetherbee, Winthrop. *Chaucer and the Poets: An Essay on Troilus and Criseyde*. Ithaca: Cornell University Press, 1984.

Wheatley, Edward. "The Manciple's Tale." In *Sources and Analogues of the "Canterbury Tales,"* edited by Robert M. Correale and Mary Hamel, 2:749–73. Cambridge: D. S. Brewer, 2005.

———. *Mastering Aesop: Medieval Education, Chaucer, and His*

*Followers*. Gainesville: University Press of Florida, 2000.

Whiting, B[artlett] J[ere]. *Chaucer's Use of Proverbs*. Cambridge, MA: Harvard University Press, 1934.

———. *Modern Proverbs and Proverbial Sayings*. Cambridge, MA: Harvard University Press, 1989.

———. "The Nature of the Proverb." *Harvard Studies and Notes in Philology and Literature* 14 (1932): 273–307.

Whiting, Bartlett Jere, with Helen Wescott Whiting. *Proverbs, Sentences, and Proverbial Phrases from English Writings Mainly Before 1500*. Cambridge, MA: Belknap of Harvard University Press, 1968.

Wiggins, Alison. "What Did Renaissance Readers Write in their Printed Copies of Chaucer?" *The Library*, 7th ser., 9, no. 1 (2008): 3–36.

Winick, Stephen D. "Proverbial Strategy and Proverbial Wisdom in *The Canterbury Tales*." *Proverbium* 11 (1994): 259–81.

Wogan-Browne, Jocelyn, with Carolyn Collette, Maryanne Kowaleski, Linne Mooney, Ad Putter, and David Trotter. *Language and Culture in Medieval Britain: The French of England, c.1100–c.1500*. Cambridge: Boydell & Brewer, 2009.

Woods, William F. "Symkyn's Place in the Reeve's Tale." *Chaucer Review* 39 (2004): 17–40.

Woodward, Daniel, and Martin Stevens. *The New Ellesmere Chaucer Monochromatic Facsimile*. San Marino: Huntington Library, 1997.

Wright, Louis B. "William Painter and the Vogue of Chaucer as a Moral Teacher." *Modern Philology* 31 (1933): 165–74.

Yeager, Stephen. "Chaucer's Prudent Poetics: Allegory, the *Tale of Melibee*, and the Frame Narrative to the *Canterbury Tales*." *Chaucer Review* 48, no. 3 (2014): 307–21.

Young, Karl. "Chaucer's Aphorisms from Ptolemy." *Studies in Philology* 34 (1937): 1–7.

# INDEX

Adages (*Adagiorum chiliades*). *See* Erasmus, Desiderius
Albertanus of Brescia. *See Liber consolationis et consilii*
Andreas Capellanus, 90, 96
Aristotle, 14, 56, 160
Arora, Shirley, 21–22
*Ars Poetica* (Horace), 14, 15–16
Askins, William, 134, 144
Athenaeus, 16
Audelay, John, 57
Augustine, Saint, 116, 162

Bahr, Arthur, 5
Bakhtin, Mikhail M., 59–60
  "Problem of Speech Genres, The," 11, 38, 60, 180n96
  "utterance," theory of, as applied to the proverb: defined, 38–39; "finalized wholeness" or "fullness of value" of, 40–41; permeable boundaries of, 37–40, 91, 106–7, 180n98; "re-accentuated" by new speaker's voice, 40, 91, 106, 111
Beaumont, Francis, 30–31
Benjamin, Walter
  "On Proverbs," 24–26, 120
  "Storyteller, The," 24–25
  on transformational power of proverbs, 24–26
Bible, Hebrew, 14, 23, 60
  *See also* Genesis; Ecclesiastes; Ecclesiasticus; Proverbs (biblical book of)
Blake, William, 29, 179n68
Blamires, Alcuin, 88, 186n46
Boccaccio, Giovanni, 89–90, 148
Boethius
  *Consolation of Philosophy*, 64, 121, 145–46, 160

Boffey, Julia, 13
*Book of Margery Kempe*, 27–28, 29
Bowden, Betsy, 34, 126
Bowyer, Anne, 34
Brathwait, Richard, 13
Burke, Kenneth, 11, 23–24, 26, 120, 173
Burke, Victoria E., 34

*Canterbury Tales* (Chaucer)
  *Canon's Yeoman's Prologue and Tale*, 38, 40, 61, 63, 79–83
  *Clerk's Tale*, 62, 164, 166
  *Cook's Tale*, 26, 36, 148
  *Friar's Prologue and Tale*, 31, 43, 62–63, 76
  *General Prologue*, 13, 52–54, 63–64, 82, 93
  *Knight's Tale*, 27, 39, 40–41, 59, 61, 71, 119
  *Manciple's Prologue and Tale*, 64, 158–61, 173
  *Man of Law's Introduction and Tale*, 18, 127, 172
  *Melibee, Tale of*, 3, 4, 15, 61, 72, 125–56, 168; contrasted with *Sir Thopas*, 8, 125–26, 128, 165; "free choys" in adopting counsels, 8–9, 147, 160, 172–73; instruction on proverb use in, 98, 102, 139, 147–52; positive reception by premodern readers, 33–34, 134–35; as a proverb collection, 126, 131, 133–52, 157; Prudence as wisdom figure in, 137–47, 152; role in *Canterbury Tales*, 152–56; structured by a Solomonic proverb, 139–41, 153–54; Thopas–Melibee link, 127–33
  *Merchant's Prologue, Tale, and Epilogue*, 33, 62, 98–102, 153–54, 164
  *Miller's Prologue*, 131–32

*Canterbury Tales* (Chaucer)(*continued*)
  *Miller's Tale*, 13, 31, 36–37, 39, 43, 59, 61, 63–64, 73, 110; microgenres in carpenter's represented speech, 64–71; one-sided wisdom contest in, 64–71
  *Monk's Prologue and Tale*, 36, 127, 140, 155, 164; proverb use contrasted with *Nun's Priest's Tale*, 8–9, 165–68, 170
  *Nun's Priest's Prologue and Tale*, 8–9, 32, 35, 55, 103, 127, 155–56, 165; fruit and chaff proverb in, 8, 35, 171–74; as Chaucer's implicit *ars poetica*, 167–74
  *Pardoner's Prologue and Tale*, 39–40; "radix malorum" proverb as central text, 154–55
  *Parson's Prologue and Tale*, 18, 33, 36, 61, 132, 160–61, 170; "good conseil" in, 136; exempla in, 161–65; "Manye smale maken a greet" proverb, 161–65
  *Prioress's Tale*, 127
  *Reeve's Prologue and Tale*, 27; "greatest clerks" proverb in, 43, 44, 49–52, 76; mediation across class lines in, 74–75; vengeful proverb use in, 72–74
  *Second Nun's Prologue and Tale*, 82, 100
  *Shipman's Tale*, 117, 127
  *Sir Thopas, Prologue and Tale of*, 74, 133, 135; contrasted with *Melibee*, 8, 125–26, 128, 131, 139; disclaimer about proverbs in *Thopas–Melibee* link, 128–33
  *Squire's Tale*, 71–72
  *Summoner's Prologue and Tale*, 43, 63, 76–79, 81
  *Wife of Bath's Prologue*, 7–8, 18, 31, 33, 34, 36, 50; as debate in proverbs, 85–117; wisdom figure, Wife as, 85, 90, 92–94, 102–7, 110
  *Wife of Bath's Tale*, 117–24; old woman as wisdom figure in, 8, 88, 104–5, 117, 119–20, 123–24; proverbs as moral instruction in, 119–124
Cannon, Christopher, 126
Carruthers, Mary, 45, 143
Cassiodorus, 137, 138
Caxton, William, 13, 67, 134
Cecil, Robert, 32
charms, verbal, 65–67
Chaucer, Geoffrey
  "Gentilesse," 122
  *House of Fame*, 3, 36
  *Legend of Good Women*, 100, 132
  *Troilus and Criseyde*, 19, 26–27, 32, 36, 37, 62
  See also *Canterbury Tales*
*Chaucer New Painted* (Painter), 34, 179n87
Chartier, Roger, 21
Christine de Pizan, 8, 88–89, 90, 100, 114–17, 146
Cicero, 137, 148, 151
*City of Ladies* (Christine de Pizan), 88–89, 90, 100, 114–17, 146
  refutation of a proverb, 115–16
Colie, Rosalie, 37–38
Collette, Carolyn P., 146
commonplace, 22
commonplace books, 2, 16, 34
compilational practices, premodern, 2, 4–5, 14, 15, 16, 32, 34, 35, 126, 135
*Consolation of Philosophy* (Boethius), 64, 121, 145–46, 160
Cooper, Helen, 57
Crane, Susan, 123

Dagenais, John, 5
Dane, Joseph A., 3
Dante, 121, 122
Davis, Natalie Zemon, 58, 59
*Dialogue of Solomon and Marcolf*, 56–63, 69, 78, 81, 92–94, 95–96, 172, 184n70
Dinshaw, Carolyn, 109–10
*Distichs of Cato* (*Disticha Catonis*), 12, 18, 65, 137, 168
*Dives and Pauper*, 94–95
*Doctrinal of Sapyence*, 67
Dolven, Jeff, 22, 159–60, 165

Ecclesiastes, 62, 88, 92, 98–99, 112, 130
Ecclesiasticus, 59, 78, 88, 92, 94, 95, 96, 103, 112, 156
Erasmus, Desiderius
  *Adages* (*Adagiorum chiliades*), 1 (epigraph),3, 71, 126, 135, 155; and English proverbs, 14, 20; Introduction, value of, 13; on marking proverbs, 16, 31; on profit and pleasure afforded by proverbs, 15–17; on proverbs as aids to memory, 45–46; proverbs, need to deliberate on, 15; on skillful use of proverbs, 40, 132; on special powers of the proverb, 29, 44, 45–46, 84
"Godly Feast, The," 132

exemplum (*ensample, exaumple*), 32, 35, 90, 154, 168
 in *Parson's Tale*, 161–65

fable, 12, 24, 32, 147, 158, 161, 165, 167, 170, 191n1
 of tell-tale crow, 159–60
 of wolf and mare, 51–52
Fein, Susanna, 90
Fletcher, Alan J., 68–69, 183n53
*Folewer to the Donet*. See Pecock, Reginald
Foley, John Miles, 22
Freedman, Paul, 55
Frost, Robert, 10–11
fruit and chaff image, 8, 35, 58, 161, 171–74
Frydeswyde, Saint, 67

Genesis, 116
Geoffrey of Vinsauf, 19
Gibson, Walter S., 6
Ginsberg, Warren, 159
Godfrey of Winchester
 *Liber proverbiorum*, 138
Gower, John, 37, 55
Gray, Douglas, 6, 181n11, 183n56
Green, Richard Firth, 119

Hanning, Robert W., 93
Hernadi, Paul, 37–38
Heywood, John, 14
Honeck, Richard P., 22, 25, 179n61
Horace
 *Ars Poetica*, 14, 15–16

*Iliad* (Homer), 46
Isidore of Seville
 *Etymologies*, 56

Jauss, Hans Robert, 37, 191n8
Jean de Meun
 *Roman de la rose*, 92, 93, 98–99, 109
Jehan LeFèvre
 *Lamentations of Matheolus*, 96–97, 116
Jerome, Saint, 20
 *Against Jovinian*, 88, 92, 97–98, 109, 111, 113

Kempe, Margery
 *Book of Margery Kempe*, 27–28, 29
Kinney, Clare R., 32
Kittredge, George Lyman, 20–21
Krug, Rebecca, 28

*Liber consolationis et consilii* (Albertanus of Brescia)
 allegory in, 136–38, 142–45
 *Melibee*, Chaucer's *Tale of*, relation to, 3, 129–30, 136, 188n12
 as a proverb collection, 126, 129–31, 133–46, 150–52
 proverbs, need to deliberate on, 15, 137, 149
*Liber parabolarum*, 12
*Liber proverbiorum* (Godfrey of Winchester), 138
*Livre de Mellibee*. See Renaud of Louens
Livy, 56, 100
Lydgate, John, 13, 57

manicule (fist, pointing hand)
 as premodern means of identifying proverbs, 2–3, 18, 173
 *See also* Speght, Thomas
Mann, Jill, 131, 153
Marcolf, fictional peasant, 56–63, 69, 78, 81, 172
 parallels to Wife of Bath, 85, 92–96, 110
 See also *Dialogue of Solomon and Marcolf*
*Matheolus, Lamentations of*. See Jehan LeFèvre
Matthew of Vendôme, 19
"Mending Wall" (Frost), 10–11
Metham, John, 13
microgenre, 35, 66, 68, 72, 76, 162
 *See also* charm, verbal; exemplum; oath, religious; proverb; sawe
*moralite* (Latin *moralitas*)
 in individual tales: *Clerk's Tale*, 164; *Manciple's Tale*, 159–61; *Monk's Tale*, 8, 164, 165–67, 168, 170; *Parson's Tale*, 161–64; *Nun's Priest's Tale*, 165, 168, 170–71, 172; *Reeve's Tale*, 51–52
 relationship to *sentence*, 158
 as explicit lesson attached to a tale, 133, 155, 158, 164–65, 167, 173–74, 191n1

oath, religious, 67–68, 76
Ovid, 13, 88, 93, 111, 148, 159

Painter, William
 *Chaucer New Painted*, 34, 179n87
Patterson, Lee, 144–45
Paul, Saint, 81, 88, 109, 161
Paulhan, Jean, 23–24, 25, 178n55

Pearsall, Derek, 30, 32
Pecock, Reginald, Bishop, 43, 44–45
　*Folewer to the Donet*, 46–49; refutation of a proverb in, 43, 44–45, 46–49, 50, 51, 68–69, 116
Peter, Saint, 65–67, 183n47
Petrarch, 148–49, 164
Plato, 14, 64
"Problem of Speech Genres, The." *See* Bakhtin, Mikhail M.
*Li Proverb au vilain*, 56
proverb-conscious reading practices, 3, 4–5, 15–16, 33–35, 72, 153, 157, 163, 173
*proverbe* and *sentence*, relationship, 17–22, 59, 87, 120, 122
proverbiality, perception of, 21, 37, 41, 63, 74, 87
*Proverbia rusticorum*, 56
proverbs
　antifeminist, 7–8, 33, 85–117, 123–24, 146
　brevity of, 37–38, 159
　as constraints on meanings in texts, 4, 8–9, 132–33, 158–60, 161–65, 168
　contradictory, 9, 35, 150–51, 165, 170–71, 173
　as "equipment for living," 26, 173
　"finalized wholeness" or "fullness of value" of, 40–41
　as frameworks for decision making, 147
　as interior decoration, 16–17
　Latin and vernacular, interchange between, 12–13, 14, 20, 32, 44, 86–87, 88, 177n13
　in mediation across class lines, 44, 74–75
　memory and, 12, 22, 45–46, 84, 99, 112, 120, 148–49
　as microgenres, 35, 37, 72
　as morals of tales (see *moralite*)
　object-like quality of, 38–39
　as peasant wisdom, 54–60
　in premodern education, 12–13, 14, 31, 32, 111, 120–21, 124, 133, 143, 158–60
　"re-accentuated" by speaker's voice, 40, 91, 106–7, 111
　transformative powers of, 11, 24–29, 49, 85, 158
　voice-permeable boundaries of, 37–40, 91, 106–7, 180n98
Proverbs (biblical book of), 18, 26, 95, 97, 140
　antifeminist uses of, 88, 92–93, 98, 106–7, 111
　numerical proverbs, 23

*Proverbs of Alfred*, 169
*Proverbs of Hendyng*, 57
Ptolemy, 18, 65, 79, 91, 185n17
Pythagoras, 14

*Queste del Saint Graal*, 93
quiting, Chaucer's dynamic of, 61, 63, 72, 75, 76
　in *Reeve's Tale*, 72
　in *Wife of Bath's Prologue* and *Tale*, 101, 108–10, 113, 117, 124

Ray, John, 14, 84 (epigraph), 86
Renaud of Louens
　*Livre de Mellibee*, 130, 134, 136–37, 139–46, 152, 153, 190n42
Rising of 1381 (Peasants' Revolt), 55
Robertson, D. W., 109
romance, medieval
　generic features, 74, 117, 119, 124, 132, 170
　as parodied in *Sir Thopas*, 127, 131, 133, 139
*Roman de la rose* (Jean de Meun), 92, 93, 98–99, 109

*sawe* ('saying'), 37, 41, 112
Schieberle, Misty, 146
Seneca, 18, 121, 134, 151, 159, 189n32
*sentence*
　denoting meaning of a word or literary form, 13, 99, 100, 103, 129
　*moralite*, relation to, 158, 166, 173
　multiple meanings of, 13, 96, 155
　*proverbe*, relation to, 17–22, 59, 87, 120, 122
　and *solaas*, 15, 128, 133, 139, 156, 165
Severs, J. Burke, 126, 134
Shippey, Tom, 21, 22
Solomon (Salomon)
　as adversary of women, 53, 85–86, 89, 92–102, 105–10, 111–113, 117
　authoritative wisdom of, 58–63, 70–71, 78, 81–82, 92–93, 96, 139, 140–42, 154–56, 159
　biblical wisdom books attributed to, 18, 60–63, 89, 92, 106–7, 185n19
　See also *Dialogue of Solomon and Marcolf*
Speght, Rachel, 33
Speght, Thomas
　editor of Chaucer's works, 1–4, 29–30

proverb-marking in 1602 edition, 1–4, 13, 29–35, 64, 65, 72, 80, 121, 125–26, 151, 157, 163, 173, 175n1, 175n4, 179n64
Spenser, Edmund, 30
Staley, Lynn, 146
Stewart, Anne W., 26
Stock, Brian, 4
Stow, John, 3, 34
*Suda*, 16, 177n25

Tabard Inn, 30
*Taill of Rauf Coilyear*, 74–75
Taverner, Richard, 14
Taylor, Archer, 19–20, 56
Travis, Peter W., 167, 171
Trevisa, John, 2, 56, 175n5

Vine, Angus, 16
Virgil, 13, 31, 43, 88

Wade's boat, 30, 179n71
Wallace, David, 146, 176n10, 189n38
Walsingham, Thomas, 55

Whiting, Bartlett Jere
 *Chaucer's Use of Proverbs*, 4, 5, 19, 20–21, 56, 59, 125, 162, 177–78n32
Whiting, Bartlett Jere, with Helen Wescott Whiting
 *Proverbs, Sentences…Mainly Before 1500*, 5–6, 18, 20–21, 33, 37, 74, 75, 86, 177–78n32, 178n42, 182n43
 "Whiting numbers," 5–6
Wiggins, Alison, 34, 134
wisdom
 clerical claim to monopoly on, 7, 44–45, 48–60, 76, 78, 80–82, 85, 102, 124, 157
 multiple forms of, 48, 52–54, 57–58, 72, 91, 105–6
 "Sophie" (in *Melibee*) as, 143–44, 147–48, 190n46
 sought by knight in *Wife of Bath's Tale*, 119
 See also *Dialogue of Solomon and Marcolf*; Solomon
Wright, Louis B., 34

www.ingramcontent.com/pod-product-compliance
Lightning Source LLC
LaVergne TN
LVHW041631060526
838200LV00040B/1531